Attack of the Monster Musical

Attack of the Monster Musical
A Cultural History of *Little Shop of Horrors*

ADAM ABRAHAM

methuen | drama
LONDON • NEW YORK • OXFORD • NEW DELHI • SYDNEY

METHUEN DRAMA
Bloomsbury Publishing Plc
50 Bedford Square, London, WC1B 3DP, UK
1385 Broadway, New York, NY 10018, USA
29 Earlsfort Terrace, Dublin 2, Ireland

BLOOMSBURY, METHUEN DRAMA and the Methuen Drama logo are trademarks of
Bloomsbury Publishing Plc

First published in Great Britain 2022
Reprinted 2022, 2023

Copyright © Adam Abraham 2022

Adam Abraham has asserted his right under the Copyright, Designs and Patents Act,
1988, to be identified as author of this work.

For legal purposes the Acknowledgments on p. vi constitute an
extension of this copyright page.

Cover design by Rebecca Heselton
Cover image: *Little Shop of Horrors* © Geraint Lewis / Alamy Stock Photo

All rights reserved. No part of this publication may be reproduced or transmitted
in any form or by any means, electronic or mechanical, including photocopying,
recording, or any information storage or retrieval system, without prior
permission in writing from the publishers.

Bloomsbury Publishing Plc does not have any control over, or responsibility for, any
third-party websites referred to or in this book. All internet addresses given in this book
were correct at the time of going to press. The author and publisher regret
any inconvenience caused if addresses have changed or sites have ceased to exist,
but can accept no responsibility for any such changes.

A catalogue record for this book is available from the British Library.

Library of Congress Control Number: 2021951473

ISBN: HB: 978-1-3501-7930-1
PB: 978-1-3501-7931-8
ePDF: 978-1-3501-7933-2
eBook: 978-1-3501-7932-5

Typeset by RefineCatch Limited, Bungay, Suffolk
Printed and bound in Great Britain

To find out more about our authors and books visit www.bloomsbury.com
and sign up for our newsletters.

Contents

Preface and Acknowledgments vi
Image Credits x
A Note on Lyrics xi

1   Skid Row: From Roger Corman's Hollywood to Off-Off-Broadway 1

2   Adaptation: How to Make a Nightmare Sing 23

3   Opening the Shop: Designers, Auditions, Rehearsals 49

4   A Monster Hit: The Off-Broadway Production 73

5   It Conquered the World: New York to London and Beyond 97

6   Audrey III: Cinematic Dreams and Disillusionment 121

7   We'll Have Tomorrow: The Curious Afterlives of a Man-Eating Musical 145

Appendix A: Comparative Song List, 1981–82 167

Appendix B: "Somewhere That's Green" Song Development 169

Appendix C: Original Casts, 1982–86 171

Notes 173
Bibliography 215
Index 225

Preface and Acknowledgments

On the twenty-seventh day of the month of July, in an early year of a decade not too long before our own, theatre audiences encountered a musical unlike any they had seen before—*Little Shop of Horrors*. Now the question is: how does an ultra-cheap, black-and-white movie from 1960 become a hit musical and a cultural phenomenon? This book is the answer. *Little Shop of Horrors* transcended its low-budget origins, thrilled New York audiences for over five years, and eventually played in Europe, Africa, and Asia. What is more, the musical launched the careers of its creators, Howard Ashman and Alan Menken, who proceeded to revive the Disney animated musical with *The Little Mermaid, Beauty and the Beast*, and *Aladdin*. But first there was *Little Shop*, the Off-Broadway show about a man-eating plant, which made it all possible.

Attack of the Monster Musical would not exist without the guidance and support of Sarah Ashman Gillespie and William Lauch. They are the Howard Ashman Estate and keepers of the flame. They donated his papers—including scripts, lyrics, correspondence, and production materials—to the Library of Congress, in Washington, DC. Further, they made themselves available for multiple interviews and shared their intimate knowledge of Ashman, his life, and his work. I am grateful to them both for entrusting me to tell this story.

The first person I interviewed for the project was Alan Menken. Just beginning my research, I did not know what I was talking about. Nevertheless, Menken graciously answered all my questions and performed snippets of lost songs. Remembering his work on *Little Shop*, he told me, "Howard was the boss." Indeed, Ashman was the author, lyricist, director, and artistic director of the WPA Theatre, where the show premiered. I thank Menken for inviting me to his studio and illuminating the creative process.

Ashman and Menken found an ideal collaborator in Martin P. Robinson, a Muppeteer with a taste for the macabre. Robinson designed Audrey II, the plant from another world, and performed the puppets on stage during the initial run (*Sesame Street* was his day job). I was thrilled to interview Robinson in his home, where he showed me his workshop and some of the original puppets (still intact). He also shared many photographs and his vivid memories of this transformative time in his life.

If you want to learn about a musical, talk to the stage managers. The writers write the show; the actors perform in it; but the stage managers watch the piece, night after night. I interviewed the original stage manager, Paul Mills Holmes, and his eventual successor, Donna Rose Fletcher. Both shared their insights into *Little Shop of Horrors*. Fletcher, in particular, is a fellow historian of all things *Little Shop*. She maintains the production reports from the Off-Broadway run (1982 to 1987)—an unparalleled resource. And she spent countless hours discussing the musical and offering helpful corrections.

Histories of musicals sometimes close on opening night. However, if the show is a hit, then opening night is only the beginning. There will be cast replacements, touring productions, international companies, the occasional rewrite. This book tracks the life of a long-running show and the lives of those involved. I had the good fortune to interview many who worked on *Little Shop of Horrors*, from the Off-Off-Broadway début to the Warner Bros. film and subsequent productions. I thank them all: Eydie Alyson, Anthony Asbury, Robert Billig, Tammy Blanchard, Joseph Church, Edie Cowan, Sheila Kay Davis, Eric Eisner, Hunter Foster, Steve Gelfand, Edward T. Gianfrancesco, Nancy Nagel Gibbs, Constance Grappo, Jonathan Groff, Lynn Hippen, Leilani Jones, Darlene Kaplan, Tom Kirdahy, Michael Kosarin, Michael James Leslie, Sally Lesser, Franc Luz, Cameron Mackintosh, Michael Mayer, Katherine Meloche, Robby Merkin, Brad Moranz, Otts Munderloh, Albert Poland, Deborah Sharpe-Taylor, Brent Spiner, Will Van Dyke, Jennifer Leigh Warren, Marsha Waterbury, Stephen Wells, and Lee Wilkof.

Further, I interviewed others who knew key participants and provided helpful background on the show and its history. I am grateful to Robert Callely, Ellen Cole, Delin Colon, Ann Dumaresq, Ron Gillespie, Dennis Green, Michael Lavine, Marsha Malamet, Harriet McDougal, Nancy Parent, John Sadowsky,

Jacky Sallow, Norman Schwartz, Jonathan Sheffer, Freddye Kaufman Silverman, Valerie Velardi, and Maury Yeston.

The book you are reading is not the first history of *Little Shop*. That honor belongs to *The Little Shop of Horrors Book*, by John McCarty and Mark Thomas McGee, published in 1988. I spoke to McGee on the phone, and he was forthright about that book's inception. He is also a wonderful raconteur, who delineated some of the practices of Roger Corman, producer and director of the original film. I gleaned further insight into Corman from conversations with Steve Barnett, Lee Goldberg, Beverly Gray, and William Rabkin.

Of course, this book is also not the first to chart the life of a single musical. An important predecessor is *Show Boat: The Story of a Classic American Musical*, by Miles Kreuger. He has been a friend for many years and remains an inspiration for his scholarly rigor and encyclopedic knowledge of New York City and its theatres. Further, I modeled this book on other studies of individual musicals, especially *Oklahoma!*, *My Fair Lady*, *Oliver!*, *Fiddler on the Roof*, *Cabaret*, *Hair*, and *Sunday in the Park with George*.

Don Hahn paved the way by charting the accomplishments of Howard Ashman in two remarkable documentaries: *Waking Sleeping Beauty* and *Howard*. In 2018, I saw *Howard* at the Tribeca Film Festival, and it rekindled my desire to write this long-gestating project. I thank Hahn for his kind advice and for his inspiring efforts to chronicle this era of American culture.

Kyle Renick was Ashman's business partner at the WPA Theatre, which Renick continued to operate through the 1990s. He died in 2019, before I could interview him. But he left his papers to the New York Public Library, and they were collated in 2020, while a global pandemic shuttered just about everything. In 2021, the library reopened, and the collection became available. So I thank Renick for this gift from beyond the grave. He saved everything: letters, contracts, photographs, every newspaper article in which the words *Little Shop of Horrors* appeared. Thanks also to Doug Reside and the expert staff at NYPL.

A few other institutions claim my gratitude. The Library of Congress is a wonder, and I appreciate Mark Eden Horowitz for answering my endless questions. The Shubert Archive also contains information on *Little Shop*, and I am grateful to Mark Swartz and Sylvia Wang for their help and persistence.

Two universities provided funding that allowed me to travel to these archives: Virginia Commonwealth University and Auburn University.

At Bloomsbury Publishing, Dom O'Hanlon has been an ideal reader and editor of this book. He is thoroughly versed in musical theatre, with a keen appreciation of the form. Further, my anonymous reviewers offered constructive feedback. Before I found my way to Bloomsbury, Laura Chasen helped to shape the proposal. Throughout the process, Tony Angeles lent his graphic-design talents and solved many problems. A few friends read early drafts and offered comments and corrections: Andrew Brownstein, Gibson Frazier, Marc Madnick, Dale Smith, Michael Weiner, and Alan Zachary. For additional support, I give thanks to Richard Kraft, Rick Kunis, Michael Marcus, and Aram Sarhadian.

Ambika Tewari has endured another book, not to mention life with a monomaniac for whom all roads lead to *Little Shop*. I endeavor to be worthy of her affection and sweet understanding. My sisters, Shara and Nina, and their respective families have brightened these difficult years with their laughter. Finally, I thank my parents, Ronald and Marcia Abraham, who raised me in a culture of musicals, with trips to Broadway and cast albums in the car. My mother always read every word I ever wrote: my first and best critic. This book is dedicated to her memory.

Image Credits

Every reasonable effort has been made to acknowledge the ownership of images included in this volume. Any errors that may have occurred are inadvertent and will be corrected in subsequent editions provided that notification is sent to the publisher. The third-party copyrighted material displayed in the pages of this book is done so on the basis of "fair use" for the purposes of criticism, teaching, scholarship, or research, in accordance with international copyright laws, and is not intended to infringe on the rights of the original owners.

Figure 1. © 1960 The Filmgroup, Inc. Figure 2. Courtesy of Norman Schwartz. Figure 3. © 1981 Shoptalk Ltd. Courtesy of howardashman.com. Figure 4. © 1981 Shoptalk Ltd. Courtesy of howardashman.com. Figure 5. Courtesy of Martin P. Robinson. Figure 6. Photograph by Edward T. Gianfrancesco. Figure 7. Source: Howard Ashman Papers, Library of Congress, Washington, DC. Figure 8. Source: Kyle Renick Papers on the WPA Theatre, 1950–2018, New York Public Library for the Performing Arts, New York, New York. Figure 9. Source: Howard Ashman Papers, Library of Congress, Washington, DC. Figure 10. © 1986 The Geffen Film Company. Figure 11. © 1986 The Geffen Film Company. Figure 12. Photograph by Adam Abraham.

A Note on Lyrics

It was customary for song lyrics in typed and printed scripts to appear in ALL CAPITALS. In the pages that follow, lyrics will appear in mixed case, for ease of reading (and so that it will not seem that someone is yelling). No punctuation has been added or removed; not a single word has been altered.

Except where noted, all quotations from *Little Shop of Horrors* refer to the edition published by Samuel French, Inc., in 1985. Each quotation is followed by the page number in parentheses.

Chapter One
Skid Row: From Roger Corman's Hollywood to Off-Off-Broadway

Some movies are made for art, some for profit, and some in order to win a bet. *The Little Shop of Horrors* falls in the third category. Perhaps it was not so much a bet as a *challenge*: could a feature-length film be shot in exactly two days? Roger Corman, an independent producer and director, said Yes. He rose to prominence in the 1950s, when the Hollywood studio system was crumbling. The federal government forced Paramount and other studios to sell off their movie theatres; families migrated to suburbia and stayed home to watch television; and the moguls who once led the system—Louis B. Mayer, Harry Cohn—were dying. The cinema audience was also getting younger, ready to rebel without a cause, more attuned to the macabre. *Attack of the Crab Monsters. A Bucket of Blood.*

Corman thrived in the changing climate. Born in Detroit, Michigan, in 1926, he was raised in the Great Depression, forever haunting his relationship with money. He studied industrial engineering at Stanford University and then English literature at Oxford before he drifted into the movie business.[1] Living in Los Angeles and working outside the system, he produced films for pennies and always turned a profit. Vincent Price called him "dead serious, humorless."[2] Corman, with sufficient preparation, could shoot a film in five or six days. "I had never thought of myself as doing Great Art," he said. "I felt I was working as a craftsman."[3]

A longtime Corman assistant, Beverly Gray, noticed "the engineer's zest for problem-solving." Actor Mel Welles, who appeared in many Corman films, observed that the director solved problems "with the greatest amount of efficiency."[4] Prolific and reliable, he became a key supplier for American International Pictures (AIP), a company formed in the 1950s by James H. Nicholson and Samuel Z. Arkoff. According to one critic, AIP "specialized in fun, hip, sexy, and contemporary alternatives to Hollywood's stuffy spectacles and mundane melodramas."[5] In the summer of 1957, for example, AIP offered *Invasion of the Saucer Men*, *I Was a Teenage Werewolf*, and *Reform School Girl*. Growing up in New Jersey at the time, Joe Dante noticed that "they were movies your parents wouldn't want you to see."[6]

AIP offered Corman $50,000 for each film he produced, plus a $15,000 advance on foreign sales. So Corman completed each film for under $65,000; every third or fourth film would be extremely cheap, thus increasing his profits.[7] Nevertheless, Corman bristled at the well-known term for low-budget Hollywood fare: "I never made a 'B' movie in my life."[8] He insisted that the B movie (the second half of a double feature) was a relic from the 1930s and 1940s, when the major studios controlled production, distribution, and exhibition. Yet in the era when color photography became affordable for the majors, AIP found a winning formula by combining two similar black-and-white pictures into a double feature: "two films for the price of one."[9]

The legend that Roger Corman produced *The Little Shop of Horrors* in two days has often been told.[10] However, Corman biographer Mark Thomas McGee argued that "the legend is a lie."[11] Here is what happened. In 1959, Corman formed his own company, the Filmgroup, which generated movies on the AIP model: fast and cheap. When offered free access to a movie set that depicted an office, Corman brainstormed ideas with a frequent collaborator, the screenwriter Charles Byron Griffith, known as Chuck. They considered a story about cannibalism but feared that it would never get past the censors. Late one night, when such ideas emerge, Griffith suggested a "man-eating plant."[12] The resulting screenplay resembles a Corman-Griffith film made earlier that year, *A Bucket of Blood*.[13] Both projects center on the same trio: a hapless loser, his love interest, and his boss. To economize, each story is built around a single workplace location (a beatnik café, a florist shop), and in each case, the loser-hero becomes an accidental murderer, thus winning attention and the love that he craves. Griffith entitled his new script "The Passionate People Eater"[14]—a variation on "The Purple People Eater," a 1958 novelty song by Sheb Wooley. In the song, a creature from another world descends to the earth and proclaims, "I want to get a job in a rock 'n' roll band." So the song blends a monster movie and rock music: a potent combination.

In December 1959, "The Passionate People Eater" went into production. Corman intended to beat his own record for speed and shoot in just two days. On Tuesday, December 22, Corman began filming at the former Charlie Chaplin Studios, on North La Brea Avenue, near Sunset Boulevard. On Wednesday, production wrapped.[15] How did he do it? He shot with two cameras simultaneously to get more coverage in less time. The actors were engaged for one week; they rehearsed for three days and shot for two.[16] All the scenes in the florist shop play out as if on stage; the editor cuts between angles, left and right. The film's interiors are high key and low contrast; indeed, these scenes look more like a multicamera sitcom than a monster movie—appropriate for Corman's blend of comedy and horror. The story also required about twelve minutes of exterior photography, which took place over four evenings, produced by a non-union crew. Since Corman was in the union, directing duties here were handled by Chuck Griffith.[17] Hence the shoot was a few days longer than the legendary two days.

"My film budgets have always been notoriously lean," Corman admitted. Beverly Gray recalled that he would "hire young unknowns who would work for almost nothing in exchange for the chance to learn their craft."[18] In *A Bucket of Blood*, the hero exclaims, "Gee, fifty dollars for something I made!" His coworker replies, "Now you're a professional." For the film that became *The Little Shop of Horrors*, the lead actor, Jonathan Haze, was paid $400 for a week of work; a prop company called Dice Incorporated charged $750 to construct four mechanical plants of increasing size and menace.[19] Multitalented Chuck Griffith earned $1,800 for writing the screenplay, acting in the film, and directing the exterior scenes.[20] A young Jack Nicholson also appeared in the film, as a masochistic dental patient. When offering the role, Corman handed Nicholson only those script pages in which the actor would appear. "That's what low budget was like," Nicholson remembered.[21] The total cost: less than $30,000.[22]

Retitled *The Little Shop of Horrors*, the film opened at the Pix Theatre, in Hollywood. Nicholson attended, and there was a strong reaction, at least to his scene: "They laughed so hard I could barely hear the dialogue."[23] Here's what the audience saw: Business is bad in a low-rent florist shop on Skid Row, run by Gravis Mushnik. He has two assistants: Audrey and Seymour. Seymour, a budding botanist, discovers a new kind of carnivorous plant, which eventually eats four people. The remarkable plant grows and attracts business to the now-booming shop; as a result, Seymour wins popular acclaim and the love of Audrey. The police, however, investigate the murders and find their way to the florist shop, but Seymour eludes them. Finally, he tries to kill the plant and dies in the process.

Cheap exploitation pictures such as this one generally did not command many reviews. But the industry journal *Variety* offered a positive notice, in 1961, months after the film first appeared. The reviewer found *The Little Shop* to be "one big 'sick' joke" but also "harmless and good-natured." Further, "Horticulturalists and vegetarians will love it."[24] On the other hand, exploitation films were lavished with colorful artwork created by publicity departments eager to sell the studio's product. A typical poster might suggest epic scope, when in fact the advertised film is nothing more than a few people running around the San Fernando Valley, occasionally menaced by a rubber monster. The poster for *The Little Shop of Horrors* is elegant and strange—clearly the artist never saw the picture. The period is now the early twentieth century. Perhaps the artist remembered the old-world charm of *The Shop around the Corner*, the 1940 M-G-M film based on a Hungarian play. A tagline on *The Little Shop* poster is adapted from a song in Gilbert and Sullivan's *The Mikado*, appended by musical notation: "the flowers that kill in the Spring / TRA-LA." So *The Little Shop of Horrors*, a horror-comedy, appears to be a musical.

Nevertheless, the Filmgroup encountered difficulty distributing the new film. It appeared as the lower half of a double bill in September 1960, paired with more elaborate Corman productions, *House of Usher* or *Last Woman on Earth*.[25] Some exhibitors refused to book *The Little Shop* because they perceived that it was anti-Semitic.[26] The major characters seem to be Jewish, and they are morally suspect. The nebbishy hero, Seymour Krelboin (or Krelboined), kills people and then feeds them to his hungry plant; Seymour's employer,

Figure 1 *A lobby card for the original 1960 film, signed by the producer and director, Roger Corman. The vocal phrase and notes at the top suggest a possible musical.*

Mr. Mushnik, fails to report the crimes because business is now profitable.[27] Nevertheless, in 1961, the film was invited to appear (out of competition) at the Cannes Film Festival. Back at home, AIP rescued the languishing *Little Shop* when the company needed a second feature to accompany *Black Sunday*, an Italian shocker that AIP acquired for US distribution.[28] By May, Corman devised a new release pattern, with a focus on art-house cinemas and "special college town campaigns."[29] Like many low-budget films, *The Little Shop of Horrors* played in smaller theatres and drive-ins before it disappeared.

But in the mid-1960s, Corman sold a number of Filmgroup pictures to television, through Allied Artists, and the movie about Seymour and his carnivorous plant found a new audience.[30] Mel Welles, who played Mushnik, discovered that "[i]t became a kind of cult film." One critic explained how the iconic plant's dialogue entered the popular consciousness: "Every time it's on television, school kids go around yelling, 'Feed me! I'm hungry!' the next day."[31]

Corman's movie appealed to slightly older students as well; Mark Thomas McGee recalled that "college kids started watching it. They'd all toke up and think it was even funnier than it was." Character actor Dick Miller, who appeared in *The Little Shop* and other Corman films, said that the director "didn't think these things would ever go anyplace." Yet, according to Welles, *The Little Shop of Horrors* "caught the imagination of the young people, the hipsters of the time."[32]

One of these young people was Howard Elliott Ashman. "I think it was past my bedtime," he recalled, when "the beat-up black and white TV was working overtime in my teenaged den of iniquity, the pine-panelled clubroom of our split-level home in Baltimore."[33] Corman's film frequently appeared on local television stations, one of many pieces of cinematic detritus filling the airwaves. *The Little Shop* made a deep impression on the young Ashman: "I thought it was maybe the wittiest thing I had ever seen at age fourteen"; further, "it was unexpected and delicious in its way."[34]

As a child, he adored horror films, but he lived and breathed musicals. Born in Baltimore, in 1950, he was the son of Raymond and Shirley Ashman. Raymond held a series of jobs, and for a time he was a wholesale ice-cream-cone salesman. Shirley was a singer, who had performed locally and loved operetta.[35] A daughter, Sarah, was born in 1953. "We grew up with cast albums," she said.[36] On weekends in the summer, the children attended Painters Mill Music Fair, where touring theatre companies performed in the round. "It was a big tent in the middle of a big field, and you could see actual, real life professional actors," Sarah remembered. "Afterward, they'd autograph our programs." The family also traveled to New York City, to see *Camelot* on Broadway.[37] When Ashman was old enough, he and a friend cut school and took the train to New York by themselves. Their destination: the Broadhurst Theatre and the original production of *Cabaret*, which opened in November 1966.[38]

Ashman's love of musicals led to performing and then writing them. "He was in every talent show, and he won," according to his sister.[39] He became involved in local theatre companies, including the Pickwick Players. A formative experience was the Children's Theatre Association (CTA), founded in 1943.[40] The company recruited young people to get involved in theatre and work with professionals to mount children's theatre productions of classic tales. Here Ashman befriended another local boy, Otts Munderloh, who recalled the company's focus on empathy. Acting exercises would ask participants to put themselves "into someone else's shoes." Further, at a time when Baltimore was still segregated in many ways, CTA was open to everyone, regardless of race. "We were ecumenical," Munderloh said.[41] Ashman also appeared in the more conventional school productions, including *Brigadoon* and *The Skin of Our Teeth*. But performing was not enough. Sarah Ashman felt that her brother was "always searching for a creative outlet." He wrote for the high school literary magazine, the *Spectrum*, and during the 1960s reign of free verse, the teenaged Ashman worked through traditional rhyme schemes and iambic pentameter. "He wasn't trying to break the mold," a friend observed. "He believed in creativity within a structure."[42] One form in which Ashman exercised his talent was the musical. He began writing musicals at the age of twelve; his first was based on Harper Lee's 1960 novel *To Kill a Mockingbird*. But Ashman did not read the novel—he read the *Reader's Digest* condensed version.[43] So it was an adaptation of an adaptation.

In Milford Mill High School, in Baltimore County, the juniors (eleventh graders) performed an assembly each year to bid farewell to the graduating seniors. Ashman and his childhood friend John Sadowsky wrote skits and song parodies, in which new lyrics append an existing piece of music. The seniors at Milford Mill performed their own annual assembly; and by the time Ashman and Sadowsky reached twelfth grade, their classmates expected them to stage the usual variety show. Ashman had a better idea: "Let's just do a Broadway musical!"[44] Rather than write a series of unconnected sketches, he adapted the folktale "Dick Whittington and His Cat," a fanciful story about a real person, Richard Whittington, who became Lord Mayor of London. Because Ashman and Sadowsky would no longer craft song parodies to existing music, they needed a composer. At a school meeting, fellow senior Norman Schwartz volunteered for the job. He had studied the guitar for two years and played in a Motown-style band.[45]

The team of Ashman, Sadowsky, and Schwartz wrote *The Brat's Meow*, a full-length musical with some twenty songs, performed at the high school in January 1967.[46] Ashman took charge of the production and directed a cast of more than thirty fellow students. "You better do what he wants," commented a

Figure 2 *Collaborators, 1967. From left to right: Howard Ashman, Norman Schwartz, and John Sadowsky, authors of* The Brat's Meow, *a high school musical.*

friend who appeared in the show.[47] Prior to the opening, Ashman told the school newspaper, "This is the rags-to-riches story of a poor London street urchin who finds fortune and true love with the aid of his faithful cat."[48]

Indeed, there is a structural similarity to *The Little Shop of Horrors*, directed by Roger Corman. Seymour, a lowly clerk, finds fortune and true love with the aid of his fantastic plant. Ashman tended to share his obsessions with others, and he invited friends to his house to watch the Corman film, which occasionally aired on Friday nights. John Sadowsky was among those invited: "I couldn't get over how great this movie was."[49] Others included Debi Linowitz and Jackie Sallow, who was then dating Norman Schwartz. Their high school was predominantly white—part of the suburban migration in the years after the Second World War—and maybe half of the students were Jewish.⁵⁰ So the exhibitors who found *The Little Shop* to be anti-Semitic were mistaken: here in Baltimore County, a group of Jewish teenagers delighted in the film. Gravis Mushnik. Mrs. Shiva and her dying relatives. Seymour Krelboin (or Krelboined or something). After *The Brat's Meow*, Ashman and Schwartz wrote another musical, *The Candy Shop*, which recalls *The Little Shop* in certain ways. The story focuses on a young man who runs a candy shop, his love interest, and a talking plant. The plant is named Ethel—after Ethel Merman, star of the 1959 Broadway musical *Gypsy*. As Schwartz remembered, "The plant made pills that got people high."⁵¹ Unfortunately, *The Candy Shop* was never publicly performed, but the collaborators shared it with some of their friends during the summer after high school. Soon, according to Ashman, it "went the way of adolescent things."⁵²

Ashman spent a year at Boston University and then continued his theatrical explorations at Goddard College, an undergraduate institution in Vermont. By this point, he was tall and slender, with tousled blond hair. He stood out among the hippies of Goddard when he arrived in 1968. In the words of a classmate, "Howard was always in a nice suit and clean-shaven and fresh-eyed." Further, his musical taste differed from that of the majority. While other students blared rock music from their dormitory windows, "he was blaring out *No, No, Nanette*."⁵³ The 1925 musical introduced the songs "Tea for Two" and "I Want to Be Happy." Ashman also fell in love, during a summer program at Tufts University. Stuart White hailed from Glyndon, Maryland, just twenty miles from where the Ashmans lived.⁵⁴ A mutual friend described him as a "prankster" and "playful"; with a "twinkle in the eye," he was "Peter Pan-ish."⁵⁵ Another friend observed that "he was very handsome in a kind of Bosie way"⁵⁶—an allusion to Oscar Wilde's fateful lover, Lord Alfred Douglas. White was known as Snooz or Snoozy.

Together, Ashman and White applied to graduate school, and they both attended the grad theatre program at Indiana University, in Bloomington.⁵⁷ They acted in a student production of *Dames at Sea*, a musical that began Off-Off-Broadway and then opened Off-Broadway in 1968. The show is a loving recreation of 1930s movie musicals—a surprise hit in the age of political assassinations and the Vietnam War. The university hired Broadway dancer Edie Cowan to direct and choreograph. She appeared in the 1964 hit *Funny*

Girl, starring Barbra Streisand, and a 1967 flop entitled *Sherry!* Cowan had to teach her Indiana students how to tap dance, and she cast Ashman as Dick and Stuart White as his best friend, Lucky.[58] In the end, each character wins the girl of his dreams (it is a musical). For his master's thesis, Ashman wrote and directed *The Snow Queen*, a musical adaptation of the fairy tale by Hans Christian Andersen. An undergraduate named Nancy Parent acted in the show, and she recalled that her director "had something to say about every aspect of the production—costume, set, choreography."[59]

Upon graduation, Ashman and White moved together again—now to New York City—and they planned to work in the theatre. Ashman landed a survival job at Tempo Books, a paperback division of Grosset and Dunlap. Editorial director Harriet McDougal described Tempo's list as "semi-respectable": sports biographies, astrology, and reprints of newspaper comic strips.[60] When Ashman became her assistant, he decided, "Well, if I'm going to be a secretary, I will be the best secretary since Rosalind Russell!"[61]

Ashman had the good fortune to live during the "Golden Age" of the American musical—roughly, the mid-1940s to the mid-1960s.[62] Theatre critics may dispute the term; Jessica Sternfeld and Elizabeth L. Wollman call it "riddled with unfair assumptions."[63] There is also disagreement on when this period began and ended. Thomas S. Hischak proposes the 1950s as "a golden age of sorts." Indeed, it may be better to identify a *form* rather than an era, as Stacy Wolf asserts: "The 'Golden Age' of musicals refers as much to a set of formal and aesthetic conventions as it does to a time period."[64] One term often used to describe this particular form is the "integrated" musical. As early as 1925, Oscar Hammerstein II claimed the importance of integrating elements in a show with "skillful cohesion."[65] Further, the integrated musical is associated with the partnership between Hammerstein and composer Richard Rodgers, which lasted from 1943 to 1959—*Oklahoma!* to *The Sound of Music*—a golden age of sorts. *Oklahoma!* was deemed "integrated" by the *New York Times* when the play first opened. Rodgers, in his autobiography, describes a kind of American *Gesamtkunstwerk*, in which all the elements cohere: "In a great musical, the orchestrations sound the way the costumes look."[66]

Whether golden or integrated, a coherent kind of book musical appealed to audiences in the mid-twentieth century. Unlike the European opera, which combines music and libretto (the words), the American musical usually combines three elements: book, music, and lyrics. The book is not only the spoken dialogue; the book is the structure, the shape of the piece. During the reign of Rodgers and Hammerstein, the Broadway musical gained sophistication and moved beyond a concatenation of songs linked together on the flimsiest of pretexts. Gerald Mast, in his compelling history of the American musical, writes, "By 1948 producers and audiences knew exactly what a book musical was supposed to be: a romantic drama of conflicting characters, alternately comic and dramatic, based on a literary source, ancient or modern, with at least eighteen musical slots."[67] Audiences in the 1940s and 1950s would recognize this form in *South Pacific*, *Guys and Dolls*, *Wonderful Town*, *The Pajama Game*, and *Gypsy*.

Songs in the book musical are not merely decorative or diverting; they advance plot or illuminate character. That is to say, music and lyrics must be particular, "appropriate to both the people and the period of the play," according to Mast.[68] Any number of Cole Porter characters could ask, "What is this thing called love?" Which musical is that from? *Anything Goes*? *Fifty Million Frenchmen*? You're not supposed to remember—you're supposed to remember the song. But only Henry Higgins, of *My Fair Lady*, could ask, "Why can't the English teach their children how to speak?"[69] At the same time, there was a tension between this particularity and the fact that popular music was meant to be popular. The shape of the musical-theatre song developed in Tin Pan Alley, in the first decades of the century. The typical song was built around a refrain of sixteen or thirty-two measures, often structured in an AABA pattern. The A section contains the hook (a catchy melody), repeated in two more A sections, so that you would remember. The B section (sometimes called the bridge or release) diverts from the A, musically and lyrically.[70] Raymond Knapp claims that the Tin Pan Alley forms dominated "Broadway, but also Hollywood, jazz, sheet music, recording, and radio."[71] Popular singers recorded songs from hit New York shows, and millions of families purchased original cast albums. The Broadway musical, for the first and last time, *was* American culture—as American as apple pie and Disneyland.[72]

A central figure in the history of the musical is Lehman Engel. He was born A. Lehman Engel, in Mississippi, in 1910. Like a modern Mozart, he wrote an opera around the age of ten. He studied music in Cincinnati and then moved to New York to work as a composer and conductor. During the Great Depression, President Franklin D. Roosevelt launched the Works Progress Administration (WPA), an agency designed to put Americans to work. Engel's contribution was the formation of the Madrigal Singers; each participant sang the music of the Renaissance and earned $23.86 per week. For the theatre, Engel wrote incidental music for plays and carved out a career as a music director of Broadway shows, often for composers such as Kurt Weill and Leonard Bernstein. A music director is responsible for coordinating and teaching music to the singers and may also conduct the orchestra. During the 1950s, Engel music directed many shows, including *Fanny*, *Li'l Abner*, and *Destry Rides Again*.[73]

But Engel was not infallible. Over the years, he rejected the chance to work on a number of hit plays. He turned down *Brigadoon*, the 1947 musical by Alan Jay Lerner and Frederick Loewe. Engel surmised that this rejection cost him the chance to conduct their next productions: *Paint Your Wagon*, *My Fair Lady*, and *Camelot*.[74] Later, he said no to *The Pajama Game*; its eventual music director, Hal Hastings, worked on many subsequent hits for producer Harold S. Prince.[75] Engel also disputed the public's taste (always risky in a popular medium) by disliking *Man of La Mancha* and *Cabaret* and listing them in a book chapter on "Failures," even though both were hits in the mid-1960s.[76] Born half a century before the Beatles, Engel hated rock 'n' roll: "It is small, repetitious, and, although ear splittingly raucous, ephemeral."[77]

By the early 1960s, Lehman Engel felt frustrated and ready for a new challenge. An opportunity appeared in the form of Broadcast Music, Inc. (BMI). This company arose during World War II as a rival to ASCAP (American Society of Composers, Authors and Publishers), which existed to collect royalties from sheet music and radio broadcasts. ASCAP protected the financial interests of its members and became a force in the music business. By 1940, with ASCAP and radio broadcasters locked in a dispute, BMI emerged as an alternative. Thereafter, ASCAP and BMI co-existed—the Coke and Pepsi of music-royalty companies. In 1961, Robert Sour, the vice president of BMI, asked Lehman Engel to lead a discussion with a group of young theatre songwriters. Engel by this time was portly, with the look of a man who enjoys the good things in life, and he was balding, with deep-set eyes and a furrowed brow. The event at BMI was so successful that everyone agreed to meet again. These talks formed the kernel of what became the BMI Musical Theatre Workshop.[78]

Eventually, Engel designed a two-year curriculum. In the first year, he would introduce types of musical-theatre songs: the charm song, the ballad, the production number, and so on. Participating composers and lyricists would then create a song of the designated type. For class assignments, Engel would rely on familiar narratives. For example, students might be asked to write a ballad for Blanche Dubois, in *A Streetcar Named Desire*, or a charm song for young Frankie, in *The Member of the Wedding*.[79] In the second year, the class would turn to the architecture of the musical and study the book. At this point, teams might begin developing their own projects. The most promising students would graduate to a third year and become, in essence, members for life. Participants did not need to belong to BMI; they simply had to audition, by performing two original songs for Engel. Workshop meetings took place once a week, usually on Monday or Friday afternoon, and lasted around two hours. And it was free.[80] For the first time, novice songwriters were given the opportunity to develop their skills and receive valuable feedback from an expert and his attentive students. Through the BMI Workshop, Engel turned himself into a vehicle for transmitting musical-theatre history; he insisted that "we will never build something worthily new" without understanding the forms of the past.[81]

In the early 1970s, the workshop enjoyed a crop of talented new members, many of whom would go on to write Broadway musicals: Judd Woldin, Edward Kleban, Carol Hall, Maury Yeston, and Alan Menken.[82] He was born in New York City, in 1949, the son of Norman and Judith Menken. Norman was a dentist, who also played piano; Judith was in the arts, as a performer, writer, and director. Early on, their son demonstrated musical ability and, like Lehman Engel, began composing at a young age. The Menkens lived in New Rochelle, north of the city, and Alan graduated from New Rochelle High School, in 1967. He attended New York University and graduated with a degree in music. In 1972, he married the former Janis Roswick, a dancer, and the couple eventually had two children. At the time, Menken's ambition was to be a singer-songwriter;

in the words of a frequent collaborator, "Alan wanted to be like Elton John."[83] BMI classmate Maury Yeston noted a cultural shift from the 1960s to the 1970s. In earlier decades, songwriters could peddle their tunes to the popular singers of the day—Frank Sinatra, Elvis Presley, Tom Jones. This was the model used by the songwriting team Jerry Leiber and Mike Stoller; they wrote many hits for others, including "Hound Dog" and "Yakety Yak." But the rise of the singer-songwriter, like Bob Dylan, disrupted this model.[84] If you wanted to market your songs in the 1970s and did not happen to be a recording star, there were fewer opportunities. But one of them was the theatre. In an earlier period, an Alan Menken might have written pop songs; instead, he entered BMI and planned to write for the stage.

He arrived at the workshop as a composer-lyricist, a next-generation Cole Porter or Irving Berlin. Menken was short and compact, with brown hair and wire-rim glasses, a bundle of eagerness and excitability. The first musical that he developed was based on the Hermann Hesse novel *Steppenwolf*, published in 1927. It did not go far. Menken wrote songs for other potential musicals as well, including *Conversations with Pierre*, which concerns the relationship between a psychiatrist and a patient.[85] His teacher and classmates were impressed. Yeston observed that a Menken song entered the world "just as beautifully and as easily as if it was always there."[86] In 1975, Lehman Engel published his definitive book on the art of lyric writing, *Their Words Are Music: The Great Theatre Lyricists and Their Lyrics*. After chapters on Ira Gershwin, Sheldon Harnick, and Stephen Sondheim, Engel concludes with a selection of "New Lyricists," drawn from his BMI Workshops in New York, Los Angeles, and Toronto. Two songs are from a budding lyricist named Alan Menken.[87] Still, the path was not easy. Menken worked various gigs through the 1970s; he played the cabaret circuit; he contributed songs to revues. As he explained, "We were all struggling to get our shows on."[88] He was talented, no doubt. He needed an opportunity.

Several people claimed the honor of introducing Howard Ashman to Alan Menken, but the one who made it happen was Maury Yeston, a friend from BMI.[89] Ashman directed an early version of Yeston's musical *Nine*, based on Federico Fellini's autobiographical film *8 1/2*. By 1978, Ashman was looking for a composer for his next musical: *God Bless You, Mr. Rosewater*, an adaptation of the 1965 novel by Kurt Vonnegut. At the time, Menken saw himself as a composer-lyricist. He was not especially interested in writing to someone else's words, but he agreed to the meeting. Alan and Janis Menken lived at Manhattan Plaza, at 400 West Forty-third Street, which offered federally subsidized housing for actors, artists, and musicians. An upright piano occupied one corner of the light-filled den, where Menken would compose; the room was decorated with potted plants. Enter Howard Ashman, in torn jeans, a bomber jacket with a fur collar, and a muscle shirt. Unshaven, he was smoking Marlboro Lights. "He was not the bright-eyed, bushy-tailed, potential collaborator that one normally meets," Menken explained. "He was another breed." The composer played his material, including such songs as "Pink Fish," in which a non-Jew first encounters smoked salmon on a sliced bagel. The potential collaborators discussed Vonnegut, and Ashman promised to get in touch soon. "He led with the tougher side first," Menken observed.[90]

Almost five years had passed since Ashman and Stuart White moved to New York City; now Ashman ran a not-for-profit theatre with state and federal funding. How did this happen? The WPA Theatre was part of the Off-Off-Broadway scene. Alternatives to the commercial New York theatres appeared in the early twentieth century in the "Little Theatre" movement; often these were amateur or social organizations based in Greenwich Village. By the 1930s, the term "Off-Broadway" entered usage.[91]

But Off-Broadway is not a place; it is a contract. In 1913, a group of New York actors formed a union, the Actors' Equity Association. Throughout history, actors were treated poorly—considered just a notch above beggars and thieves. Equity, as the name suggests, would determine fair and equitable salary and work conditions. Through the union's bargaining strength, Broadway producers agreed to adhere to an Equity contract, but the union also made provision for smaller theatres (Off-Broadway) that met certain criteria. For those artists who found Off-Broadway a little too mainstream, there emerged an Off-Off-Broadway movement, in the 1960s, represented by small venues such as Caffe Cino and LaMaMa Experimental Theatre Club.[92] Elizabeth L. Wollman describes companies that "pushed the boundaries of what was considered theatrically appropriate."[93] Again, Actors' Equity created a path: its members could appear in what was called an Equity Showcase, which would limit the number of seats in the theatre and limit the number of performances. This was a model for producing shows Off-Off-Broadway.

The cost of entry was low. For a fifty-dollar filing fee, you could found a not-for-profit company in the State of New York. Three partners—Virginia Aquino, David Gale, and Harry Orzello—incorporated the WPA Theatre and filed on November 24, 1970.[94] The name recalled Franklin Roosevelt's WPA of the 1930s, but now the letters stood for Workshop of the Players Art Foundation, Inc. Through the early 1970s, the WPA would mount seasons of plays, usually autumn to spring, with a mix of revivals and new works. In 1976, the company presented *Dreamstuff*, an update of *The Tempest*, with music by Marsha Malamet, lyrics by Dennis Green, and book by Howard Ashman. Malamet and Green were members of the BMI Workshop; they participated from 1974 until 1976.[95] Further, Malamet achieved a piece of eminence denied to the young Alan Menken: she recorded as a singer-songwriter, with a début album, *Coney Island Winter*, released by Decca Records in 1969. James Dennis Green, known as Dennis, conceived the idea of a musical about contemporary Americans who "sail through the Bermuda Triangle and end up on Prospero's island." At BMI, Malamet and Green developed the show and presented a number of songs. A friend named Otts Munderloh, who knew Ashman from Baltimore, connected Ashman and the *Dreamstuff* team.[96] James Nicola directed the piece at the WPA, on the Bowery. But the show encountered an unfriendly review from Clive Barnes, in the *New York Times*, who wrote that "it never quite comes together."[97]

Stephen G. Wells was a "fledgling producer" who added enhancement money to *Dreamstuff*. When he was eighteen, his father, a Wall Street attorney, died, leaving young Wells an inheritance with which to play.[98] He hoped to launch *Dreamstuff* in a commercial run Off-Broadway, but the *Times* review made this difficult. Then something unexpected happened. Harry Orzello and his partners decided they were done. The New York City Fire Department shut down the WPA Theatre; the cost to upgrade the space was prohibitive. In lieu of monies owed, Orzello offered the WPA to Stephen Wells: here's a not-for-profit theatre with some funding and a good reputation.[99] So, in 1977, a new WPA Theatre was born in the shell of the old. Wells admired Ashman's work and invited him to be the artistic director. Ashman made a counter-proposal:

he wanted to be co-artistic director with his romantic partner, Stuart White.[100] Dennis Green, who was friendly with both, thought that it was an attempt to save their relationship. Once in New York City, White's wild side emerged: "constantly drinking, seeing other people," as Ashman complained.[101] The WPA would give them something to do together. White could exercise his talents as a director; Ashman could write new plays and musicals. They asked another friend, Kyle Renick, to operate the theatre day to day. Born in 1948, he had light brown hair, a round face, and high cheekbones. His two great loves were the opera and automobiles.[102] If Ashman and White were artists, visionaries, then Renick was the businessman, "the backbone of the operation."[103] He would find the money so they could play.

With the space on the Bowery condemned, the collaborators needed a new home. They found it at 138 Fifth Avenue, a four-story building near the corner of Nineteenth Street. This was not Fifth Avenue as depicted in films and television—fashionable, with high-end shops and imposing hotels. This was *lower* Fifth Avenue, a dump in the 1970s and "scary at night," in Renick's words.[104] At this point, another founding member joins the tale: Edward T. Gianfrancesco, whom Sarah Ashman called a "master carpenter."[105] Born in Providence, he attended the University of Rhode Island, where he studied fine arts and adopted a curious nickname, Hawk, which derived from *Up the Down Staircase*, a 1964 novel. Through Kyle Renick, Hawk arranged to meet the co-artistic directors in their apartment, in Chelsea, and presented his portfolio. Comparing himself to Ringo Starr, he said, "I came along at the right time." Ringo became a Beatle in time for a recording contract, Beatlemania, and global success; Hawk joined the WPA when it was time to build. The second floor at 138 Fifth Avenue was available—a loft, around twenty-five by one hundred feet. "This would be a perfect space for a small theatre," Hawk said. "We went in and completely gutted the entire space, from stem to stern, and I designed a new theatre." He built a black-box theatre space, with ninety-eight seats—then the Equity maximum for an Off-Off-Broadway contract—as well as dressing rooms, rest rooms, and offices. Facing Fifth Avenue, with oversized windows, was a rehearsal space.[106] To ascend to the second floor, you could take the stairs or "a rickety rackety elevator."[107] The top floor of the building was occupied by Chopsticks Health Club, which was in fact a brothel. Hawk remembered Korean women in pink, sheer outfits. Others who rode the elevator noticed the shy glances of the Chopsticks patrons, going up or going down.[108]

Kyle Renick secured donations to get the new theatre underway, including five thousand dollars from LuEsther T. Mertz, an owner of Publishers Clearing House. Renick and his five co-founders—Ashman, Hawk, Wells, White, and lighting designer Craig Evans—contributed their work at the start.[109] They were able to mount a full season of plays in 1977 and 1978, beginning with a revival of *The Ballad of the Sad Café*, an Edward Albee adaptation of the Carson McCullers novella, which began performances in the new space on October 13, 1977. This all-important first production was directed by Stuart White. In the words of Stephen Wells, "he had very strong proclivities for the Tennessee Williams/William Inge axis of American drama. He was masterful at evoking mood."[110] This was the kind of theatre the new company could produce: small, spare, intimate, compelling.

The next production surprised everyone: *Gorey Stories*, based on the work of American gothic writer Edward Gorey, who specialized in Victorian parlors and dying children. A team of commercial producers decided to mount the show on Broadway, and it re-opened a year later at the Booth Theatre.[111] Sarah Ashman admired the can-do spirit of these early productions, which she described as "Hey, kids, let's put on a show!" As the WPA grew, others arrived to join the effort. One was Paul Mills Holmes, also from Maryland, who became a stage manager: "We were all just a bunch of kids trying to figure out what show business was." Further, as Sarah explained, the WPA "was a wonderful incubator."[112] As a not-for-profit, non-commercial entity, the theatre was spared the capitalist urge to make money. Subscribers and donors underwrote the cost of producing all the shows. But if a given play had potential, it could move to a commercial theatre, on Broadway or Off. This was the model of *Hair* and *A Chorus Line*; both were Broadway musicals that began in small, non-commercial venues, which invited experimentation. Both shows proved their commercial viability and ran for years—and earned cash for the original producing organization, the Public Theater.[113]

In the second WPA season, it would be Howard Ashman's turn; he would write and direct a musical adaptation of *God Bless You, Mr. Rosewater*, as an

Equity Showcase. He turned to his *Dreamstuff* songwriting team, composer Marsha Malamet and lyricist Dennis Green, and proposed the novel as their next collaboration. This time, Malamet said no. She had just signed an exclusive music-publishing deal with Herb Alpert's company, which she believed prevented her from working on outside projects.[114] So Ashman went shopping for a composer and found Alan Menken. Menken and Green began writing the score; Ashman would write the book and direct the show at the WPA.

By the time the songwriters had finished three or four songs, Ashman asked to meet with Green and pitched the idea of collaborating on the lyrics instead. "I was a little taken aback," Green recalled. But he added, "I could read between the lines." He understood that Ashman "wanted to test his lyric-writing skills." Further, Green had less enthusiasm for *Rosewater* and felt that other Vonnegut novels were better, such as *Cat's Cradle*, from 1963.[115] So Green offered to step aside; Stephen Wells called him "one of the most amenable people you'll ever meet."[116] As a result, Green earned a credit for "Additional Lyrics" and a corresponding royalty. Two Menken-Green songs remained in the score: "Thank God for the Volunteer Fire Brigade" and "Since You Came to This Town."[117]

So a new songwriting team was born. Alan Menken and Howard Ashman were a study in contrast: Menken was short, straight, married, the bourgeois son of a New York dentist; Ashman was tall, gay, bitingly sardonic, from a working-class family in Baltimore. "In my collaboration with Howard, I consider myself to be a very powerful catalyst," Menken said. "But Howard was the driving wheel. No question." In their first creative meeting, they worked on "I, Eliot Rosewater," the final song in the show. Menken sat at the upright piano in his apartment and read the typed lyrics before him. "I sort of commented on a structure," he recalled, but Ashman's long forefinger reached over his shoulder and pointed at the words on the page: "Look, just—just set what's there, and then we'll talk about it."[118]

Another collaborator who worked with Ashman argued that everything was right there on the page: "he had thought of the rhythm; he had thought of the pacing; he had structured the songs."[119] Sarah Ashman, who observed the new partnership as it developed, explained that "Alan was malleable and was willing to listen to Howard and willing to say, 'Oh, you want to do a pastiche?

Great, we can do this!'"[120] Later, Ashman complimented his new writing partner in the following terms: "a very patient and willing and adaptable composer."[121] However, Ashman's relationship with Stuart White did not survive the development of the new musical. White ceded the WPA terrain to Ashman and producing partner Kyle Renick. "It was like a divorce," a mutual friend said.[122] Thereafter, White would pursue other projects and occasionally return to direct a play at the theatre they all built together.

God Bless You, Mr. Rosewater is a novel about money. It concerns one of the largest fortunes in the United States, which some clever lawyers transfer to a charitable foundation in order to avoid taxes.[123] The book's hero, Eliot Rosewater, revels in giving money away, first from his offices in New York City and then from his family seat, the depressed and dispossessed county of Rosewater, Indiana (Vonnegut's home state, where Ashman and White went to grad school). Giving money away, he must be crazy, so another lawyer decides to sue Eliot Rosewater on behalf of a neglected branch of the family. The obvious question is this: why adapt *God Bless You, Mr. Rosewater*, out of all the books and stories in the world? The novel was published in 1965, around the time that Ashman discovered *The Little Shop of Horrors*. He recalled that he read the book when he was seventeen.[124] Both stories captured his young imagination. In the case of *Rosewater*, Menken identified a "classic structure"; the protagonist "has something he wants to do that everyone is against, and he finally accomplishes it."[125] Further, there is the coincidence of name: Ashman's middle name was Elliott (his parents chose this particular spelling). "I think what Howard fell in love with was that character," his sister added. "I always think Howard had a lot of Eliot Rosewater in him."[126] In a conversation with his wife, the title character articulates a mission statement for the rest of his life. "I'm going to be an artist," he says.

"An artist?"

"I'm going to love these discarded Americans, even though they're useless and unattractive. *That* is going to be my work of art."[127]

The musical version of *Rosewater* opened at the WPA Theatre on May 17, 1979, Ashman's twenty-ninth birthday. Tickets cost three dollars each.[128] During rehearsals, when he was pressed for time, the director asked Dennis Green to work on the occasional lyric; in this way, Green contributed to two more songs.[129] An important step was the approval of Vonnegut himself. He attended a presentation at the WPA, ascending to the second floor and finding an open seat in the black-box theatre. "He sat through it with kind of a poker face," Green recalled. But at the end, the novelist literally skipped up the aisle.[130] Embracing the adaptation of his book, Vonnegut later hosted an opening-night party for the cast and crew, a party that Menken remembered well. "I discovered this drink called the White Russian," he said; the result was "the first time I ever got roaring sick in my life."[131]

Off-Off-Broadway productions such as this one did not always command reviews. There were many little theatres producing little shows. But twelve days after the opening, the *New York Post* ran a glorious review by Clive Barnes, who had dismissed *Dreamstuff*, when he worked for the *Times*. Now writing for the *Post*, he begins, "Once in a while something utterly beguiling and surprising happens on the New York stage." After praising the performances, "the cheerful music and supple lyrics," the review concludes, "This show should find some appropriate Off-Broadway theater and settle down for a happy while."[132]

Kurt Vonnegut agreed. He assigned the commercial rights to his daughter Edith, assisted by an attorney, Donald C. Farber, who wrote a book on how to produce shows.[133] They staged a backers' audition at the WPA and raised $400,000 to re-mount *Rosewater* Off-Broadway, as Barnes suggested. Warner Bros., the Hollywood film studio, invested $100,000 on behalf of its theatrical division, run by Claire Nichtern.[134] The producers settled on the Entermedia Theatre, on Second Avenue and Twelfth Street. Formerly a Yiddish theatre and previously known as the Phoenix and the Eden, the Entermedia was where *The Best Little Whorehouse in Texas* played in 1978, prior to its own move to Broadway.

However, after running his own company, Ashman did not enjoy the interventions of his new producing team. "Too many people were talking to him," Sarah Ashman said, "and he lost his own vision."[135] In particular, the director clashed with Claire Nichtern. His assistant at the time, Nancy Parent (recent graduate of Indiana University), observed the conflict. Nichtern was a generation older than Ashman; she worked in the theatre in the 1950s and 1960s and expected a certain amount of deference. "He wasn't a good placater," Parent explained, "because he knew he was right." Eventually, Nichtern wanted to fire the director, who proved to be so intractable.[136] Menken recalled one meeting between the opponents, in which "Howard sat there popping valiums, very, very openly and expansively." The composer said that "Howard needed to be in control."[137]

Previews began in September 1979, with an opening night in October. The musical did not change much from its first incarnation at the WPA. One song was cut; a new song, "Plain, Clean, Average Americans," added humor to the second act. But the show that was so appealing got lost in the new space. Menken described the Entermedia as "a big, Broadway-size house"; Renick ultimately felt that it was "the wrong choice for an intimate musical."[138] At the WPA, *Rosewater* was "bright colors and high energy," Sarah Ashman remembered. At the Entermedia, "there was a lot of wood in the set, and it was very dark," according to Nancy Parent. "It just didn't resonate."[139]

God Bless You, Mr. Rosewater closed in November. Despite its success at the WPA, the first musical by Ashman and Menken was a commercial failure. "We were both depressed," Ashman said. "I decided that the next show we worked on would have to be something that was *fun*."[140]

Chapter Two

Adaptation: How to Make a Nightmare Sing

Damn Yankees, a musical about baseball, opened on Broadway in 1955. The show is a modern retelling of *Faust*: a man makes a deal with the devil (or some equivalent demon) to become younger and play ball for the Washington Senators, a team frequently defeated by those damn Yankees. Twenty-five years later, New York must have seemed ready for another baseball musical. A sportswriter named Robert W. Creamer approached Frederick Coffin, the actor who had portrayed the lead in *God Bless You, Mr. Rosewater*. Creamer was the author of a 1974 biography, *Babe: The Legend Comes to Life*. As it happens, Coffin bore a striking resemblance to the legendary Babe Ruth, a player for the Boston Red Sox and the inevitable Yankees. Coffin agreed to take on the baseball project, and he recommended the songwriting team responsible for *Rosewater*: Howard Ashman and Alan Menken.[1]

Babe, as their next musical was to be called, already had a bookwriter attached, whom "Howard could not stand," according to Menken. Ashman called this writer "a mean drunk."[2] Nevertheless, Ashman and Menken wrote five songs for *Babe* as they developed the project as a starring vehicle for Fred Coffin, who was so winning in *Rosewater*. Ashman had no fondness for baseball; Menken and his wife, Janis, took him to a game just to give him a feel for it.[3] But Ashman's assistant, Nancy Parent, mentioned "a nostalgia for the time period."[4] Further, he was intrigued by the story of Babe Ruth as a working-class man from an immigrant family in Baltimore who achieved eminence because of his unique gifts. One of the songs, "Hero," develops the idea that Ruth was in some ways commonplace, an everyman:

> He wasn't always a hero.
> He was nineteen once like you and me.
> Yeah, he was green once
> And fresh out of Baltimore, MD.[5]

Another highlight of the musical-in-process was "Growing Boy," with a lyric that revels in culinary detail: "candied yams," "crown roast of pork," "biscuits," and "cherry sauce." Ashman himself was an excellent cook, who enjoyed preparing stews and roasts—comfort food—for guests.[6] He would continue to look for song opportunities about food and cooking and feeding.

Around the same time, he suggested a different idea to Menken. Ashman wanted to write a musical with "some sort of large gimmick sitting in the middle of it"—something to distinguish their next musical from all the other shows playing in New York.[7] It was at this point that Ashman remembered the low-budget film about Seymour and his carnivorous plant: "*Little Shop* came back to me." He identified the project's appeal: "The plant is a lot of fun, and it's the plant that attracted me to it." Further, he explained, "I don't think anybody else has done a monster movie for the stage. We've had horror pieces for the stage."[8] *Sweeney Todd*, by Stephen Sondheim and Hugh Wheeler, opened on Broadway in 1979, billed as "A Musical Thriller." *The Rocky Horror Show*, which premiered in 1973 and then became a perennial midnight movie, blends a haunted-house narrative with B-movie science fiction, as explained in its opening number, "Science Fiction Double Feature."

But Ashman was thinking about another cultural phenomenon: the Muppets. Jim Henson's Muppets reached a wide audience through *Sesame Street* and then *The Muppet Show*, which began syndication in 1976. Miss Piggy, performed by Henson's protégé Frank Oz, was beloved. She appeared on magazine covers—a fashion icon like her near namesake, Twiggy.[9] Ashman connected the Muppets to his ambition for *Little Shop of Horrors*: "The very first conceptual thing we started with was the plant was to be Miss Piggy. The plant was to have very, very human qualities; the plant was to have a funny, hip, smart personality; the plant was to sing and dance; the plant was to be the star of the show."[10]

Kyle Renick, producing director of the WPA, contacted Roger Corman about the rights on April 5, 1980: "I am writing to request your permission to present a small, intimate musical adaptation of your film, THE LITTLE SHOP OF HORRORS, as one of the five productions of the WPA Theatre's 1980–81 Season." Renick mentioned the theatre's track record; a recent production, *Nuts*, would soon transfer to a Broadway run.[11] Nine days after this letter, Corman himself responded: "I have no objections to your presenting a musical adaptation of THE LITTLE SHOP OF HORRORS; however, before you proceed any further, a written proposal should be submitted to our attorney, Ms. Barbara Boyle." The filmmaker added that he had received a similar request from a theatre company in Paris, although the French adaptation was never realized. He also felt that such a show would be "better suited for a New York audience."[12] Negotiations between the WPA and Corman's company took over a year, so plans for *Little Shop* were postponed until the following season.

In the meantime, Ashman and Menken worked on a revue, *Real Life Funnies*, based on a *Village Voice* comic strip. Ashman wrote the adaptation, Menken the music and lyrics. The show opened at the Manhattan Theatre Club in February 1981 and earned a savage review from Frank Rich in the *New York Times*: "The listless score that accompanies this material is the work of Alan Menken, who collaborated with Mr. Ashman last season on the flop musical version of Kurt Vonnegut's 'God Bless You, Mr. Rosewater.'" The review found *Real Life Funnies* to be inferior to the work of Stephen Sondheim and, worst of all, not very funny.[13] Menken's manager, Scott Shukat, referred to the notice as "the Frank Rich review that just about drove Menken out of the theater."[14] At this point, the collaborators would need to carefully consider what to write next. In baseball terms, they now had two strikes. Three and you're out.

While mulling over possibilities for his next musical, Ashman set up a screening for some friends to introduce them to Corman's film. In attendance were his agent, Esther Sherman, of the William Morris Agency; Nancy Parent; her boyfriend, Michael Serrian; Sarah Ashman; and her boyfriend, Ron Gillespie. Gillespie had a real-world job, at IBM, and he lived with Sarah on West 55th Street, in midtown Manhattan. "We were the first on the block, so to speak, to have a Betamax," Sarah said of their videocassette player. "We got the tape."¹⁵ So a party was held at Ron and Sarah's to watch *The Little Shop of Horrors*. The screening did not go well. "We just thought it was awful," Nancy Parent recalled. "We all said, 'You're crazy. Don't do this!'" Ashman explained the film's unusual provenance: "It was made in two days on a bet in 1960 on the set of another film."¹⁶ Sarah understood that *The Little Shop* was "campy and silly," but "we were all just worried because *Rosewater* had hurt, and he got hurt." She continued, "None of us wanted to see him get hurt again." However, "this just seemed like a bad idea." They discussed the challenge of presenting the plant on stage. Gillespie thought that it could be invisible, like the rabbit in the 1944 Broadway play *Harvey*: a "presence that we tacitly acknowledge." Ashman had a better idea. "Are you familiar with the Muppets?" he asked. Gillespie feared that Ashman was "dragging this further down into the sewer."¹⁷ Esther Sherman, the agent, thought that her client was "out of his mind." She couldn't imagine selling this show to a producer. "All I can say is it's a good thing you've got your own theatre."¹⁸ So Ashman shared his passion for this bizarre little movie, and they rejected it. A frustrating experience. But he was undaunted.

Looking at Corman's film, they couldn't see what he saw. Something about *The Little Shop* captivated Ashman's attention as a child and resonated with him years later. Menken thought that *Babe* and *Little Shop* "were equally good," but the disagreeable collaborator made the baseball project less appealing. For *Little Shop*, Howard Ashman could write the book and lyrics, direct the show, and produce it in his own theatre. He would have control.

It is curious to observe that Ashman and Menken's dueling projects of 1981 divide the essential elements of *Damn Yankees*: baseball and Faust. *Babe*, despite Ashman's limited love of the game, would necessarily be an homage to the all-American sport, and *Little Shop* features a young man who makes a pact with a devilish plant in order to achieve his desires. In choosing *Little Shop*, the songwriters selected the Faustian side of *Damn Yankees*. *Babe* was left to languish as the team began to focus on the monster musical.

Their first task was one of adaptation: how to turn Corman's nasty little shocker into a musical with characters who sing. American musicals of the "Golden Age" and thereafter are typically adapted from some other medium—a book, a memoir, a collection of short stories. For example, seven of the nine

Broadway musicals by Rodgers and Hammerstein are based on something else: novels, plays, or the life of Maria von Trapp and her singing stepchildren.[19] Films were adapted less often, and there are three reasons why. In the mid-twentieth century, the motion picture was still a newer medium, lacking the cultural authority of print. Second, there were literally fewer movies available in, say, 1950, than in subsequent decades. Third, and most important, films were ephemeral. You could not hold them in your hand or place them on the shelf, as Andrew Sarris explains: "We went to the movies and came back home. The movies themselves came and went and almost never returned."[20] Nevertheless, there are exceptions: *Silk Stockings*, a 1955 Cole Porter musical, was adapted from the romantic comedy *Ninotchka*; *Sweet Charity*, from 1966, drew inspiration from Federico Fellini's *Nights in Cabiria*. By the early 1970s, the dark satire *All about Eve* was transformed into *Applause*, and Ingmar Bergman's *Smiles of a Summer Night* became the Sondheim-Wheeler collaboration *A Little Night Music*. All of these cinematic sources are, in various ways, good. Yet in 1958, Walter Kerr wrote an unfavorable review of the musical *Oh, Captain!* and suggested, "Perhaps they should try making Broadway musicals out of bad movies." Lyricist Tim Rice agreed that a kind of topsy-turvydom may be at work: "if someone says, 'Hey, what a great idea for a musical!', it usually isn't."[21] In 1981, Ashman and Menken embarked on this peculiar challenge: to adapt a work that is woefully, willfully inept.

Ashman had already musicalized William Shakespeare and Kurt Vonnegut, so he had clear ideas about what works. "Adapting is like reading and talking to your friend about what you read," he suggested. "Adapting is saying: this is what struck me about that thing I saw, about that thing I read, about this story that appeals to me."[22] *The Little Shop of Horrors*, by Roger Corman, is no masterpiece. But Ashman wanted to share his teenage enthusiasm for it: he saw *The Little Shop* "as hip and funny and smart in a certain way." He continued, "I want you to have the experience that I had when I saw that film, so I transform it."[23]

To transform *The Little Shop* for the stage, Ashman and Menken had to choose an approach and decide where to begin. The perennial musical-theatre question is: which came first, music or lyrics? Lehman Engel recommended that writers begin with an outline; indeed, Ashman began by writing a few.[24] He watched the Corman film once again, this time with a lined, yellow notepad in front of him. He proceeded to sketch out the story beats one at a time, without judgment—an act of transcription. Names are unstable in the 1960 film. There is no list of character names on screen, and producers of low-budget fare generally did not offer press kits to share such relevant data. On the page, Ashman recorded the name "GRAVIS MUSHNIK," the owner of the florist shop.[25] But in the film, the sign outside the store reads, "MUSHNICK'S FLORIST." Apparently, this spelling is incorrect, "because the movie's art director didn't know any better."[26] Ashman would write "Mushnik" or "Mushnick" hereafter. More confusion surrounds Seymour's last name, which has variously appeared as Krelboin and Krelboined. Ashman wrote, "KRELLBORN"—an interesting variant.[27] Now Seymour is born of a "krell," which resembles *krill*—tiny crustaceans that are devoured by whales. Otherwise, this outline follows Corman's film rather closely. In one instance, Ashman misheard or changed a location. Seymour, in the film, claims that he found his unusual plant on Central Avenue, a street in Los Angeles. Ashman wrote, "2nd AVE," which is on the east side of Manhattan.[28] Now the story takes place in New York.

There are three more early, handwritten outlines of uncertain date. Ashman was fond of scribbling down ideas and doodling in the margins, but did not make note of *when*. One of these outlines is the opposite of the plodding list of beats from the 1960 film. As an experiment, Ashman rethought and reimagined *The Little Shop*. To escape the tyranny of his source material, he changed the names of the characters: Seymour became Bernie, another nebbishy name. His boss, Mushnik, was rechristened Mr. Bush, rhyming with *Mush* and perhaps inspired by George Herbert Walker Bush, recently installed as Vice President of the United States: "The boss is sadistic to Bernie + boss is a slumlord creep à la Bush." Audrey also acquired a new name, Myra, and a career trajectory unmentioned in Corman's film. According to the outline, she worked in a kosher dairy restaurant, which has closed. In the same location, there appears a new establishment, the "Pussy Palace," and Myra works there. Further, this outline opens with a question: "Where does the plant come from? Bernie sends away for things—inflatable women, shrimp, cheese, medals + answered an ad for a living grapefruit tree. Instead, he got this weirdo. ('You're a weirdo, too, Bernie,' it seemed to sing to me)." This last parenthetical is somewhat obscure, but it does suggest a musical moment. In any case, the outline ends with a three-way confrontation: man, woman, and plant. "He confesses to her about the murders. She confesses to him about working in the Pussy Palace. The plant uses insidious psychological tactics + pushes Bernie over the edge. He kills Myra." Ashman would soon abandon these invented names—Bernie, Bush, and Myra—but the character of Audrey would retain the complexity of Myra's hidden past.[29]

Another outline, just one page, reduces the story to eight major beats, sketched out in cursive and then redrafted in all capital letters. Now Ashman was thinking in terms of musical theatre; song titles appear, including "Grow for Me" and "Worse He Treats Me." However, the first three beats hew closely to the Corman original: "1. Prologue. 2. Shop. 3. Sey[mour]'s house." The penultimate beat in this outline generates a potential climax when Seymour is tempted by "TV offers, chain of stores, etc. and Audrey." Another innovation is that Audrey gains a boyfriend; in Corman's film, there is no rival for her affections. This new character is merged with the thief in the 1960 film (played by screenwriter Charles Griffith). Ashman wrote, "Boyfriend attempts a robbery because store is now so successful." The result? "Seymour feeds 'bf' to plant."[30]

Next, a three-page outline expands the story into thirteen beats and thirteen musical numbers. Again there is a prologue, followed by "FIRST SHOP SCENE," which begins, "Mushnik about to fire Seymour. Seymour secretly loves Audrey. Mushnik may have to close the shop, even. Sey. is given his one last chance—he'll bring plant in." The third beat in this outline develops the main character's motivation. Seymour speaks to his plant, "I'm a zero—help me, huh?" At this point, Ashman wrote the phrase "All the things I want," and the last two words are heavily underlined. "I Want" is a key phrase in musical-theatre construction, and the authors would continue to focus on what Seymour and Audrey want. This same outline contains potential song titles and moments. On the first page, Ashman queried, "SONG: SKID ROW?" Other song titles appear throughout: "MY SON," "SEYMOUR'S SOLILOQUEY [sic]," and "DOLLY SONG AUDREY!" In these early versions, Ashman conceived of a song similar to the title number in *Hello, Dolly!*, the 1964 Jerry Herman musical. Later in the evening, there would be a "MONEY + POWER SONG" and a

"LOVE SONG."[31] Ashman claimed to enjoy this part of the process: building a musical through story beats and song ideas. "It's a puzzle," he said.[32]

But he was not just sketching a theoretical musical on the page; his intention was to produce the show at his own theatre. To accommodate the near-zero budget of the WPA, Ashman addressed cast size, characterization, and plot. The film is to some extent theatrical: the majority of the story takes place in the florist shop. Corman himself commented, "That is why this became such an easy film to adapt to the stage."[33] In fact, Corman's budgetary limitations would lend themselves to those of the WPA. Then there was the issue of cast size. *Rosewater* had a cast of fourteen (plus understudies), which added to the weekly running costs when it played Off-Broadway. Ashman decided to craft his next show with a smaller ensemble. On the three-page outline mentioned above, he jotted a list of key characters:

MUSH.
~~2 GIRLS~~
SEYMOUR
AUDREY
~~PLANT VOICE~~
2 COPS
~~MOM~~
1 GARDEN SOC[IETY]. LADY
~~DENTIST~~
CUSTOMER

Note that he crossed out four items on the list (some of these would return).[34] To those familiar with the film, it is striking how many characters Ashman removed. The stage play dispatches with Seymour's mother, Burson Fouch, Hortense Fishtwanger, Wilbur Force, two police officers, a prostitute, and a local yenta named Mrs. Shiva (although her name is mentioned in the play).[35]

Ashman focused his narrative on four principals: Seymour; his boss, Mr. Mushnik; coworker Audrey; and the plant, Audrey Junior.[36] Curiously, Ashman changed her name to Audrey II—now she is a sequel, like *Jaws 2* and *Smokey and the Bandit II*, the imaginative successor to an original.[37] One minor character that Ashman expanded is the dentist, Phoebus Farb, whom Ashman renamed Mervin Goldsmith, then Orin Goldsmith, and finally Orin Scrivello, DDS. In the three-page outline, Ashman crossed out the phrase "Audrey in love w/dentist"—a story beat that would be saved for later.[38] The dentist in Corman's film appears in a somewhat irrelevant set piece; Seymour has a toothache and goes for a checkup. In the show, Orin would become the abusive boyfriend of the heroine—a monster in human form and an obstacle to Seymour's love.

In the Corman film, all the characters are white. Ashman wanted a cast that was more representative of the urban experience, as he remembered it from his childhood in Baltimore, as he lived it in New York City in the 1970s. Half of the performers would now be African American. Menken recalled that the film has "two ponytailed teenagers," who become Seymour's groupies; they incessantly hug him and cheer his success.[39] Ashman turned them into two African American women, later expanded to a trio. The plant, in the film, was voiced by screenwriter Charles Griffith, standing off-camera. In a whiny, high-pitched tone, he uttered, "Feeeeed me!" Menken countered that "[w]e wanted the plant to have a deep, New Orleans, funky kind of sound."[40] So there is a musical impetus behind these choices, but there is a sociological one as well. As a gay man, Ashman was in tune with those who felt excluded by the WASP hierarchy: women, African Americans, aliens from somewhere else. His musical version would sympathize with the downtrodden denizens of Skid Row.

Inevitably, Ashman noticed the flaws in his source material: "The plot of the film of *Little Shop of Horrors* is all over the place and falls apart in the second half. It's funny as all great get-out when you're twelve" (or "stoned and still in college").[41] He complained that the film "descends into a lot of silly chase sequences." For the stage, he said, "the story had to be more coherent."[42] Ashman observed that the characters who die and get fed to the plant are tangential, with little emotional connection to Seymour himself. The first is a homeless man (in fact, an undercover police officer); the second is the dentist; the third is a criminal who tries to rob Mushnik's shop; the fourth is an aggressive prostitute. Each death is played for laughs, in a darkly comic vein. For example, Seymour wanders the streets at night and looks for a victim to feed to his ravenous plant. He tosses a rock in the air; it lands on the head of streetwalker Leonora Clyde and kills her. Instant plant food!

Ashman's innovation: "The people in the show who die are closer and closer to Seymour."[43] First his rival (Orin Scrivello), then his boss (Mr. Mushnik), then the woman he loves (Audrey), and then himself. In Corman's film, the murders are random, silly, inconsequential. The musical digs deeper. Ashman noted "the Faustian undertones" of "the little guy who sells his soul to the devil."[44] Seymour will gain what he wants—but at a terrible cost. In the three-page outline, Ashman wrote, "The good things flood him. CBS? Movie deals? Rosebowl [sic]? Lecture tours? Chains of florists'? An agent? And finally, Audrey 1!"[45]

To write this Faustian story, the authors settled on a gothic musical idiom; "it was more like Brecht and Weill," according to Menken.[46] Again, *Sweeney Todd* may have been an influence. Much of Sondheim's score is dark and brooding, like its protagonist, a barber who seeks vengeance on the world. The first draft of *Little Shop* opens with a prologue, spoken by an off-stage voice "NOT UNLIKE GOD'S": "On September twenty-first, nineteen fifty-eight—life on Planet Earth came to its inevitable conclusion. All human existence was utterly destroyed. This is the story of how that strange occurrence came to be."[47] So the show has not even begun, and everyone is dead. Here is the opening of one of the earliest songs written, its melody filled with foreboding:

On the day that it started
All our sources confirm
Ike was out on the golf course
Mamie was having a perm
No-one told the First Lady
As she had her hair curled
That September 21, 1958
Was the start of the end of the world![48]

This song, originally called "On the Day That It Started," was renamed "All Gone." It also transitioned from opening number to closing number. A grim, final stanza was to be sung by the ensemble:

We don't pilfer the till no more
No sick dentists to drill no more
Cause they're gone

Now
We don't give in to greed no more
No Skid Row do we need no more
Cause we're gone
All gone!⁴⁹

Other early numbers recall scenes in the Roger Corman film. Audrey Junior's lament, "Feeeeed me," became a quotable catchphrase for teenagers in the 1960s. In Ashman's handwritten list of beats from the movie, he emphasized this moment: "Feed me—plant speaks for first time. Tries to squeeze more blood—Feed me <u>more</u>!"⁵⁰ Perhaps it was inevitable that Ashman and Menken would write a song entitled "Feed Me." Before the collaborators settled upon a bluesy, New Orleans sound for the plant, Menken would perform this number in a voice that resembled the whiny delivery of Chuck Griffith:

Feed me
I'm hungry
Feed me
I'm starving
Feed me
I'm fading and fast!⁵¹

But at the same time, the collaborators wrote songs such as "Audrey II," which seems to be the "Hello, Dolly!" moment identified in the outlines. This is a production number that finds Menken at his tuneful cheeriest. Ashman's lyric begins:

When it's time to pick a pet flower,
Who's the shrub we love?
Who's the potted plant of the hour?
Who's our bush, when push comes to shove,
And who rakes in that cash, those kudos,
Look Ma, who came through—
Not Audrey Hepburn or Audrey Wood,
Tho' both of them may be well and good
They're dismal failures beside the beautiful Audrey II.⁵²

Despite the merit of any one of these numbers, the early songwriting did not cohere. Menken admitted that "we did go through a long period of outlines and song styles that we discarded."[53] Ashman agreed that they "wrote the show in fits and starts."[54]

Little Shop of Horrors—as the play would be called, without the *The*—needed a musical language of its own. Ashman thought back to 1960, when the film was new. "It's about a pop-culture phenomenon," he argued. "It's about B-horror movies of 1960. So when you're looking for a musical style, you say, 'What's the music of that period?'"[55] *Little Shop of Horrors* is also a memory play of sorts: Ashman was remembering how the movie tickled his teenage imagination. In order to recapture that feeling, he decided, the play should *sound* like the popular music of the early 1960s—after the formative rock of Bill Haley and His Comets but before the British Invasion. According to Greil Marcus, "If you were looking for rock 'n' roll between Elvis and the Beatles, girl groups gave you the genuine article."[56] Indeed, Ashman grew up listening to the girl groups of the period: the Crystals, the Ronettes, the Chiffons, the Shangri-Las. For research, he began to revisit records by Phil Spector, the Bronx-born music producer who was, according to Tom Wolfe, "The First Tycoon of Teen."[57] Spector pioneered the "wall of sound": a dense musical tapestry that doubled, tripled, and quadrupled the guitars and rhythm and included backing vocals, handclaps, brass, and strings. In the recording studio, Spector would demand take after take from his musicians. Rather than use the first take or two, when the musicians were still fresh, he wanted the twentieth, the thirtieth. After hours in the studio, their playing lost much of its personality; the musicians merged into a single unit, machine-like.[58] In Ashman's view:

> I heard—something I hear to this day—something very dark and horrifying and scary as hell in the Phil Spector sound. There's a BUNK-BUNK-BUNK-TSCH, BUNK-BUNK-BUNK-TSCH. There are chains and whips in the background. There's real dark, nasty stuff going on under some of these very innocent lyrics. And if that doesn't sound like a horror movie, I don't know what does.[59]

Ashman brought a record by the Crystals to Menken's place, in Manhattan Plaza, where they usually worked by the piano. Ashman announced that this would be the sound of their show; he called it "the dark side of *Grease*." "We started over again," Menken conceded.[60]

Phil Spector's songs were not noted for the urbane sophistication of their lyrics, a criticism with which Spector himself was familiar: "why doesn't anybody write lyrics like Cole Porter anymore"?[61] Da doo ron ron ron, da doo ron ron. This was something that Ashman could bring to the form: blending the "teen-age sexual" energy of pop with musical-theatre craftsmanship.[62]

He decided to write a title song as an opening number. He may have been drawn to the phrase "Little Shop of Horrors" because it contains an internal conflict. There is something petite, and it is a "shop"—a British idiom, not even as grand as an American "store." Yet this is a shop of "horrors."[63] What could that possibly mean? Do they sell *horror*? The whips and chains required by Phil Spector? On lined, yellow paper, Ashman began to shape an opening song:

Little shop
Little shop 'o' horror
At the shop[64]

On a separate page, he made note of potential rhymes for *shop*: *chop*, *drop*, *lop*, *cop*, *hop*, *pop*, *bop*, *stop*, *top*, *mom and pop*.[65] Then he crossed out the third line above and wrote:

~~At the shop~~ Bop shoo bop

That's it! In a moment, he cracked the song. It is at once something horrifying and also bubble-gum rock: bop shoo bop. This contrast conveys the kind of evening the audience was in for. He sketched a first stanza:

Little shop,
Little shop 'o' horror.
Bop shoo bop
What a cropa terror.
Little shop
Gotta stop the horror
Oh-oh-oh-oh-no[66]

The song also deserves recognition for rhyming the nonsense syllables "shang-a-lang" with "sturm and drang," a German phrase suggesting revolutionary fervor, the heightened passions of storm and stress.[67] Again: there is a contrast between the cheerful and the morbid.

While some songs recreate the style of early rock 'n' roll, others focus on particular models; Ashman called it a "pastiche of pop music." The second number in the show, "Skid Row (Downtown)," is "a direct inversion of the Crystals' 'Uptown,'" he said.[68] Produced by Phil Spector, this song hit the pop charts in 1962. (Ashman added that his inspiration "has nothing to do with Petula Clark."[69]) The Crystals' song begins:

> He gets up each morning, and he goes downtown,
> Where everyone's his boss and he's lost in an angry land.
> He's a little man.
> But then he comes uptown . . . .

Menken's music resembles that of the original, but the collaborators reverse the polarity. Now "Downtown," Corman's Skid Row, is home. Ashman himself lived downtown, in New York's Greenwich Village, not far from the WPA Theatre. In the new song, "uptown" becomes the angry land where our downtown dwellers are subjugated:

> Uptown you're orderlies and chambermaids
> Uptown you're porters, thieves, and nurse's aides
> Your jobs are really menial
> You make no bread
> And then at five o'clock, you head—
>
> By subway—
>
> Downtown . . . .[70]

"Skid Row (Downtown)" seems like an opening number, but it was displaced by "Little Shop of Horrors." Like an opening, "Skid Row" introduces major characters and the world of the show. Ashman and Menken experimented with a number of different interludes for the song, to investigate even more terrain. The first was given to Mr. Mushnik, who offers his perspective on how Skid Row has changed over time: "Once, the neighborhood was nice down here. / We had no roaches and no lice down here."[71] His friends have abandoned the city for "the suburbs where their grandchildren play"—a migration that occurred in the years after World War II.[72] The next attempt at an interlude shifted from the sociological to the personal. Now this section was given to Seymour, who sings, "No-one seems to know I exist / Disrespected, discarded, dismissed."[73] Still unsatisfied, Ashman rewrote the interlude once again, simplifying it, getting to the heart of the matter, in plaintive language that Seymour himself might use:

> Poor!
> All my life, I've always been poor!
> I keep asking God what I'm for,
> And He tells me,
> "Gee, I'm not sure...."
>
> (19)

The songwriters continued to develop the character of Seymour in two solos: "A Little Bit Anemic" and "Grow for Me." "Grow for Me" is a 1950s-style song of loving devotion—except that it is sung by a man to a plant.[74] The form is AABA; each A ends with the song's hook and the phrase "grow for me." The time signature is 12/8, and Menken's opening piano riff uses straight eighths, resembling a doo-wop number. But "Grow for Me" advances the story as well: Seymour discovers that Audrey II is a carnivore. In the film, when the hero accidentally cuts his hand, the little pod opens its leaves. "Blood? You like blood?" Seymour asks. To write lyrics for this horticultural number, Ashman generated a list of relevant terms: "misting," "reflection + floods," "Southern exposure," "indirect light," "repotted," "pinching," "cutting back," "sunshine," and "shade."[75] An early handwritten version of the B section (the bridge or release) incorporated some of these ideas, while carefully building to the reveal, with a series of words that rhyme with *blood*:

> I've given you south[ern]. exposure.
> To get you to bud
> I've pinched you back hard, like I'm s'posed ta
> But you're still a dud.
> I've given you levels of moisture
> From desert to mud.
> I've given your growlights + minerals—
> What do you want from me? Blood?[76]

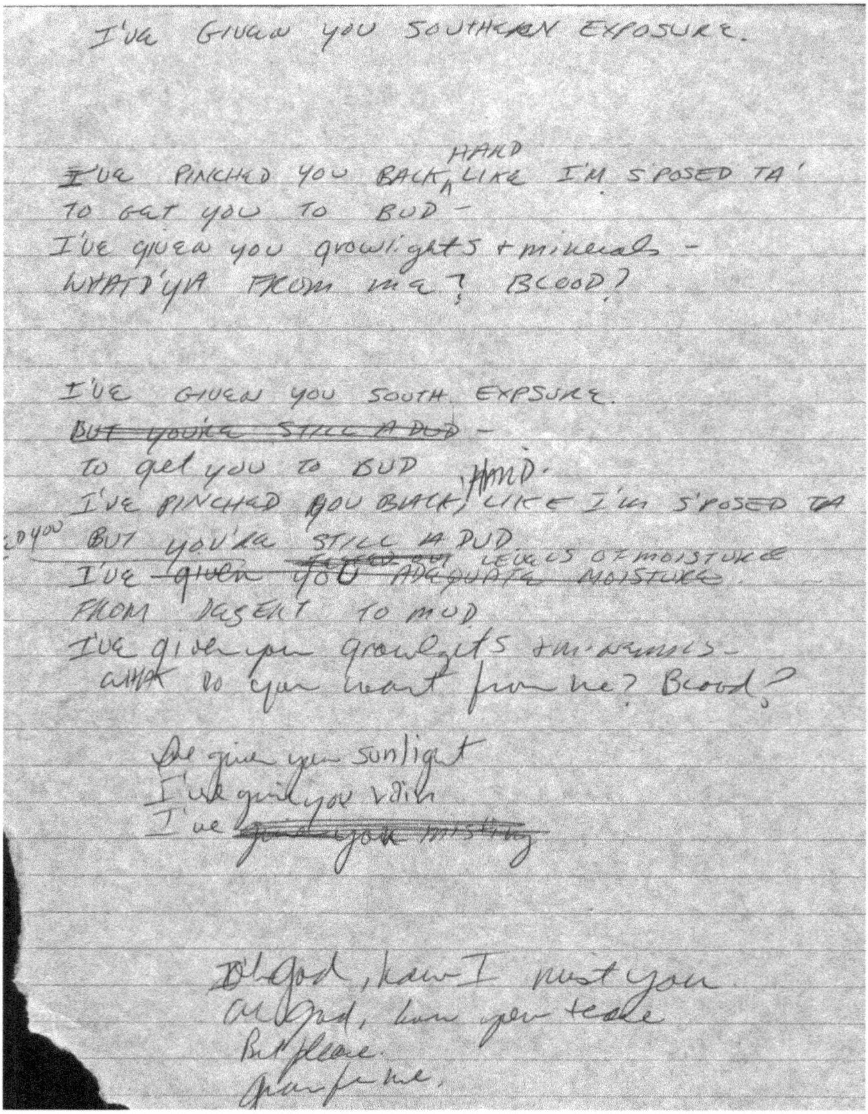

I'VE GIVEN YOU SOUTHERN EXPOSURE.

I'VE PINCHED YOU BACK, HARD LIKE I'M S'POSED TA'
TO GET YOU TO BUD —
I've given you growlights + minerals —
WHAT'D'YA FROM me? BLOOD?

I'VE GIVEN YOU SOUTH. EXPSURE.
~~BUT YOU'RE STILL A BUD~~ —
To get you to BUD
I'VE PINCHED YOU BACK, LIKE I'M S'POSED TA
TO YOU BUT YOU'RE STILL A BUD
I've ~~given you ADEQUATE~~ LEVELS OF MOISTURE
FROM DESERT TO MUD
I've given you growlights + minerals —
WHAT do you want from me? Blood?

I've given you sunlight
I've given you rain
I've ~~got you misting~~

Oh God, how I need you
Oh God, how you tease
But please
grow for me.

Figure 3 Howard Ashman's work-in-progress lyric for "Grow for Me," sung by Seymour to his plant, Audrey II.

Ultimately, Ashman decided that the bridge overemphasized the *ud* sound of *blood* and *dud*—too silly, too cartoonish. The revised lyric reads as follows:

> I've given you southern exposure
> To get you to thrive
> I've pinched you back hard,
> Like I'm supposed ta,
> You're barely alive
> I've tried you at levels of moisture,
> From desert to mud.
> I've given your grow-lights and mineral supplements.
> What do you want from me?
> Blood?
>
> (27)

During this developmental stage, the authors sought a musical language for Audrey as well. Ashman held strong views on this character, initially clarified when he called her Myra. To an interviewer, he described Audrey thus: "She's an ex-hooker with bleached-blonde hair and a black eye 'cause her boyfriend is not nice to her, and she's secretly in love with Seymour."[77] Jackie Joseph, who played Audrey in the 1960 film, was surprised when she heard this assessment: "Never in a million years did I suspect that I might look like a hooker."[78] Ashman and Menken wrote a song that focuses on Audrey's relationship with her abusive boyfriend, and the wellspring was yet another track by the Crystals, "He Hit Me (And It Felt Like a Kiss)," from 1962.[79] It is one of the darker Phil Spector recordings—already identified by Ashman as horror shows. In the *Little Shop* variation on this idea, Audrey sings:

> The worse he treats me
> The more he loves me
> It sounds unusual, I know
> But when he hurts me,
> That's how he tells me
> That he would never let me go.[80]

Sarah Ashman, who loved everything her brother wrote, felt that this number was "offensive."[81]

Besides the pop nightmares of Phil Spector, another influence was the New York–based girl group the Shangri-Las. "I already knew the Shangri-Las were funny in 1964," Ashman boasted.[82] On the very first page of the first draft of *Little Shop of Horrors*, there is a stage direction that reads, "Shouted, a la the Shangri-La's."[83] The line that follows, in the show's opening number, is drawn from one of the girl group's signature hits, "Leader of the Pack." Audrey, terrified by something, cries, "Lookout, lookout, lookout, lookout!" (This remained in the show, although in subsequent drafts it is assigned to someone else.) Other sly references follow. Later in the first draft, Audrey defends her dentist boyfriend: "Folks are *always* putting him down"; the other women on stage echo, à la the Shangri-Las, "Down, down, down."[84] These latter two lines from "Leader of the Pack" were eventually dropped. However, when audiences finally meet Orin Scrivello, DDS, he is introduced thus: "Here he is, girls, the Leader of The Plaque" (42). So *Little Shop of Horrors* recreates the popular music of the late 1950s and early 1960s and sees the world through the prism of doo-wop records and girl-group patter.

In choosing this retro musical style, Ashman and Menken would have recognized that nostalgia was in vogue. At the height of the 1960s counterculture, the earlier, Eisenhower era was already bouncing back (a counter-counterculture). Sha Na Na, the mock rock group who sang close harmony and dressed as if it were forever 1959, performed at Woodstock.[85] They sang "At the Hop," "Duke of Earl," and other outmoded numbers to the long-haired hippies on the lawn. In the 1970s, George Lucas directed *American Graffiti*, a love letter to the earlier era; Michael D. Eisner, as the vice president of ABC Television, programmed *Happy Days*, a show about growing up in the 1950s; and the musical *Grease* proceeded from Off-Broadway's Entermedia Theatre (then called the Eden) to Broadway and the big screen, in 1978, starring John Travolta and Olivia Newton-John.[86]

Ashman and Menken also recognized that they were writing an Off-Off-Broadway musical for a ninety-eight-seat theatre. They could not compete with the spectacle of a Broadway show such as *Barnum* or a West End production such as *Cats*. Three of the songs originally written for *Little Shop* contain the word *little* in their titles, to suggest the scale of the WPA and its budget: "Little Shop of Horrors," "A Little Bit Anemic," "A Little Dental Music." Yet Ashman perceived that little shows may have particular strengths. "Off-Broadway musicals have a history of handling genre satire very well," he claimed. In an interview, he mentioned three important predecessors: *The Boy Friend, Little Mary Sunshine* (*little* once again), and *Dames at Sea*.[87] Two of them—*Little Mary Sunshine* and *Dames at Sea*—were Off-Broadway hits. *The Boy Friend* began its life in London, at the Players' Theatre, an intimate venue, before the show conquered the West End and Broadway and introduced the world to the young Julie Andrews. What all three musicals have in common is that they are retrospective: each looks back at an early musical style and mode of performance. *The Boy Friend* and *Little Mary Sunshine*, from the 1950s, remember the musicals of the 1920s; *Dames at Sea*, from the 1960s, reclaims the spirit of 1930s movie musicals such as *42nd Street*. So the delay is roughly three decades. By the time of *Little Shop*, the delay is only *two* decades: the early 1960s revived in the early 1980s. Life was moving faster.[88] For Ashman and Menken, *Dames at Sea* was an important model, in part because it turns a cinematic experience into a theatrical one. (Recall that Ashman performed in the show as a grad student.) As John M. Clum explains, "*Dames at Sea* was a product of the 1960's discovery and worship of old movies, including the rediscovery of Busby Berkeley musicals."[89] Furthermore, *Dames at Sea* accomplishes a great deal with very little. With a cast of three men and three women, the show recreates the rehearsal process of a fictional Broadway musical and then a performance on a battleship. As Ashman quipped, "I was trying to write the *Dames at Sea* of horror movies."[90]

So Ashman and Menken's creative choice was a savvy commercial one as well. Audiences bought records and enjoyed films that exploited nostalgia for recent decades of Americana, and intimate musicals excelled at genre parody. *Little Shop of Horrors* would evoke an earlier era and its music with playful irreverence, yet the show would treat its characters with sympathy. Despite the rock influence on the score, Ashman believed that *Little Shop* would be "an old-fashioned musical"—the form perfected by Rodgers and Hammerstein and their successors in the mid-twentieth century. Ashman said, "It just happens to be about a man-eating plant from outer space."[91] This is the essence of *Little Shop*: a story of murder and mass annihilation, seen through the eyes of innocence. Like those that watched a flickering film on a black-and-white TV, late one night in Baltimore.

As a teenager, Howard Ashman had inadvertently plagiarized *The Little Shop of Horrors*. "Now I was all grown up," he observed, "and could probably acquire the rights and do it for real."[92] Kyle Renick, the producing director of the WPA, recalled that "[t]here was no wrangling."[93] Roger Corman was known for pinching pennies on his films, yet he now cast himself in the role of benevolent patriarch. "I was helping these young guys out," he said. "Maybe I should have been tougher."[94] What Renick and the WPA did *not* know was that Corman did not actually own the rights to his 1960 film entitled *The Little Shop of Horrors*. When producing his ultra-low-budget movies, he never bothered to copyright them. Corman did not wish to pay the filing fee or the cost of an additional print for the Library of Congress.[95] Longtime assistant Beverly Gray commented, "He came from an era where movies were considered to be disposable, like Kleenex," and Mark Thomas McGee summarized the prevailing attitude: "This is all junk anyway. Who is gonna want this two minutes after?"[96] Indeed, no one in the early 1960s imagined that *A Bucket of Blood* or *Last Woman on Earth* might have underlying rights with value in other media. Dick Miller, who appeared in *The Little Shop*, said of Corman's film: "It was public domain from the minute he made it."[97] Nevertheless, Renick negotiated in good faith with New World Pictures, Corman's latest company, and completed a deal for the stage rights on October 23, 1981.[98] A month later, the WPA sent New World the agreed-upon fee of five hundred dollars.[99] Thereafter, Roger Corman would earn one percent of the weekly box-office gross.[100]

While negotiations continued, Ashman and Menken wrote much of the show between September and November 1981.[101] "Once we found the right approach to it," Ashman recalled, "we finished it in about eight weeks."[102] During this period, they performed songs-in-progress at the BMI Workshop, founded by Lehman Engel, where Menken was a longstanding member. It was here that Ashman and Menken presented a complete draft of their new musical, with Menken at the piano, in front of Engel and his class of student-songwriters—the very first audience for *Little Shop of Horrors*. Ashman read the stage directions, rapidly, and played many of the characters himself, singing

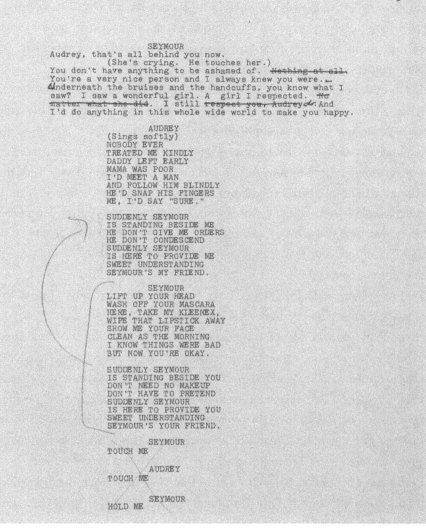

Figure 4 *An early draft of "Suddenly, Seymour." Note that the order of Audrey and Seymour's stanzas was different. The arrow indicates the corrected version. There is also a fragment of a discarded bridge, beginning with "Touch me / Touch me / Hold me."*

and acting the roles of Audrey, Mr. Mushnik, and more. Menken sang a few numbers and read opposite Ashman in the scenes. Essentially, the two writers performed the entire show that day—no actors, no sets, no costumes, no rock band, no monstrous puppet. Just two men singing at the piano. The teacher and fellow students listened politely.[103]

A number of songs would be heard for the last time: "A Little Bit Anemic," "A Little Dental Music," "The Plant Who Loves You." But the show was basically *there*. Business is bad in Mushnik's florist shop, on urban Skid Row. Seymour, an amateur botanist, offers to display his latest horticultural find. This lures new customers, but there is a catch. The plant is a carnivore. Seymour feeds the plant human flesh; it thrives and grows. It wins him public acclaim and the love of his coworker Audrey, but the body count grows as well. When Seymour can countenance no more, he tries to kill the now-gigantic monster but gets eaten alive. The authors concluded their presentation with the finale, "All Gone," and all of the characters dead.

Mild applause. Silence. Then Lehman Engel attacked the show. "This is just constant nihilism," he announced to everyone in the room. "I don't think you can do that; I don't think you can possibly get away with that." He complained about Menken's music: "I thought it was just endlessly like itself." Engel cited "the same percussive quality" and found that "one song melted into the other without relief." Further, he did not care for the title song; in fact, he preferred the previous opening number, "Skid Row." He went on for minutes. Voluble Howard Ashman was strangely silent. But Engel was the teacher, and this was his class. Menken agreed that there was some similarity in the 1950s-style accompaniments.

The other members of the class chimed in. They were not quite as harsh—but not quite enthusiastic. One mentioned that "it's certainly a grim fairy tale." The group discussed the 1978 remake of *Invasion of the Body Snatchers*, with its apocalyptic ending. Another student compared *Little Shop* to *The Twilight Zone* but argued that Rod Serling always had a "moral point" at the end of each episode. *Little Shop* seemed to lack any such message. A woman in the audience was distressed that "the hero was a murderer." In this version, Seymour kills Orin Scrivello in cold blood. Another woman suggested that the show must be "a metaphor about the end of the world." She mentioned "a neutron bomb." Ashman jumped in. "Oh, God, it's not that!"

He proceeded to tell the story of *Little Shop* from the point of view of Audrey II: "The plant came from another planet specifically to take over the world by playing upon the innate greed and nastiness of mankind." In corporate terms, "it's a very easy takeover, because all I have to do is offer the guy a Chevy and a girl, and he will do *anything*." So *Little Shop* is not a musical about Audrey or Seymour or the human characters; it is about an alien plant who wants to eat *us*. "By the end you ought to know the story I just told. If you don't, I have a problem." Ashman was frustrated with his initial audience. "That's not the show that you heard." Then: "It's terribly important to me."[104]

Most writers who get a reaction like this would be devastated. *They hated it.* The only sensible decision would be to throw it in the garbage. Or start over. Or write a musical about Babe Ruth. Everyone loves Babe Ruth, right? A normal person would be discouraged. Howard Ashman was indomitable. He knew the show he wanted; he would make them see it. Thankfully, he ran his own theatre and did not have to hold backers' auditions in order to raise the money. Sarah Ashman explained, "That was the beauty of the WPA, because you could fall on your ass, and it would run for a couple of weeks. And that was it; you were done."[105] Ashman didn't need to please Lehman Engel or a producer like David Merrick or the chiropractor from Poughkeepsie who was writing a check for ten thousand dollars. *Little Shop of Horrors* would open in the spring of 1982. As artistic director of the WPA, Ashman could schedule and direct the musical—he had creative control. But he wanted the show to be *great*.

He stuck to his vision and focused the material over the next few months as he prepared to head into rehearsals. There were three key takeaways from the presentation at BMI. First, to make it clearer that the musical was "a cautionary tale," Ashman added an unambiguous moral to the story.[106] "All Gone" was out. He and Menken wrote a new finale, with a hit-you-over-the-head title: "Don't Feed the Plants."

> They may offer you fortune and fame
> Love and money and instant acclaim
> But whatever they offer you,
> Don't feed the plants!

(95)

Next, they added more humor and energy to the piece. The two teenagers, Crystal and Ronnette, were joined by a third, Chiffon. (In various drafts, including the published edition, Ashman spelled his character Ronnette—a slight variation on the Ronettes.) All three were named for girl groups from Ashman's childhood.[107] Menken explained that the trio "functions as a Greek chorus, commenting on the action."[108] They would now sing the opening number, originally meant for the entire ensemble, and much of a new song, "Don't It Go to Show Ya Never Know." With an infectious Menken melody, this song is punctuated by onomatopoeia words straight from a 1960s comic book: BANG! CRASH! KERPLUNK! In fact, Ashman built one stanza around the unlikely rhyming sound of *unk*:

> Seymour was
> In a funk
> He was number zero
> Who'da thunk
> He'd become a hero?
> Just a punk
> He was a forgotten so and so
> Then one day
> Crash! Kerplunk!
> Don't it go to show ya never know?
>
> (31)

Third, and perhaps most importantly, the authors added emotional weight to the story. "I care about what people want and don't have," Ashman told a newspaper reporter. "That touches me."[109] Audrey's solo, "The Worse He Treats Me," was cut from the show. Ashman explained the problem: "Some people pointed out that the song made it seem that Audrey being beaten by someone was actually funny." In fact, "she is an abused woman."[110] After the presentation at BMI, Ashman and Menken wrote a new song for the character, "Somewhere That's Green." At first it was to be a duet, with Seymour, but the collaborators decided to delay the Seymour-Audrey duet until the second act.[111] Now the essence of the cut song is rendered in a couplet:

I know Seymour's the greatest
But I'm dating a semi-sadist.

(34)

Again, Ashman was thinking in terms of the Broadway shows of his childhood. "In the classic American musical," he said, "in the third slot in the show, the girl, the leading lady, has a song where she expresses her wish for something that she doesn't have."[112] In "Somewhere That's Green," Audrey expresses that wish in terms that she understands: the consumer culture of postwar America.

A matchbox of our own
A fence of real chain link
A grill out on the patio
Disposal in the sink
A washer and a dryer and
An ironing machine
In a tract house that we share
Somewhere that's green

(34–35)

"[I]t makes me cry," Ashman confessed.[113] Notice how this first stanza, which could have been treacly, is grounded by the concrete, unpoetic rhyming of "link" and "sink." In the last two lines, the internal rhyme of "share" and "Somewhere" catches the listener off-guard; the sound arrives before we anticipate it and propels the song forward—hastening toward her desire.

The bridge does not stray far; it continues to insistently rhyme with *green*: "between," "fifteen," "screen." Now Audrey imagines the comforts of domestic life:

Between our frozen dinner
And our bed-time: nine-fifteen
We snuggle watching Lucy
On our big, enormous
Twelve-inch screen

(35)[114]

There is irony here, of course, but the song does not laugh at Audrey. She is sincere in her desire: this is what she *wants*. Earlier musicals include examples of an "I Want" song, for instance, "Waitin' for My Dearie," in *Brigadoon*, and "Wouldn't It Be Loverly," in *My Fair Lady*.[115] But Ashman specialized in the form. He talked about the mundane hopes of his *Little Shop* characters: "from our sophisticated distance we might find their dreams a bit pathetic, but I hope we don't find it silly," he emphasized. "What other people want and can't seem to get is not always of their own making and that's something that moves me. That's what I write about."[116] His assertion stands at the core of *Little Shop of Horrors*: the show surprises with its ability to humanize anyone, from an extraterrestrial plant to a sweet if damaged woman like Audrey. Her dream is at once specific, with references to Betty Crocker and *I Love Lucy*, but also timeless in her desire for home, stability, and a loving partnership. To be boring and bourgeois with the person you love.[117]

Now the revised version of the musical was ready. It was early 1982. Ashman, Menken, and the WPA Theatre needed to find a cast, a choreographer, an orchestrator, and someone who could build a convincing and terrifying Audrey II for just a few thousand dollars.

Chapter Three

Opening the Shop: Designers, Auditions, Rehearsals

Marty Robinson loved monsters. "I was a horror-movie addict," he confessed. As a teenager, he saw *The Little Shop of Horrors* on television, and he was smitten. He developed the habit of watching a movie and then sketching what he saw. He drew Seymour's plant in its smallest form, when it lives in a can of instant coffee. Since Robinson's father drank Maxwell House, the son used one of the cans as a model. From this love of monster movies, Robinson segued to Halloween—season of the uncanny, the undead. "Best day of the year," he boasted. He wanted to extend Halloween all the year round, so he began dabbling in "makeup special effects," creating gashes, wounds, and monsters.[1]

Born Martin Patrick Robinson, in Michigan, in 1954, he grew up in Wisconsin and appeared in school plays. But he was always cast in character parts: "the gnomes, the Evil Eye Fleagle from *Li'l Abner*, the Luther Billises." When he was accepted at the American Academy of Dramatic Arts, in 1972, he moved to New York City—in part to escape the Midwest. Nevertheless, his acting options were limited; he was the "six-foot-two, affable Wisconsin white boy." Through puppetry, he discovered, he could play anyone: "animals, vegetables, minerals." "It was still just acting," he said. "Through an object."[2]

Robinson booked a job touring with Nicolo Marionettes; the main qualification was a driver's license. "You could either go mad, or, you know, you learn how to work a puppet," Robinson explained. "I kind of did both." Next, he worked for puppeteer Bil Baird and admired his "wonderful sculptures come to life." It was at this point that Robinson "got excited about puppetry." Anyone working with puppets in the 1970s would be aware of the Muppets. In 1981, Robinson attended an open casting call at the Ansonia Hotel, in the Upper West Side of Manhattan. He was one of the few left standing after five grueling days and got to audition for Jim Henson. Ultimately, Robinson was cast in the role of Mr. Snuffleupagus, on *Sesame Street*, replacing the original performer, Jerry Nelson, who had injured his back.[3] (Puppetry may be hazardous to your health.)

By early 1982, the not-for-profit WPA Theatre was in the market for a puppeteer. Kyle Renick recalled that three or four people interviewed.[4] One was Julie Taymor, a stage director who incorporated masks and puppetry in her work; as it happened, she was represented by Esther Sherman. Taymor recommended Martin P. Robinson.[5] She had worked with him on *The Haggadah*, produced at the Public Theater for the Jewish holiday of Passover. Soon Howard Ashman met Marty Robinson on the empty stage of the WPA. Born four years apart, they had "a similar energy and a similar excitement," Robinson observed. And they both had a "childhood obsession with the same project"—Corman's 1960 film. Ashman even mentioned his abandoned plagiarism, *The Candy Shop*. During the meeting, he talked about scenes he had in mind for the play. In the song "Don't It Go to Show Ya Never Know," he wanted Seymour to pick up the plant and move it from one spot to another, but he couldn't figure out how to make this work. Would they need two puppeteers—or three? "Just do the old fake-hand routine," Robinson replied. This was new to Ashman. Robinson explained that the actor would wear a jacket with a fake arm; underneath, his hidden hand would operate the potted plant as a puppet. Ashman loved the idea. He ended the meeting: "I think we should just get married and do this!" But Robinson was not ready to say yes. Days later, he was back on the set of *Sesame Street*, where he encountered composer Alan Menken, who had written a song for that week's episode. Menken was all enthusiasm: "Are you gonna do it? Are you gonna do it?" Robinson admitted that "Alan closed the deal."[6]

Sesame Street shot on a six-month schedule: three months in the autumn, three in the spring. During the winter break, Robinson began work on *Little*

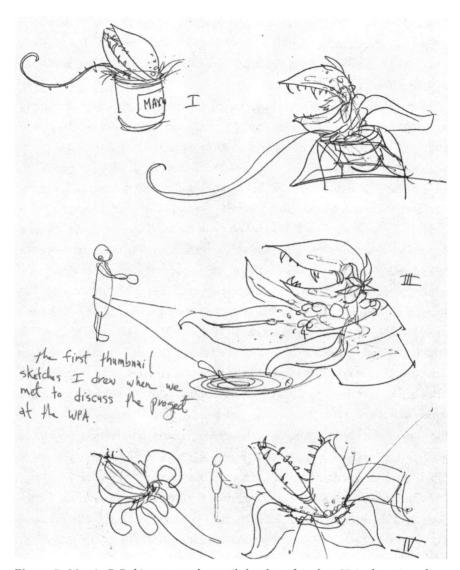

Figure 5 *Martin P. Robinson, rough pencil sketches of Audrey II, in four sizes, from a baby pod in a Maxwell House coffee can to a gargantuan monster.*

Shop of Horrors. Flush with television money, he purchased the required materials—costing around two thousand dollars, which the WPA Theatre eventually reimbursed. "I think we chipped in," Menken noted. For designing, building, and performing Audrey II, Robinson was paid a flat fee of $350.

Researching plant life for inspiration, he stumbled on a picture of a Himalayan orchid. He loved "the magentas and the purples" and "the dark greens going into the light greens and the yellows." "That's it!" he exclaimed. He found the look he wanted for Audrey II.[7]

In *The Little Shop of Horrors*, directed by Corman, the plant appears in four incarnations of increasing size. Robinson followed this model and built four puppets. "The plant starts out very cute; its face is small and blunt—it's kind of like a puppy," he explained. However, "Audrey has no face, really," he said. "She's all mouth."[8] The two smaller Audreys were traditional hand puppets. For the next two, Robinson would climb inside; they would be larger than life.

He built the smaller Audreys in his place on East Seventeenth Street: a typical downtown apartment, "with the bathtub in the kitchen and the toilet down the hall." This became Robinson's workshop. These puppets were made of Celastic, which happened to be toxic. Another puppeteer described this material as "canvas impregnated with glue" and applied "like papier maché."[9] Robinson assembled the larger puppets at the WPA. Plant No. 3 was constructed with rattan, a lightweight material used for the interior of Snuffleupagus. Robinson described the process: "It's a reed that you soak and then form in shapes, and it dries and retains the shape." He covered the rattan with chicken wire and foam, which he painted. Plant No. 4 was "bigger, heavier, more dangerous." To paint all the puppets, he used Krylon. The colors were brilliant, but the paint was toxic; yet Robinson did not wear protective gear. "I'd blow my nose, and, you know, jungle green and sunset orange." He added, "It took years off my life."[10]

While looking for a puppeteer, Ashman decided that he would not be the director. He said to Menken, "I don't want to direct this one."[11] After wearing many hats on *Rosewater*—author, lyricist, director, and artistic director of the theatre—he thought that he would share the duties with someone else. Ashman and Menken interviewed some contenders and settled on Grover Dale, a dancer and choreographer with Broadway credits. In the 1950s, he appeared in the original casts of *Li'l Abner* and *West Side Story* (as one of the Sharks). Then he delved into choreography and eventually directed Stephen Schwartz's 1974 Broadway hit, *The Magic Show*.

The future collaborators met perhaps three times. Ashman and Menken performed their musical for Dale (much as they did at BMI), and he pitched some ideas.[12] He proposed that the stage should be divided into "three different layers of reality": celestial, earth, and hell.[13] It soon became clear that Dale's vision clashed with the tone and spirit of the show as written. As Ashman recalled, "He thought that the plant should look like a big umbrella."[14] Disaster loomed. When Ashman found himself in this awkward relationship and didn't know how to end it, Menken offered a solution. "Just disagree with Grover on something," the composer said. "He won't be able to take it, and he'll go." Menken continued, "He's very thin-skinned that way."[15] So Ashman followed this advice and quarreled with Dale over a suggestion. To formally end the collaboration, Kyle Renick telephoned Grover Dale to say that it would not work out.[16]

On January 16, 1982, Ashman sent a letter of explanation to Dale, who did not handle the breakup well. That same day, the director typed a reply, which he copied to his agent, Renick, Menken, and Esther Sherman. Wounded in the extreme, Dale wrote the following:

> You twice mentioned "respect for my work" and the possibility of working together on a future project. If you're serious about either subject, how do you explain the capricious manner in which you aborted our collaboration over a single scenic issue? How do you explain denying yourself (and me) the opportunity of solving the first collaborative problem we encountered? How do you explain, once the problem got to the table, why I never heard from you again until someone on your behalf (Kyle) called two days later informing me of your decision to terminate our collaboration?[17]

Despite the grievances, the letter proves that one person knew that *Little Shop of Horrors* would be a great big hit: Grover Dale. He was laying the groundwork for a possible lawsuit and claiming certain "material" as his "exclusive property."[18] Three weeks later, on February 7, Dale sent another letter in which he sketched out "THE PLANT SCENARIO." Presumably, these pages represent his directorial ideas, although he admitted that "Ideas cannot be protected."[19]

After the Grover Dale episode, Ashman resumed the role of director. "There are some writers who are not directors and some directors who are not writers," he clarified.[20] He believed that the important criterion was the ability to see a work in its entirety. According to one observer, "Howard was the big-picture guy," while Menken focused on building a strong music department.[21] For music director and vocal arranger, they chose Robert Billig, known as Bob. Billig conducted the national tour of *The Magic Show* and served as assistant conductor on *Annie*, in 1977. Next, he worked on *The Best Little Whorehouse in Texas*, which moved from Off-Off-Broadway to Off-Broadway's Entermedia Theatre and then landed on Broadway, in 1978. Billig signed with manager Scott Shukat, who connected him with another client, Alan Menken.[22]

To create the orchestrations, Menken hired Robert Merkin, known as Robby. Born in Brooklyn, in 1951, Merkin dropped out of New York University after a Vietnam War protest. He continued his education at Queens College, where he earned a BA and MA in music. The music department in turn asked him to teach its very first course on rock. With no interest in or affinity for theatre, Merkin began to orchestrate dance and theatre pieces because he needed the money. In the early 1980s, he music directed a revue based on the songs of Carole King, entitled *Tapestry*. Merkin arranged her music for a ten-piece band, and the show premiered in New York City at Symphony Space, a one-night event for Broadway backers and producers.[23] Also in the audience was Alan Menken. At the end of the performance, he raced down the aisle: "Robby, Robby, Robby! I want you to orchestrate my next show!"

"Oh, hi, Alan," was the unenthusiastic response.[24]

They had met before. When Merkin attended NYU, he assumed that he was "the hot piano player on campus." But he soon heard talk of a rival, an upstart, named Menken—also short and Jewish and from New York. Robby Merkin decided to hear this wunderkind for himself. At the time, Alan Menken sang and played piano in a rock band of fellow students, and they needed a bassist. Since Merkin also played the bass, he showed up unannounced at one of the band's rehearsals. Seated at the piano, Alan Menken observed the newcomer without question or comment. "He looks up, and he's clearly stoned," Merkin recalled. The band played through some early Menken compositions, which Merkin admired but found too facile. So when Alan Menken asked Robby Merkin to orchestrate a new musical, Merkin did not jump at the opportunity. But Menken kept calling on the phone: "I want you to come to my apartment so I can play you this show."[25]

So Robby Merkin ventured to Manhattan Plaza, where Menken shared a rent-controlled apartment with his wife, Janis. The composer played and talked through the score of *Little Shop*; but "he's doing all the voices, and I can't follow," Merkin complained. "Eventually, his energy became infectious." Merkin recognized the sound of his childhood: "doo-wop harmonies, early rock 'n' roll harmonies." Most of all, he was impressed by "Skid Row (Downtown)," which he described as "this sophisticated combination of Motown and girl-group stuff and Phil Spector." And yet the song "clearly functioned the way a classic musical-theatre production number should." Merkin was ready to commit to the project.[26]

Reaching 138 Fifth Avenue, he took the bumpy elevator up one flight. "On the floor, on all fours, is this long guy with an enormous mane of hair," Merkin said. It was Marty Robinson, who offered "a huge grin." Merkin stepped over alien tentacles to find his way to the rehearsal room, with windows overlooking Fifth Avenue. There he saw Menken at an upright piano, Ashman lingering behind.[27]

In that first session, they refined the song "Git It" (sometimes called "Feed Me"). This number replaced the earlier "Feed Me" song, based on the whiny, Charles Griffith voice. Effectively, they were workshopping the songs before rehearsals began. Indeed, "Git It" is a model of musical-theatre songwriting; it's a miniature one-act play, with three movements. First, temptation. Second, indecision. Third, decision. The first movement begins with the plant's two-note melody on the words "Feed me!"—as emphatic and memorable as John Williams's two-note theme for another carnivore in *Jaws*. The subsequent lyrics show Ashman's mastery of musical-theatre songwriting as rhetoric: the plant wants to persuade Seymour to do something. Indicative of the plant's rhetorical power is the use of three rhymes in a row: "car," "Jack Paar," "Hedy Lamarr"; or "putz," "King Tut's," and "guts" (51). The second movement, Seymour's solo, returns to the 12/8 time signature associated with the character in two earlier songs, "Grow for Me" and "Da-Doo." Finally, Audrey and her boyfriend appear on stage. He abuses her, curses at her, slaps her in the face. This event seems to prove the plant's argument: "Alotta folk deserve to die!" (53). So the most implausible notion—that Seymour could become a killer—is now logical, necessary.

Menken imagined a four-piece ensemble, with piano, bass, and drums at the core. He would play his own piano part, and the other instrumentation would develop around it. Robby Merkin developed a triple-keyboard part: electric piano, portable organ, and synthesizer. Steve Ferrera joined the band as its drummer, and Elliot Sokolov played bass as well as saxophone (in a few numbers).

While Merkin prepared orchestrations, Ashman formed his own team, including an assistant director and a choreographer. Kyle Renick told Ashman, "I think the lighting designer's assistant wants to direct. We should meet her."[28] This was typical of the WPA's open and welcoming atmosphere—and its interest in promoting from within. *The Whales of August* was revived by the WPA in February 1982, with lighting by Phil Monat. His assistant, Constance Grappo, known as Connie, was born in Cuyahoga Falls, near Akron, Ohio. She moved to New York City in 1977 to pursue acting and studied with Uta Hagen. Vibrant and petite, with short-cropped, boyish hair, Grappo appeared as "ingénues" in plays by William Inge and Anton Chekhov before turning her sights on a directing career. In her first meeting with Ashman, she found him "super smart, fun, and a little bit snarky." Even though she had no love of musicals, she thought that she could learn more about her craft by assisting him on *Little Shop*. "I didn't go just get coffee," she explained. "He confided in me."[29]

For choreography, Ashman thought of hiring Mary Kyte, from *God Bless You, Mr. Rosewater*, but she was unavailable.[30] Then Ashman had another idea. He remembered his time at Indiana University and the production of *Dames at Sea*, directed by Edie Cowan. She taught Ashman and Stuart White how to tap dance and made them look good. "I'd get non-dancers to dance," Cowan explained.[31] Older Broadway musicals might have a singing chorus and a dancing chorus, but Ashman had to do more with less. He could not assume that he would find Broadway-caliber dancers—he needed people who could act, sing, and originate the characters that were on the page. So he reconnected with Edie Cowan, who was unfamiliar with his work as a playwright; she knew him as a graduate student. Since that time, she appeared in the New York and national touring companies of *Annie*, which opened on Broadway in 1977. She read the *Little Shop* script and met with Ashman and Menken in Manhattan

Plaza, where they sang through the score. After three or four numbers, Cowan required no more persuasion: "I'm in!"[32]

However, there was one song that she believed was weaker than the rest: Orin Scrivello's "Just a Hobby," which Ashman performed at BMI with an Elvis Presley snarl. "This is high school boy humor," she insisted.[33] In the song, Orin recounts his early history, with reference to erections and masturbation. There was also some confusion about Orin's identity: he is a leather-wearing sadist but also, in Audrey's terms, "a professional" (25). Why not introduce him in one guise and then reveal the other? Responding to the challenge, Ashman and Menken wrote a new song for Orin Scrivello. An early version begins:

> When I was younger, just a bad little kid,
> My mama noticed funny things I did,
> I'd shoot at puppies with a B.B. gun
> I'd poison guppies and when I was done
> I'd pluck the parakeet until it was dead—

Naturally, he would become a dentist.[34]

With pre-production underway, Ashman and Menken negotiated their contract with the WPA Theatre. The two writers were offered $350 total for a month of performances. The WPA retained the right to transfer the piece to a commercial theatre, at which point the authors would earn 6 percent of the weekly box-office gross (7.5 percent after the producer recouped initial costs). The authors' share was divided: two-thirds to Ashman, for writing the book and lyrics; one-third to Menken, for composing the music. So if the show moved to Broadway or Off-Broadway, then the authors would reap the rewards.[35]

In February 1982, the casting process began. Again, *Dames at Sea* was an important model. That musical was performed with three men and three women. In an early outline, Ashman wrote, "3 MEN/3 WOMEN."[36] This was eventually increased to four men and four women, plus a puppeteer: nine total. Menken observed that unlike *Rosewater*, with its large cast of characters, *Little Shop* "was meticulously planned to run."[37] The WPA production would be an Equity Showcase, which allowed producers to employ Equity actors for a limited term. There would be a maximum of twenty-four performances and ninety-eight seats in the house. Further, the rehearsal schedule had to be flexible, allowing performers to keep their day jobs and audition for other work. Stage manager Paul Mills Holmes explained, "You'd get a check that would cover transportation." In New York City, this meant the subway, and one-way fare at the time cost seventy-five cents. According to Menken, "Actors get paid very little, but they had to be reviewed. So you can't escape the *New York Times*."[38]

Casting was handled by Darlene Kaplan, who joined the WPA in the late 1970s. Ashman's friend and former assistant Nancy Parent left her position as literary advisor, so Kaplan, after finishing her BA at Yale University, took the job. She read script submissions and got involved in the audition process. Casting announcements for *Little Shop* appeared in the middle of January 1982; agents submitted clients who might (or might not) be appropriate. After a week of open calls (required by Equity), auditions were by appointment. Each actor would sing a prepared song and maybe read a book scene. When it was time to offer the role, there were no negotiations; the Equity showcase was a take-it-or-leave-it proposition. Kaplan would call the agent and ask: does your client want to do this? Because of the WPA's strong reputation, many actors were inclined to say yes: "they knew they were getting involved in something special."[39]

Auditions took place in the WPA rehearsal room; at the table sat Ashman, Menken, Kaplan, music director Bob Billig, and assistant director Connie Grappo. One round focused on the characters Crystal, Ronnette, and Chiffon, known collectively as the "urchins." This name derives from the script. In the very first scene, Mushnik scolds them, "You! Urchins! Off the stoop!" (16). They would be the only performers required to dance during the audition process. Edie Cowan choreographed around twenty measures of the opening song, "Little Shop of Horrors," which she would teach as a tryout piece. She described her choreography as "girl-group movement" but more "theatrical." Billig would look for a range of voices who could handle his vocal arrangements.[40]

The strongest contenders were Jennifer Leigh Warren, Sheila Kay Davis, and Leilani Jones. They hailed from all around the country before arriving in New York City to work in the theatre. Warren was from Dallas, Texas; Davis from Miami, Florida; and Jones was born in Hawaii. Unlike previous generations of Broadway hopefuls, all three were university-educated: Warren went to Dartmouth College, in New Hampshire; Davis attended Spelman, an HBCU (Historically Black College or University), in Atlanta; and Jones earned a BA in music theory at the University of Hawaii. During the auditions, Bob Billig was impressed by Jennifer Warren's vocal range; he kept testing how high she could go. Eventually, she sang the highest parts; Davis took the lower notes; and Jones was usually in the middle.[41]

Movement took place during callbacks. Women were formed into groups of three, then they learned and danced Cowan's routine. Sheila Kay Davis remembered, "Howard was fixated on me. I was in a trio of very talented girls, but he didn't take his eyes off me." She noted that she did not audition with Warren or Jones; they met later on. Davis was a bit more worldly than her fellow urchins; she was already married and lived with her husband, on East Thirty-first Street. Appropriate for the musical in which she was about to appear, her neighborhood was a kind of Skid Row. Prostitutes worked the street, and they knew everyone's schedule, the comings and goings of those on Thirty-first Street. One night after a performance, Davis hurried home, and a streetwalker announced, "You're late tonight, little showgirl."[42]

Unlike Warren and Davis, Leilani Jones was more of a dancer; she served as dance captain for a revival of the 1944 musical *Bloomer Girl* at Goodspeed Opera House, in Connecticut, where she met Edie Cowan. Needing a strong dancer to anchor the choreography, Cowan encouraged Jones to audition for *Little Shop*. However, Jones had an earlier audition that same day, for the role of a flight attendant, so she showed up in an outfit that was a bit too Pan Am. She plowed into her prepared material—a song by Rodgers and Hart and a song by Rodgers and Hammerstein—"Where or When" and "Honey Bun." "I didn't even know it was a 1950s vibe," Jones pleaded. Realizing that she was blowing it, she promised to return next time dressed as an urchin. Granted a callback, she showed up in sneakers, jeans, a sweatshirt, with her hair in a ponytail. This time she chose a period-appropriate number and belted, "Does he love me? I wanna know!" From behind the table, Ashman and Menken sang spontaneous backup: "Is it in his eyes?" Jones continued, "Oh, no, he'll make believe." Now she felt more confident: "This is a good audition—when they're singing with you!"[43]

For the speaking and singing voice of the plant from another world, Marty Robinson wanted to audition. "I can do it all!" he insisted. This connected to his training with Jim Henson: the Muppeteers perform the voice *and* the manipulation of a given puppet—it's holistic. "I took singing lessons, private singing lessons," Robinson explained. He worked hard to prepare for the day when he would sing "Git It" for the authors of the show. But Ashman was unconvinced. Letting Robinson down gently, he said that he and Menken really wanted "a big bluesy singer." However, if they were "casting the plant as Nosferatu," then Robinson would get the role.[44]

Ashman and Menken's ideal arrived in the form of Ron Taylor, an African American actor and singer, born in Galveston, Texas, in 1952. Growing up, he was known as Sugar Bear. Taylor looked more like a linebacker than a Broadway gypsy, yet he had appeared in *Jesus Christ Superstar* and the national tour of *The Wiz*, the 1975 Broadway update to *The Wizard of Oz*, as the understudy to the Lion. Deborah Sharpe was the understudy to Dorothy. On tour, she and Taylor fell in love. "Dorothy and the Lion got married," she explained—a different ending to the narrative. Back in New York, Taylor's agent sent him to the *Little Shop* audition. By coincidence, he and Marty Robinson had been classmates at the American Academy of Dramatic Arts. When Taylor joined the show, Deborah Sharpe-Taylor noticed how her husband was "mesmerized" by "the wonderful work Marty was doing."[45] Taylor would travel from his home in the Bronx to Robinson's apartment on East Seventeenth Street, where they practiced merging their performances. Robinson believed that this "symbiosis" would be required for a successful Audrey II: "It takes time. And it takes trust." Essentially, the two performers had to synchronize gesture and sound. Performing the larger plants, which moved more slowly, Robinson had to anticipate Taylor's next utterance: "You gotta go for it, knowing that he's gonna be there."[46] This became the model for Audrey II: two performers, one performance.

Casting the four principals offered a different set of challenges. "There was always a limited amount of old Jewish guys," complained Darlene Kaplan.[47] So the theatre was fortunate to sign Michael Vale to play Mr. Mushnik, owner of the eponymous shop. Heavyset, with a broad mustache and a double chin, he looked like a character actor, and he was recognizable from a series of television commercials in which he played Sam Breakstone for a New York–based dairy company, Breakstone's. Typecast in food preparation, Vale next appeared in many commercials for Dunkin' Donuts; he played a character eventually known as Fred the Baker, who, like Sisyphus, is bound to repeat the same task, over and over: "Time to make the donuts." Assistant director Connie Grappo felt that Vale was the only viable Mushnik to audition, and Robby Merkin agreed: "He was believably an old-world Jew; he was believably someone who had no patience for the younger generation."[48]

Among that younger generation was Orin Scrivello, DDS, the leather-wearing dentist who abuses his girlfriend, Audrey. Because the show would be performed by a cast of eight (plus puppeteer), Ashman conceived of this character as a shapeshifter, one who could play many roles, from a shop customer to a theatrical agent to an editor's wife (in drag). Frank Luz (his name at birth) was born in Cambridge, Massachusetts, and grew up in an Irish and Italian neighborhood. His parents hoped that he would work in road construction because, they argued, "the state never goes broke." He tried the job for one summer but did not enjoy his coworkers, who were conservative, Nixon voters, with a tendency to spit. So Luz ventured as far away as he could get—to New Mexico State University, where he studied psychology and theatre. Without earning a degree, he returned to Boston and landed a job in summer stock. On the national tour of *The Robber Bridegroom*, Luz replaced Barry Bostwick. While riding the bus from one town to the next, the company manager dabbled in numerology: he discovered that if Luz changed a single letter in his name, the actor would change his career trajectory from middling to lucrative. Acting is a competitive field, and Luz decided that he would exploit every possible advantage, even mystical ones. So Frank Luz became Franc Luz. Despite his working-class background and incomplete education, he "was always cast as a professional." He said, "I was either a doctor or a lawyer." Tall and fiendishly handsome, he looked like the "boyfriend of the week" on a television show—a role he often played.[49] At the audition for *Little Shop*, Luz demonstrated a range of roles. Kaplan commented, "He was so funny and so outrageous in so many ways."[50]

Casting Seymour Krelborn—Ashman's final version of the name—was more difficult. It came down to two contenders: Nathan Lane and Lee Wilkof.

Nancy Parent sat in during these auditions and was impressed by Lane's performance. She could imagine him as young Finch in *How to Succeed in Business without Really Trying*, the hit 1961 musical, although *Little Shop* would be a different kind of workplace success story. Lee Wilkof, who had limited musical-theatre experience, was, in Bob Billig's terms, "a little quirkier."[51] After the final callbacks, Ashman rode uptown in a taxi with assistant director Connie Grappo. "I just don't know," Ashman grumbled. "I can't decide." The two performers were completely different. He turned to Grappo: "What do you think?"[52] She replied, "I think as a woman, I would be more inclined to—I would feel the love and, you know, whatever, *desire* from Lee more than from Nathan." Grappo argued that the show was built around "Seymour's love for Audrey," his "worship of Audrey"; "I would believe that coming from Lee more than I would believe it coming from Nathan."[53] Wilkof got the part.

Ironically, he was planning to audition for the dentist. Born in Canton, Ohio, in 1951, Lee Wilkof grew up in a "tightknit Jewish community." Like Ashman and Robinson, he was corrupted by *The Little Shop of Horrors* in his youth. On Friday nights, a Cleveland television station offered a show hosted by Ghoulardi (real name: Ernie Anderson), who introduced classic horror films. "He dressed crazy," and "he wore a fright wig," Wilkof remembered. "I think he was probably high." Roughly three times a year, Ghoulardi would screen *The Little Shop*.[54] After attending Temple University, in Philadelphia, and the University of Cincinnati, Wilkof became an actor. In 1977, he appeared Off-Broadway in *The Present Tense*, with music written by Alan Menken, among others. The show was produced by Roger Ailes, a sometime political operative, who wanted to manage Wilkof's career. Even then, at twenty-six, Wilkof was balding. By the time he reached Los Angeles, to work in film and television, he had taken cover in a toupee.[55] In LA, he received a phone call from Darlene Kaplan, who told him about her next production: "You gotta audition for this!" They first met when her boyfriend, Steve Zuckerman, directed Wilkof in a play in Colorado. A fan of the original film, Wilkof flew to New York at his own expense for the chance to appear in the musical version of *Little Shop*.[56]

When Wilkof arrived at the WPA rehearsal room, Menken noticed the rich, brown hair. Remembering Wilkof as bald, he laughed.[57] Then Ashman sized up the diminutive man standing before the casting table: "You weren't a dentist even with the fucking wig on." The director had another idea: "Seymour—look at Seymour."[58] So Wilkof removed the hair piece and read for the starring role. He sang his prepared song, "Smile," composed by Charlie Chaplin. "We were all pretty blown away by it," said Grappo.[59] When Kaplan phoned Wilkof to invite him to a callback, he asked, "Who was that girl? Who was that woman next to Howard?" It was Connie Grappo, assistant to the director. "I noticed her," Wilkof said.[60]

During the callback, he was paired with a young performer named Faith Prince, who was offered the role of Audrey.[61] But she had booked an industrial that conflicted with the *Little Shop* schedule. The industrial offered more money, which Prince was willing to forgo, but the producers "wouldn't let her out," as Grappo recalled.[62] Ashman was obliged to recast. On the callback sheet, two women, listed as "Late Audreys," did not audition with the rest: Didi Conn and Ellen Greene.[63] "Howard had Ellen in mind when he wrote it," Grappo argued. Greene had auditioned for *God Bless You, Mr. Rosewater*. She wasn't cast, but Ashman remembered her.[64] Nevertheless, Faith Prince, taking the character in another direction, changed his mind. Once she left the project, Ashman said, "I gotta go back to my original idea."[65] Greene appeared for a separate audition, with Ashman, Menken, Grappo, and Kaplan around the piano. In a moment that must have seemed like destiny, Ellen Greene tried out "Somewhere That's Green." Ashman admitted that "it was just the way it sounded in my head."[66]

Her father was a dentist with musical inclinations (as was Menken's). "He'd sing while he drilled," the daughter mentioned.[67] Greene's first Equity job was a bus-and-truck tour of *George M!*, the 1968 musical inspired by the life of George M. Cohan.[68] In 1976, she starred in the film *Next Stop, Greenwich Village*, an account of bohemian life in the 1950s. She also appeared in two Broadway flops (*Rachael Lily Rosenbloom* and *The Little Prince and the Aviator*), and was nominated for a Tony Award in 1977 for a revival of *The Threepenny Opera*. But Greene had a reputation as a troublemaker.[69] Still, Ashman was willing to ignore the theatrical gossip and hire her.

While casting was underway, designers created the look of the show. For set and lighting design, Ashman chose two of WPA's founding members: Edward

T. Gianfrancesco (aka Hawk) and Craig Evans. Hawk discussed the scenic-design process, in which a designer works with a director and manages multiple contingencies: "You're interpreting a piece of art; you have someone who's telling you their interpretation of a piece of art; you have a space where it has to fit; you have a budget." Working in the WPA, a black-box theatre, Hawk planned a unit set, with movable pieces: "I came up with this segmented-screen approach, which was on a curved track in the front of Mr. Mushnik's shop." A series of panels would close, to represent the street; or they would open, and we're inside the shop. The only missing element was Orin's office. Hawk conferred with Ashman: "Howard, I think I can make the dentist office come up out of the floor." Indeed, he designed a dentist's chair that would rise from under the stage. Since the depth below stage was around thirty inches, the chair would fold and then expand, like a collapsible bed. A few flats representing Orin's torturous tools round out the location. Suddenly, we are in the office of Orin Scrivello, DDS.[70]

For costumes, the WPA Theatre did not have a resident designer. Darlene Kaplan suggested Sally Lesser. Lesser was married to director Steve Zuckerman; the relationship ended, and he began dating Kaplan (they later married). So Lesser was surprised by Kaplan's telephone call: "We're not friends. Why would you want me at your theatre?" Kaplan answered, "Because I think you're the right designer for this project." At her costume shop, located on East Seventh Street, in the East Village, Ashman interviewed Sally Lesser. He said that the look he wanted was "harmlessly gritty." "There was very little money," Lesser understood; therefore, costumes were not designed and built; they were scrounged, gathered, assembled. She began with a series of questions: "What do the actors have in their closets? What do I have in my collection?"[71]

An early dispute involved the look of the urchins. Lesser grew up in Hempstead, New York, with a large African American population. "We went to high school with these girls," she said. She viewed Crystal, Ronnette, and Chiffon as "funky girls; they were not at all glamorous." However, choreographer Edie Cowan had different ideas. She saw the urchins in "matching outfits," sweater sets, with circle pins. Lesser disagreed: "That is just too white."[72] To complete the look, each of the urchins wore a wig, in styles of the early 1960s and the girl groups that Ashman admired. In the second act, each dons another wig.⁷³ Lenora Brown, known as Cookie, maintained all the wigs, and Lee Wilkof remembered her well: "she was just always laughing and loved her work and was a dominatrix by night."⁷⁴

Ellen Greene also wore a wig, in her role as Audrey. She explained, "We went through about five wigs before Audrey became a cornsilk blonde."⁷⁵ To a large extent, Greene developed her take on the character through the appearance: the wig and the clothes. In the Corman film, Jackie Joseph is a brunette, and she wears her own outfits—this is a low-budget picture.⁷⁶ Greene drew inspiration from Billie Dawn, the character made indelible by Judy Holliday in the 1946 Broadway play *Born Yesterday* (and the 1950 screen version) as well as "the B-movie heroines who were Audrey's role models"—at once innocent and damaged.⁷⁷

In a flea market, Sally Lesser found the perfect dress, which she bought for three dollars. She adjusted it, added sequins, and lowered the neckline. As Lesser explained, "The character doesn't have a lot of money. And she just adds different tops." So Lesser's costume design saved money but was also true to the lived reality of Audrey's situation; she would not have a Broadway designer building her fabulous clothing. In the second act, Audrey appears in a white nightgown, also vintage, costing around two dollars. To cover the costume change, Lesser added a yellow raincoat; Greene wore the nightgown underneath.⁷⁸ Ashman appreciated this kind of economy. "You know what? I'm gonna add thunder," he said.⁷⁹ This was the WPA Theatre at its best: economic limitations and imaginative solutions.

After three months of pre-production, rehearsals began at the end of March. When Ashman showed up for the first day of rehearsal, he was tall, rail thin, his blond hair short and wavy, with a touch of gray, a soft mustache over his lip.⁸⁰ Menken found Ashman the director to be "very organized" and "very clear." Grappo, as Ashman's assistant, agreed that "he knew what he wanted" and yet he "didn't always know the best way to bring it out." Stage manager Paul Mills Holmes said that Ashman's method was "guiding without being dictatorial"; "he had a great love of actors." On the other hand, Merkin, the orchestrator, saw a different side; he described Ashman's point of view thus: "There's a right way for every moment in this show. And if it isn't self-evident to you, I'm gonna hammer it into you. But it should be self-evident."⁸¹ Yet the script was not sacrosanct; the director was willing to improve any scene, moment, or song. Actors sometimes improvised variations on their lines, and Ashman incorporated some of the changes. When Audrey denies that she could ever date coworker Seymour, she says, "Oh, we're just friends. I could never be Seymour's girl. I've got a past." Chiffon replies, "Who ain't?"[82] In rehearsal, the actor playing Chiffon, Leilani Jones, offered a suggestion: "And who amongst us has not?" (34)[83] The line went into the script. Lee Wilkof also improvised dialogue for Seymour. Before Audrey II's first utterance, Seymour bids farewell for the night by saying, "I'm gonna go get some dinner now, Twoey."[84] Wilkof suggested a variant: "I'm gonna run down to Shmendrik's and get a bite to eat" (49). "That's better!" Ashman decided.[85] Among the cast, Jennifer Leigh Warren appreciated Ashman's openness. "There was no hierarchy," she said of his attitude. "He made everyone feel the same."[86]

Actors noted that their director knew his material very well: indeed, Ashman had been dreaming of this musical, consciously or otherwise, since childhood, when he saw the Roger Corman film and reinvented it as *The Candy Shop*. A band member who watched many rehearsals found that "Howard was able to enact every role in the show."[87] Of course, he had played many of the parts himself, when presenting the material at BMI or for potential collaborators. This chameleon quality aided him in the rehearsal room. Leilani Jones explained, "He could jump in and do an urchin; he could do Audrey; he could do Orin; he could do anybody. And it was hysterical the way that he would just melt into whatever character. If he wants something a certain way, he would just become that character."[88]

Since he knew the piece so well, he helped the actors develop backstories—identities that may not be perceived by the audience but may help the actors perform. One might think the urchins are merely a backup group, who sing "da-doo" and "shang-a-lang" a lot, but Ashman argued that they are "very intelligent." He said that the urchins "know what's going to happen, the consequences." Crystal is the one "everyone loves"; Ronnette is "big mama"; Chiffon, the "big sister." For Chiffon's backstory, he proposed that she attended Wilfred Beauty Academy and is preoccupied with hair and nails. Further, she is "from the street but doesn't want anyone to know." Like Audrey, Chiffon has "a past."[89] And who amongst us has not?

Imagining the piece for so long, Ashman was clear-eyed about the kind of performances he wanted from the actors. *Little Shop of Horrors* may be funny, but it is no joke. An early draft includes a note that reads, "Although the piece is a parody, it is to be played as innocently and straight as possible."[90] Again, his models may be some of the "little" musicals that evoke earlier moments of cultural history: *The Boy Friend* and *Little Mary Sunshine*. In the published script of *The Boy Friend*, the original director, Vida Hope, describes a conversation with author Sandy Wilson: "I wanted to do it as a serious reproduction of a period and not a burlesque." This objective carried into rehearsals, when Hope told the actors, "[I]n no circumstances would I tolerate any attitude of laughing at the Twenties."[91] The "AUTHOR'S NOTE" in Rick Besoyan's *Little Mary Sunshine* offers a similar injunction: "It is absolutely essential to the success of the musical that it should be played with the most warmhearted earnestness." Furthermore, "the characters, one and all, should appear to believe, throughout, in the perfect sincerity of their words and actions."[92] This was Ashman's view of *Little Shop*: the most extraordinary events transpire, but the characters believe. They do not observe their own performances from the outside, with ironic distance. They *believe*.

Rehearsals were typically five hours a day, from 12:00 pm until 5:00 pm or 5:00 pm until 10:00 pm.[93] Early on, a pattern developed in which Ashman met with some actors at the WPA while Edie Cowan worked with the urchins in a small dance studio around the corner, between Fifth and Sixth Avenues. Bob Billig taught vocal arrangements and played piano at Cowan's dance rehearsals; "we were like a separate unit in a sense," she said. Ashman and Cowan would meet in the morning to plan the day and then reconvene at the end. "We would all go back to the WPA. And we'd show Howard what we'd been working on, and he'd show us what he'd been working on," Cowan remembered. "You could see we were all on the same page."[94] For example, on Tuesday, March 30, according to the rehearsal schedule, "Edie + girls" rehearsed from 1:00 to 4:30. At the WPA, Ashman directed Mushnik, Seymour, Audrey, and Orin scenes, from 12:30 to 4:00, and then "PLANT SCENES" from 4:00 to 5:00.[95]

For the first few weeks, the director was obliged to use the WPA rehearsal room, because the season's previous production, *What Would Jeanne Moreau Do?*, was still on the stage.[96] Incidentally, this was the last play that Stuart White directed for the WPA. The show opened on March 11 and closed on April 4. Strike and load-out were scheduled for the next day, and then Hawk began building the *Little Shop* set.[97]

Schedules and call sheets do not tell the full story. "That first rehearsal process was fraught," Grappo stated. Lee Wilkof agreed: "not an easy birth." The source of much of the tension was Ellen Greene. "Rehearsals at the WPA were dominated by Ellen," Grappo admitted. "She knew what she wanted to do, and she knew what she needed." Greene had "great ideas" but also "very directorial instincts."[98] Paul Mills Holmes qualified that "her instincts, nine times out of ten, were always correct." Among the designers, Sally Lesser was surprised that Ashman never reined her in, but Grappo thought that "he was trying to manage this situation."[99] During rehearsals, Holmes found Greene difficult to handle: "She wants what she wants." Marty Robinson described her as "crazy like an artist," someone with a "vision and don't mess with it because she knows how something should be done."[100] To her credit, it was always about the work. "I just don't think we're getting it right," Greene would say.[101] Her concerns were not about billing or a larger dressing room. In fact, at the WPA, there were two dressing rooms: one for men, one for women. Audrey shared with Crystal, Ronnette, and Chiffon.

Ashman had five weeks to stage a complex musical with nine performers, a four-piece band, four carnivorous plants—and now this. Fortunately, he found a way to direct this demanding performer. Whenever he wanted to offer a note or suggestion, he would coax her in the right direction so that each adjustment would "seem like it was her idea." But the process was exhausting. One observer defended the director's manipulative approach: "Howard made her feel comfortable so that she could perform without any problems."[102]

Greene staked her terrain in the first week of rehearsal. Choreographer Edie Cowan's task was to work with the urchins, and she created movement for numbers such as "Little Shop of Horrors" and "The Meek Shall Inherit." But she also wanted a number for the entire company, and this became "Skid Row (Downtown)."[103] Even the puppeteer (Marty Robinson) and the voice of the plant (Ron Taylor) would be included, as drunken citizens of Skid Row. Ashman asked Cowan to stage the number, and it was scheduled for Wednesday, March 31.[104] At one point, Cowan asked Ellen Greene to step out of the shop and move downstage. The performer wanted a motivation, to which Cowan replied, "I don't want to put that boundary on you." Greene offered this: "Edie, in structure there is freedom. Tell me what you want—tell me what you're looking for, and I'll figure out how to do it."[105] So Cowan demonstrated a walk downstage. Greene then reproduced the walk, "and of course she made it her own," strolling pensively, in an Audrey-like manner.[106] A simple piece of stage direction was devouring too much time.

In other words, Ellen Greene did not require a hit musical to arrive at diva status—she was already there. Theatre historian John M. Clum offers his definition of a diva: "the woman who defies conventional notions of gender and plays out the parodic, larger-than-life performance of gender the musical privileges." Clum mentions Ethel Merman, Bernadette Peters, Betty Buckley.[107] A diva may be adored by audiences but unloved by colleagues.

The low point arrived when Ellen Greene banned Lee Wilkof from rehearsal. This occurred when Ashman was staging the death of Audrey, in Act Two. Greene preferred to work on the scene with Ashman alone; Wilkof could be added later. It is a breach of protocol for a director to take directions from actors, but "Howard was getting tired of the fight," Grappo commented. The feeling was: "Let's just get it done."[108] By the end of April, the schedule indicates separate rehearsal days for Seymour and Audrey.[109]

Franc Luz, in the role of the dentist, believed that he, Wilkof, and Greene "were all flopping around, trying to figure it out." Any one of them could have been fired. Luz managed to capture the menace of Orin Scrivello but not the show's humor. At last, Ashman offered a piece of direction that helped: "You know what I need you to do? I need you to put your comedy ears on."[110] Meanwhile, the ostensible star of the show, Lee Wilkof, felt neglected. "Ellen took up a lot of air," he complained, and Ashman "was not getting through to me."[111] Wilkof's performance suffered through the rehearsal period. Grappo remembered that "Lee didn't really know how to ask for or get the help that he needed." About a week before technical rehearsals, Ashman devised a solution. He asked the assistant director to work privately with Wilkof; over the next few days, Grappo met with the actor at the theatre, before or after rehearsal. As she recalled, "I would coach him through his scenes, and I would play all the other parts."[112] Wilkof admitted that he had a tendency to "rely on characterization rather than emotion." He played a nerd rather than exploring the character's "emotional life." Drawing on her training with Uta Hagen, Grappo was able to help him craft a richer performance.[113]

The backstage romance is a cliché, depicted in many a Hollywood film, but it happens nevertheless. By coincidence, Wilkof and Grappo grew up thirty minutes from each other, in Ohio. He saw this geographical fact as the signature of fate. However, Grappo kept her professional distance, for a while: "we were buddies; that's how I saw it." In a tiny theatre company, secrets are not held for long, and others soon learned about the growing relationship. "Ellen was very jealous that I had happiness," Wilkof remarked.[114] But she, too, would find love in *Little Shop of Horrors* at the WPA. While building the two larger plants, puppeteer Marty Robinson practically lived in the theatre and was present during auditions and rehearsals: "I fell in love with Ellen almost immediately. How could you not?" In the show, after Audrey is consumed by Audrey II, the actor playing Audrey is obliged to linger in close quarters with the puppeteer. So Greene and Robinson spent time together. One evening, she had a spare ticket for the Off-Broadway production of *Torch Song Trilogy*, and he joined her. After the performance, they walked along St. Mark's Place and kissed in the rain.[115]

Another show-biz cliché is that musicals are rewritten at the last minute, with late-night cups of coffee and the pounding of piano keys in hotel rooms or tenement flats. But *Little Shop of Horrors* was so carefully developed by Ashman and Menken in 1981 and early 1982 that the script that went into rehearsal was remarkably close to the finished product. They tweaked lines here and there, polished lyrics. Only one song became a casualty of the rehearsal process: "We'll Have Tomorrow," a pretty ballad sung by Seymour and Audrey, late in the second act. Cowan commented, "Most writers think that everything they've written is golden," but Wilkof noted that Ashman and Menken "cut one of the most beautiful songs ever written."[116] Ashman was philosophical about the loss: "the ballad has been disappearing for fifteen or twenty years." Older shows, he said, had five or six ballads in a single evening. *Little Shop* has only two ("Somewhere That's Green" and "Suddenly, Seymour"). "There ain't no time anymore to sit on the sofa and *moon* and *June* about things," Ashman quipped. "We're living at a different pace than people lived

Figure 6 *The original WPA company, between two performances, in 1982. (Back row, standing, left to right): Carole Finley, Michael Vale, Beth Anne Kushnick, Leilani Jones, Elliot Sokolov, Ron Taylor, Martin P. Robinson (in the plant's mouth), Ellen Greene, Paul Mills Holmes, Franc Luz, Jennifer Leigh Warren, Sheila Kay Davis, Steve Ferrera. (Middle row, sitting, left to right): Lee Wilkof, Constance Grappo, Robby Merkin, Sarah Whitham, Robert Billig, unidentified, Lenora Brown, Elizabeth (Betsy) Nicholson, Donna Rose Fletcher, unidentified. (Front and center, left to right): Howard Ashman, Alan Menken, Edie Cowan.*

thirty years ago."[117] He knew what a contemporary musical needed, as audiences would discover.

Performances were to begin on April 29, 1982, but the schedule was delayed by one week. The first performance (a preview) would take place on Thursday, May 6. In each of the four previous seasons, one or two WPA productions moved to a larger venue—either Broadway or Off-Broadway.[118] Ashman and Menken's previous collaboration, *God Bless You, Mr. Rosewater*, was one such transfer. Could *Little Shop* be next?

Chapter Four
A Monster Hit: The Off-Broadway Production

"We got to that first performance, and people fell out of their bucket seats." This is how stage manager Paul Mills Holmes described the first preview, on May 6, 1982. He watched the show from the booth, alongside two light-board operators and a follow-spot operator. He shared glances with the lighting crew: "We thought it was funny, but we didn't think it was *this* funny."[1] Ashman perhaps was unsurprised. "Howard always knew where the laughs were," Connie Grappo asserted. "He planted them there." Menken summarized his collaborator's accomplishment: "where he excelled was finding a stylistic vocabulary for a dramatic piece and then getting all the elements to marry to that stylistic choice." Ashman's sister, Sarah, agreed that "everything kind of coalesced."[2]

Among the earliest audiences was Lee Wilkof's friend and fellow actor Brent Spiner, who described *Little Shop* as "one of those rare theatrical experiences where you leave the theatre filled with joy."[3] Edie Cowan's mother was also among the WPA audiences; she attended the first matinee, on Sunday, May 9, and she told her daughter, "You have nothing to worry about." Further, "It's the first time in years I've actually sat forward to listen to the lyrics."[4] The coup de théâtre came at the end. During the finale, "Don't Feed the Plants," just before the blackout, a series of boxes overhead opened, and alien tentacles descended onto the audience below. It was tactile, visceral: Audrey II was able to reach out and touch everyone in the house as if the plant had taken over the building. The effect was that of a 3-D movie—but better. "Nobody would expect to go to a tiny, hole-in-the-wall theatre and, you know, have their minds blown," offered Leilani Jones. Another urchin, Jennifer Leigh Warren, added, "I knew we had a hit when limousines were driving up." Soon *Little Shop of Horrors* became "the hottest ticket in town," according to Wilkof. Menken noted that "we had lines around the block."[5] The performance schedule was somewhat irregular: twenty-four shows over four weeks, usually Thursdays to Sundays. Tickets were seven dollars each.[6]

One reason for the show's success was Ellen Greene, who was so difficult during rehearsal. Grappo explained that Greene was "a real technician"; she "finds what works and then she really analyzes it and understands *why* it works and how to repeat it."[7] One actor who observed her performances remarked that she was a master of inhabiting a character and "giving the audience exactly what they paid for, every time." The great challenge and threat to the vitality of a theatrical performance is repetition: it's always the same. Yet Greene had the ability "to rediscover something, over and over, hundreds of times"; indeed, "it *was* the first time with Ellen" because she was "insanely present."[8] Menken thought that her process, though challenging, was worth the trouble: "I honestly don't know if the show would be as successful as it is without her perfectionism." Once Greene fully realized the character on the page, Ashman claimed, "I think Ellen is Audrey the way Carol Channing is Dolly."[9]

Another strength of the production was that the composer played the score; he was one of four band members, who sat in the house, to the right. "Whenever the composer plays the show, it's just a certain energy," insisted Sheila Kay Davis, who created the role of Ronnette. "Every note of the music is in their heart."[10] Next to Menken, with his triple-keyboard setup, was former NYU classmate Robby Merkin. A misfortune, at least for Alan Menken, was that at the end of a given performance, audience members would approach Robby Merkin to commend the music: "Congratulations, Alan!" As Merkin explained, "We're both about the same height; we both wear glasses." Cheerfully, he responded to such compliments, "Oh, thank you very much." The real composer was not amused: "You can't do that!"[11]

Ron Taylor also found reason to be disgruntled amidst the happiness of everyone enjoying a fresh success. During performances, he hid behind

Mr. Mushnik's shop and held a microphone, into which he spoke and sang as diabolical Audrey II. From here, he could watch the movement of the puppets and the other actors. But, as Taylor confessed, "I am used to being on stage."[12] When he appeared for a curtain call, nobody knew who he was. Then he engineered a remedy: he printed a shirt with the words "FEED ME" stamped on the front, in bold capitals. Now his identity was clear; he was the voice of Audrey II, the guy who sang, "Feed me!"[13]

Taylor and his fellow cast members performed at their best during three midnight performances, scheduled in the spirit of cult films and midnight movies. These Saturday nights were "electric" and "wilder than *The Rocky Horror Show*."[14] As Holmes remembered, "You could not get a seat to save your soul." He felt the atmosphere of a carnival, the house "filled with carny trash. So, you know, you're gonna have the best audience in the world."[15] At one midnight show, director Tommy Tune and "his posse" showed up. Because there were no more seats, they sat in the middle aisle. Those evenings in May and June were hot, and the theatre had no air-conditioning. So men removed their shirts; women opened their blouses. "You thought you were in the best gay bar ever in the history of the world," laughed Holmes. "And this was our show." According to actor Franc Luz, it was after midnight that "we found our swagger."[16]

Although audiences embraced the show, critics were slower to acknowledge the downtown triumph. Broadway musicals get reviewed as soon as they open, but an Off-Off-Broadway theatre like the WPA had to wait till the ink-stained journalists were good and ready to wander to a distant outpost like the corner of Fifth Avenue and Nineteenth Street. Four days after the official opening night (May 20), the *New York Post* ran a review: "Alan Menken's sensational malt-shop score is a celebratory anthology of the '50s musical idioms." The reviewer, Marilyn Stasio, added that Howard Ashman "seems to be the resident genius behind the delightfully warped project."[17] Yet Ashman and Menken dreaded the judgment of the *New York Times*: "the boys didn't want the *Times* to come," explained Holmes. "They specifically did not want Frank Rich to be there." (He wrote that unpleasant review of their previous collaboration, *Real Life Funnies*.[18]) Instead, the paper sent Mel Gussow, who delivered a genial rave on May 30. He described "a Faustian musical about a timid clerk who sells his soul to a man-eating cactus"; notably, he compared the play not to other plays but to films: *Dr. Strangelove* and *Invasion of the Body Snatchers*. Television reviewer Katie Kelly was even more enthusiastic. "I nearly died laughing," she reported. "This show is a non-stop romp from start to finish!"[19] Among the well-wishers was twenty-eight-year-old Donna Rose Fletcher, who joined the production during technical rehearsals and became a light-board operator. Approaching the director after a performance, she ventured, "It looks like you've got a hit." Ashman remained skeptical: "Eh, I've had hits before."[20]

His producing partner, Kyle Renick, was more sanguine. He predicted that one show from the 1981–82 season would transfer to Broadway or Off-Broadway. And then it happened. Songs from *Little Shop* were featured in a presentation at BMI for an invited audience. As Renick remembered, "Within half an hour after the conclusion of the program, my telephone started to ring." Ten theatrical producers expressed interest in the musical, and then the number increased: "I had received twenty-six offers to transfer the show for a commercial run."[21] Negotiating the various offers was more than he could handle, so he telephoned Stephen Wells, the board member who reorganized the WPA when he took over from the original founders before he in turn handed the reins to Renick, Ashman, and Stuart White. "Help, I'm swamped," Renick pleaded.[22] Attorney Jeremy Nussbaum also fielded some calls. This activity began while the show continued its run at the WPA. "We'd convene every day or every other day," Wells recalled. "Producers were coming out of the woodwork, right and left." Because space was limited at the theatre, Wells worked from home. Renick sometimes directed the most annoying suitors to his fellow board member, who said, "I've always had the ability to tolerate assholes."[23]

The "most insane offer," in Kyle Renick's view, came from Paramount Pictures, the Hollywood studio purchased by Gulf+Western in 1966.[24] A Paramount executive offered Renick 7.5 percent of the Gulf+Western building, on Columbus Circle, in New York. There was a movie theatre in the basement; the idea was to convert this space into a legitimate theatre and run *Little Shop* as its maiden production. Paramount estimated that the cinema occupied 7.5 percent of the company's New York footprint. Of course, Renick and Wells hesitated to align their modest production with corporate America; they did not want a "business interest to come in and destroy the aesthetic." The best way forward, they decided, was to find a theatre owner to "anchor" the commercial production. Howard Ashman agreed. "He didn't want just somebody with a checkbook who would leave him alone," Wells argued.[25] Ashman thought strategically: it's not only about *Little Shop of Horrors*; it's about the next show and the one after that. He wanted to work with the best, the Tiffany brand or Mercedes—not the Roger Corman of the New York theatre scene but rather a Louis B. Mayer, a Samuel Goldwyn, the best in the business.

Three companies owned the vast majority of Broadway theatres: Shubert, Nederlander, Jujamcyn. "Nederlander wasn't interested," Wells explained. So it became a duel: Shubert versus Jujamcyn. The latter company was the youngest of the three, its curious name derived from the grandchildren of its founder—Judith, James, Cynthia. The Shubert Organization was built by the brothers Shubert, from Syracuse, New York, and refocused in the 1970s when the company's attorneys, Gerald Schoenfeld and Bernard B. Jacobs, took over the firm. "Jujamcyn was totally in my domain," Wells recalled, and he communicated with president Richard G. Wolff, who "always wanted to beat Bernie"—that is, Bernard B. Jacobs.[26] At the same time, Renick decided that *Little Shop* would need a general manager, who would be responsible for budgets, contracts, and day-to-day operations. So he called Albert Poland. Baby-faced, with blond hair, he became an expert in Off- and Off-Off-Broadway productions. In 1980, Poland expressed some interest in an earlier WPA show directed by Ashman, *Put Them All Together*, as a potential Off-Broadway transfer. "So what do you want for this?" Poland asked, after watching the intimate play. Renick replied, "I want six thousand dollars."

"How did you pick that figure?"

"We need new air-conditioning, and that's how much it costs."[27]

Put Them All Together never moved, and the WPA Theatre survived without air-conditioning. So when Renick telephoned Albert Poland in the spring of 1982, the general manager groaned, "Oh, he wants new air-conditioning!" On the phone, Renick's voice was all excitement: "Albert! It's Kyle Renick. I've been trying to reach you. I have a show down here; twenty-five producers are running after it." So that night, a Thursday, Poland went to see *Little Shop of Horrors*: "it was a hit from the very first note."[28] After the show, he telephoned a friend, Cameron Mackintosh. Born in London, in 1946, Mackintosh worked as a stagehand and produced his very first musical at the age of twenty-three, a revival of the 1934 hit *Anything Goes*. By the 1970s, he launched a revue of Stephen Sondheim songs, entitled *Side by Side by Sondheim*. A more ambitious project, the musical *Cats*, which Mackintosh co-produced, opened in London in 1981. But it was after midnight in the United Kingdom when Albert Poland called, and Mackintosh was asleep. He slowly awakened to the sound of American enthusiasm: "Listen, Cameron, I've just been to the WPA to see a tryout of a little show, which I think you would like; and you should really get the rights for London." Mackintosh was unfamiliar with the Roger Corman film, so Poland pitched the story of *Little Shop*. Mackintosh said, "Fuck London. I want to produce it in New York."[29] He concluded with a piece of advice: "Call Bernie."[30]

Indeed, on the following day, Poland telephoned Bernie Jacobs, of the Shubert Organization. Urged by Albert Poland, Jacobs agreed to see *Little Shop* that evening. He attended the performance with his wife, his daughter, and her husband.[31] Choreographer Edie Cowan knew Jacobs from her time as a Broadway dancer, and she spotted him. He thought that the WPA arranged "a really hot audience" to laugh and applaud at all the right moments in order to impress the Broadway theatre owner. Cowan disabused this notion: "Bernie, this was the worst audience we've had!"[32] The next day, Poland spoke to Jacobs, who began, "Well, it wasn't my cup of tea." Poland deflated; *Little Shop* would not be a Shubert production after all. Then Jacobs continued, "But if you want us to come along, we might consider it." Poland could not decipher the phrase "come along"; perhaps it meant a small investment. On Monday, the general manager called Bernie Jacobs one more time. When they connected, Poland heard these words: "Albert, I have David Geffen on the line. We want the show."[33]

Geffen was friendly with Ashman's agent, Esther Sherman; they had worked together at William Morris. Geffen went on to form his own management company and founded Asylum Records and, later, Geffen Records. He had a talent for finding the right thing at the right time, and his musical acts included the Eagles, Joni Mitchell, and Donna Summer. He also worked in film and ventured into theatre, co-producing the hit musical *Dreamgirls* with the

Shubert Organization in 1981. When Geffen first learned about *Little Shop of Horrors* as a musical, he called it "the worst idea I ever heard."[34] Nonetheless, he agreed to see the WPA production that same weekend, although he never showed up.[35] Now he wanted to produce the musical with the Shuberts: hits have their own momentum. During the phone call, Poland contended, "We have to put Cameron in," since the English producer told Poland to call Bernie Jacobs in the first place. "I had completed the deal to bring *Cats* to New York," Mackintosh explained, and his partners were David Geffen and the Shubert Organization (along with the Really Useful Group).[36] And so a triumvirate was born: David Geffen, Cameron Mackintosh, and the Shubert Organization.

While negotiations were underway, Ashman met with Bernie Jacobs, at the Shubert offices, and Richard Wolff, at Jujamcyn. "Now I know there's someone crazier than me," Ashman said of Wolff.[37] In some ways, the Jujamcyn offer was preferable: the WPA Theatre would retain 40 percent of the net profits; the Shubert contract offered only 35 percent.[38] But one deal point proved to be decisive: the "Unilateral Move Clause." The WPA determined that the commercial producers could not move *Little Shop* to another theatre without the WPA's consent. As Steve Wells recalled, "Howard was the most vehemently insistent on that." Wolff demurred, while the triumvirate conceded this point.[39] When Bernie Jacobs asked how much it would cost to produce *Little Shop* Off-Broadway, Albert Poland invented a number—$350,000—a rather good guess.[40]

Now the WPA secured a trio of commercial producers to launch *Little Shop* into the wider world—beyond an Equity Showcase in a ninety-eight-seat house with actors who are paid in subway fare. All they needed was a theatre. Marty Robinson remembered theatre shopping with Ashman; they looked at the Kit Kat Club, a downtown nightspot named for the location in the musical *Cabaret*. But Albert Poland believed there was only one venue that would work: the Orpheum.[41]

Named for Orpheus, a mythological figure associated with music and poetry, the Orpheum Theatre, at 126 Second Avenue, served as a Yiddish theatre from the early twentieth century. In 1959, it hosted the premiere of one of *Little Shop*'s important predecessors, *Little Mary Sunshine*, Rick Besoyan's nostalgic evocation of 1920s operetta. Because of the show's success, more musicals followed in the 1960s: *Madame Aphrodite*; *Half-Past Wednesday*; *Jo*, based on *Little Women*; and another Besoyan effort, *Babes in the Wood*.[42] What is more, an earlier WPA drama, *Key Exchange*, also transferred to the Orpheum. The building was near the corner of Second Avenue and St. Mark's Place—a neighborhood of punk rockers and piercings, vintage clothing stores and shady hotels, kosher restaurants and dive bars. Opposite the Orpheum stood Gem Spa, peddling candy and cigarettes and a famous egg cream; this store was a hangout for real-life urchins. For *Little Shop*, Connie Grappo believed that the neighborhood was part of the attraction: "the East Village *was* Skid Row."[43]

However, Paul Mills Holmes found the Orpheum to be strange because "it looked like a bowling alley." The house was narrow, with a long aisle down the middle. "The Orpheum Theatre was kind of a derelict space," according to scenic designer Edward "Hawk" Gianfrancesco. "So I got the job of redesigning it." The set moved from the WPA; because the Orpheum was narrower, some adjustments were needed. But Hawk focused on the building.[44] The theatre held 299 seats, and the *Little Shop* producers decided that more seating would make the show financially viable. So Hawk upgraded the theatre balcony by adding more seats to bring the total capacity to 347.[45] In the orchestra, he raised the back rows to improve sight lines, and he installed refurbished seats to replace their tired predecessors.[46] A crawlspace beneath the stage was blasted out to create a green room, with a sofa and a few chairs. Because space was so limited, the fourth and largest of the plants would hang above the stage until it was time to take over the world, in Act Two.[47]

While Hawk renovated the Orpheum, its backstage area remained joyfully *un*renovated. Each dressing room—again, one for men, one for women—was "smaller than a small bathroom."[48] When the cast moved to the new theatre, Sheila Kay Davis discovered a "dirty, cramped dressing room." Again, the urchins shared with Audrey: "four grown women in a dressing room, with the costumes, mind you." Davis continued, "The three of us sat on one side, and Ellen sat on the other side." Jennifer Leigh Warren mentioned the building's curious layout: "to get from one side of the stage to the other, we had to walk through the men's dressing room."[49] And the women's contained the one and only shower.[50]

The backstage area may not have been an improvement over that of the WPA, but *Little Shop of Horrors* was now a business, a commercial enterprise, designed to make money. Geffen, Mackintosh, the WPA, and the Shubert Organization formed a partnership, and Albert Poland registered the Little Shop Company as a legal entity.[51] *Little Shop* at the WPA closed on Sunday, June 6; eight days later, Poland prepared a budget and an estimate of weekly running expenses. At the time, a large Broadway musical might cost between three and five million dollars; Poland initially budgeted *Little Shop* at $300,000. Part of the production expense was a $25,000 payment to the WPA for its cost-to-date.[52] Earlier in the year, Renick budgeted the Equity showcase at $30,000; well-practiced in the ways of Off-Off-Broadway, he brought the show in *under* budget.[53]

Poland admitted that the eventual Off-Broadway budget ran higher than his first estimate of $350,000, but as Ashman had hoped, the show was designed to *run*.[54] Fixed weekly expenses were estimated at $20,500. In addition, the Little Shop Company would have to pay the theatre rental and royalties to key participants. Ashman and Menken would earn 6 percent of the weekly box-office gross until recoupment; Roger Corman earned 1 percent for the underlying rights; Edie Cowan would get 1.5 percent; and so on. Calculating all the numbers, Poland found that *Little Shop of Horrors* would show some profit when it grossed around $30,000 a week—then it could begin to pay back its production cost.[55]

As the show headed into rehearsal, Cameron Mackintosh decided to travel to New York to look after it. A well-established figure in the London theatre scene, he had produced only one previous play in the US: *Tomfoolery*, based on the satirical songs of Harvard mathematician Tom Lehrer. This show opened in December 1981, and the cast included Jonathan Hadary, of *God Bless You, Mr. Rosewater*. In the summer of 1982, Mackintosh perceived that *Little Shop* could be a practice run before his next American venture: the Broadway premiere of *Cats*, scheduled for October.[56] Ashman arranged two weeks of rehearsal to get *Little Shop* ready for the Orpheum, and Mackintosh would observe the musical then.[57]

In theory, this transition from the WPA to a commercial run was the moment when the producers could recast the show with minor celebrities who (presumably) would sell a few tickets. TV personality Scott Baio, of *Happy*

Days, could appear as Seymour Krelborn, and Bea Arthur could take on the role of Mr.—or Mrs.—Mushnik. But this was not the way Kyle Renick operated. Darlene Kaplan, the casting director, admired his loyalty: "He was very good and very devoted to people," and he wanted WPA productions to move "intact."[58] However, two cast changes were necessary before the musical re-opened that summer.

Michael Vale, who played Mr. Mushnik, "was never really in love with the show."[59] Further, Robinson believed that the actor "did not want to work that hard."[60] Vale was already successful from TV commercials; he lived on Central Park West and did not need the pittance that *Little Shop* could pay. He had his fans, including Robby Merkin, who noted, "you missed him when he was eaten." However, Holmes explained that the decision came down to billing; Vale demanded star billing, even though his character was secondary.[61] To replace Michael Vale, the producers found Hy Anzell, known as Hymie. One actor called him "High Anxiety": "the most nervous human being I have ever seen." Lee Wilkof, who would play opposite Anzell, used the terms "coarse and nervous and needy and not-great hygiene." Robinson agreed that the newcomer was "overweight and kind of smelly and sweaty," but these qualities worked for the character: he was a credible Mushnik, the smalltime business owner at 1313 Skid Row.[62]

Another original cast member who would miss the Off-Broadway premiere was Leilani Jones. During and after the WPA run, she auditioned for other roles: "I worked *all* the time," she said. Actors could earn good money performing in industrials—live or filmed entertainments for American corporations. One such industrial prevented Faith Prince from originating the role of Audrey at the WPA. Later, Jones was cast in another, for John Deere, the manufacturer of tractors and agricultural equipment. It was to be a live event, staged in New Orleans: "we were riding tractors and singing and dancing." Only a three-week job, "it was very lucrative," she added. However, her new gig conflicted with the scheduled Off-Broadway opening of *Little Shop*: July 27. Yet the producers decided to hold the role of Chiffon for her. "They could have said 'Well, see ya!'" Jones explained.[63] A performer named Marlene Danielle covered the part for two weeks. Edie Cowan taught her the dances, and Danielle played Chiffon until Jones returned to New York, in August.[64] Months later, Danielle opened in the Broadway company of *Cats* and never left—a long-standing member of a long-running show.[65]

The next change that took place was the ownership of Audrey II, the plant from another world. Late one night at the WPA, while a bleary-eyed Marty Robinson built his puppets, Renick asked him to sign a contract; "I had signed away all rights to the plant," Robinson learned. Ashman later resolved that the deal was unacceptable. Typically, a musical is comprised of three component parts: book, music, and lyrics. Ashman determined that *Little Shop*— exceptional in so many ways—had four parts: book, music, lyrics, and plant. "When it became obvious that we were going someplace," Robinson recalled, "Howard sat me down with his agent." On the Skid Row set one night after a performance, the lanky, long-haired Muppeteer met the compact, fiery William Morris agent. Esther Sherman lectured the young man on the ways of the theatre and the ways of the world, and Robinson mumbled something about working for art, not money. Sherman had no patience for such innocence. "I'm sorry," she said, "you're an asshole." She conveyed that *Little Shop* was going to earn a lot of money, and Robinson deserved a share. Ashman and Menken both surrendered a portion of their author royalties to give Robinson one half of one percent: "Every two dollars that *Little Shop* makes worldwide, I get a penny." Because Ashman felt that Robinson's contribution was vital to the show's success, the puppeteer earned a piece of the author royalties of gross receipts—not profits—in perpetuity, or as long as copyright exists. Robinson would share in any potential film or television deal, cast album sales, productions at home and abroad, and more.[66]

While Esther Sherman negotiated a deal for her new client, Marty Robinson, Albert Poland worked on contracts for the rest of the cast. "The negotiations for Ellen's contract went on for a very long time," he said. When he thought the deal was complete, Greene's agent surprised him with "We haven't yet discussed the doll"—that is, the inevitable Audrey action figure. Poland was again surprised when Actors' Equity, the all-powerful theatrical union, made a ruling on the contracts for Crystal, Ronnette, and Chiffon: "Equity, in their infinite wisdom, declared the three girls to be chorus contracts."[67] Warren, the original Crystal, commented, "You have three Black women, and people automatically assume in America, 'Oh, here's your chorus.'"[68] Indeed, the principals would sign one contract and the urchins another, the "pink contract." "It was pink because it was humiliating," Poland suggested.[69] Ashman was "annoyed"; he wrote a letter to protest Equity's decision. "To him, there was no chorus in this show," Warren submitted. He shaped her belief that "these women were probably—maybe—the ones in charge of this whole story."[70]

Poland also supervised the creation of the show's advertising art. David Edward Byrd, who generated the posters for other WPA productions, "was a '60s person," Poland said.[71] Because Byrd lived in Los Angeles, he did not see *Little Shop* at the WPA. Instead, the producers sent him an audiotape. Listening to the score, the artist managed to capture the spirit of the piece. In an early draft, there are three central elements: Seymour, Audrey, and Audrey II. Poland's friend Bruce Mailman happened to be at the offices of Great Scott Advertising on the day this artwork arrived; Mailman cut Seymour out of the frame. The corrected version went back to the artist, who then painted the final image.[72] Appropriately, it evokes both a B movie and a roadside haunted house; the colors are primary, childlike—red, green, and burnished gold. At the bottom is Audrey, who has fainted, her blonde hair flowing, pre-Raphaelite. The word *Horrors* drips in bloody red, much as it would in a vintage movie poster about a cannibal cult or a diabolical doctor; in contrast, the words *Little Shop* flaunt a cheerful 1980s font, with geometric shapes and polka dots, like the logo for a store at the mall, where you buy stonewashed jeans or a piano necktie. We are in the present and the past.

Little Shop of Horrors began as a film, and it was filmed again, in the form of a thirty-second advertising spot for television. The director, Thomas Schlamme, was an expert in Off-Broadway; he previously directed commercials for *Tomfoolery, Marry Me a Little,* and *One Mo' Time*.[73] The *Little Shop* cast performed for Schlamme during one long day at the Orpheum Theatre, before Hawk installed the new seats.[74] Leilani Jones, still in New Orleans, missed the shoot, even though the show's producers offered to fly her to New York for one day; she could have told her current employer, John Deere, that she was ill. So Marlene Danielle took her place in the commercial—and earned residuals thereafter.[75] Like Byrd's poster art, the commercial draws on the monster-movie tradition that inspired the musical. An end-of-the-world narrator intones, "It's bone chilling; it's spine tingling; it's a musical." Then the catchy opening number concludes the spot. In the 1970s and 1980s, Menken wrote advertising jingles, and "Little Shop of Horrors," in this context, sounds like another jingle—a welcome, an invitation to a store or a new musical. Now on television, the song "Little Shop of Horrors" becomes a postmodern artifact: an advertisement for itself.

As Ashman prepared his cast for the Off-Broadway opening, the staging did not change much from that of the WPA. Cowan generated new choreography for the song "Mushnik and Son," and Ashman re-staged the finale.[76] Marty Robinson built a slightly larger plant No. 1 and improved the branches for the fourth and final plant.[77] Opening night arrived: Tuesday, July 27, 1982. Unlike a Broadway musical, *Little Shop* did not hold previews; the WPA run effectively tested the material. Because it was summer, most theatre critics were out of town, in the Hamptons or some cooler clime. That night, before the show, Albert Poland met David Geffen at the Orpheum. "I'm a nervous wreck," said the LA-based producer. Poland beamed confidence: "Well, you have nothing to worry about." They met again at intermission, and Geffen's mood had changed: "Albert, it is a great big smash!"[78] During that first performance, there was only one major mistake: the dentist's chair failed to rise out of the floor as it did at the WPA. Hawk blamed the company that moved the set from one theatre to another. After the show, "there was a wine-and-cheese party in the lobby of the Orpheum Theatre," Poland recalled. "The Shuberts spared no expense."[79]

New York audiences in the summer of 1982 could choose from a range of musicals: *Annie, A Chorus Line, Dreamgirls, Evita, 42nd Street, Joseph and the Amazing Technicolor Dreamcoat, Nine, The Pirates of Penzance, Sophisticated Ladies, Sugar Babies, Woman of the Year*. At the Orpheum, *Little Shop* performed eight times a week, from Tuesdays to Sundays. However, one half of the performances were on the weekend: two on Saturday and two on Sunday. The top ticket price was $22.95 (the top price at *A Chorus Line* was $40). Over that summer, a new round of reviews appeared. The *Daily News* referred to the story's "Faustian pact," and *Women's Wear Daily* noticed "a grotesque but hilarious treatment of the Faust legend."[80] Mel Gussow was quoted again, on August 22, 1982, when he opined that "the scene-stealer is that people-eater"—a phrase that recalls the film's original title, "The Passionate People Eater."[81] In the same issue of the *New York Times*, Walter Kerr proved crankier, in an article that lamented the contemporary theatre's reliance on special effects, which he disliked: "It so happens that I was not as enamored as many of my colleagues were of the new musical at the downtown Orpheum, 'The Little Shop of Horrors.'"[82] Curiously, he recalled the title of the Roger Corman film, not the musical he just saw.

The most cogent review appeared in *Time* magazine, entitled "When Trash Is a Treasure" and written by a film critic, Richard Corliss. "In the popular arts, these are glory days of trash," the review begins. It explains how fiction, nonfiction, film, and theatre all borrow from the past, and the formula, for Corliss, is clear: "the way to make a hit is to recycle pulp into pop." Corliss raises the essential question: "So why shouldn't a musical comedy be spawned from one of the trashiest, cheapest B movies ever made?" Next, he describes the Corman film and its unusual genesis, and he praises actor Lee Wilkof and "Alan Menken's pastiche of infant rock 'n' roll." Ron Taylor, the voice of Audrey II, "sounds like Paul Robeson crossed with an air-raid siren." Corliss concludes with a rapturous assessment of Ellen Greene's Audrey: "a sweet, sexy, slightly dizzy blond with an Elmer Fudd lisp," who happens to be "the wildest force of nature on the Orpheum stage."[83]

Still, audiences did not fly to the theatre and buy all the tickets. On August 8, 1982, Sarah Ashman married her boyfriend, Ron Gillespie. Howard Ashman attended his sister's wedding; feeling pessimistic, he foresaw that *Little Shop* would not last a year. "Oh, it will," countered his newly minted brother-in-law.[84] David Geffen, also growing nervous that same month, called a meeting with his fellow producers. "I want all the money to be spent on ads," he insisted. Poland, a veteran of many Off- and Off-Off-Broadway shows, counseled, "David, it's a waste of money. It's not gonna change anything."[85] New York theatre was traditionally a seasonal business, from September to June, like an academic year. With the advent of electrical air-conditioning, theatres could stay open, but summer was still the off-season. Theatre audiences were at the beach, on vacation, or simply not in the mood for a singing-and-toe-tapping extravaganza. Poland predicted that business would improve in the autumn. In other words, wait.[86]

More notices greeted *Little Shop* in September, including the *New Yorker*; the *Wall Street Journal*; and the dreaded Frank Rich, of the *Times*. The *New*

Yorker's Edith Oliver called *Little Shop* "a musical comedy that is both musical and comic," and Edwin Wilson, in the *Journal*, calculated that it was "part 1930s melodrama," "part 1950s rock and roll," and "part horror show." (Or, in the words of Tommy Tune, who enjoyed the show at the WPA, "Old plus old equals new."[87]) Rich attended the musical, and his column at the start of the fall season, on September 9, 1982, conveyed his thoughts on *Little Shop*.[88] He makes reference to recent Broadway shows, such as *Sweeney Todd* and *Dreamgirls*, and claims that *Little Shop* is superior to that earlier exercise in musical nostalgia, *Grease*, which guided Ashman and Menken when they decided to create the antithesis: *Grease* is the cheerful flip-side to *Little Shop*'s darker vision. Further, Rich enumerates "the requisite references" to 1950s culture and describes "Somewhere That's Green," Audrey's solo, as "the archetypal Eisenhower-era romantic fantasy." Playing Audrey, Ellen Greene leaves her audience "ravenous for more."[89]

As Poland predicted, business improved, and *Little Shop* enjoyed its first sellout week a month later, in October. Mackintosh remembered that "everyone and his wife just came down and said, 'What an amazing little gem.'"[90] At the end of each performance, the stage manager would record notes in the form of a production report: which actor missed the show, what went wrong, and who was in the audience. In that first year of performances, a wide selection of celebrities ventured to Second Avenue to experience *Little Shop of Horrors* for themselves and possibly have a picture snapped for the benefit of the gossip pages of New York's daily newspapers. Here's a partial list: Harry Belafonte, Candice Bergen, Christie Brinkley and Billy Joel, Carol Burnett, Carol Channing, Cher, David Copperfield, Jamie Lee Curtis, Erik Estrada, Ruth Gordon and Garson Kanin, Joel Grey, Gene Hackman, Jim Henson, Gregory Hines, Dustin Hoffman, Celeste Holm, Jeremy Irons, Alan Jay Lerner, Norman Mailer, John McEnroe, Bette Midler, Ann Miller, Bernadette Peters, Sidney Poitier, Robert Redford, Linda Ronstadt, Barbra Streisand, Gwen Verdon, Shelley Winters.[91] On February 27, 1983, Broadway legend Ethel Merman arrived for a matinee, with "an entourage of beautiful young men."[92] Ashman, of course, admired her work and adored *Gypsy*: his talking plant in *The Candy Shop* was named Ethel.

Some of the celebrities agreed to a photo shoot after the show; some appeared alongside or in the jaws of Audrey II. In January 1983, gossip columns ran the story that Lucille Ball attended a performance.⁹³ Memorably, her iconic TV show is cited in the course of the evening—"We snuggle watching Lucy"— but now Lucy was watching Ellen Greene. As it happened, Greene, a brunette, looked nothing like her character without the wig. She could walk out of the theatre, and "no one would know, ever."⁹⁴ On some occasions, she would greet her admirers in full makeup and wig—a kind of drag performance. With platinum-blonde hair, she was Audrey, the girl who imagines "Somewhere That's Green"; otherwise, she was plain Ellen Greene, from Brooklyn, an actor of mild renown. Greene admitted, "It takes me about an hour to get out of that character."⁹⁵

In the first year, rumors circulated that *Little Shop* would return to the screen, now propelled by the lyrics and music of Ashman and Menken. Franc Luz, who was so winning as Orin Scrivello, DDS, could not help but notice fellow actors Kevin Kline and Steve Martin in the Orpheum audiences. "They were all eyeballing my role for the movie," Luz lamented.⁹⁶ On November 13, 1982, Robin Williams, who was married to Ashman's college friend Valerie Velardi, attended the late performance, at 10:00 pm. This time, Lee Wilkof detected the star in the house. Peering through the set of the shop, he whispered to Franc Luz, "You know who's out there? Robin Williams. You know *why* he's out there? Orin."⁹⁷ Beyond such well-known actors, a number of filmmakers also joined the audiences. Earlier that year, on August 31, two directors showed up on the same Tuesday night: Steven Spielberg and Roger Corman—the one who started it all by trying to shoot a feature film in two days rather than a more leisurely schedule.⁹⁸ "I thought the stage version was wonderful," Corman remarked. "It caught the spirit and youthful energy of the film."⁹⁹ He also appreciated the fact that when you walked outside afterwards, you were on Skid Row.¹⁰⁰

That summer, as New Yorkers and tourists and Hollywood personnel discovered the show, the Orpheum actors entered a studio to record the cast album. Ashman, like so many others, grew up to the sounds of the American musical through vinyl records—dreaming of Broadway from Baltimore or Dallas or Des Moines.¹⁰¹ When an interviewer asked Ashman how to interest young people in musical theatre, he replied, "You have to strap them to chairs and make them listen to *Gypsy*."¹⁰² Notice the word *listen*. He did not say watch or attend a performance—surely desirable. No, the key was to listen. This, of

Figure 7 *Past and present. Roger Corman attended the musical at the Orpheum on August 31, 1982. Richard Corliss's* Time *magazine review is in the background. (From left to right): Howard Ashman, Alan Menken, Roger Corman, Catherine Corman, and Julie Corman.*

course, suggests a recording, such as the Original Cast Album of *Gypsy*, released by Columbia Records in 1959; it thrills from the overture to Ethel Merman's eleven o'clock number, "Rose's Turn." *Little Shop of Horrors*, as a recording, could join *Gypsy* and other musicals on the record shelf in a local store—an honor denied to the first Ashman-Menken collaboration, *God Bless You, Mr. Rosewater*.[103]

Yet a Broadway cast album was often the work of one day: the day off, no less, when the exhausted cast and weary musicians arrive in a recording studio to preserve what they had created in the theatre. Only a few takes per song would be customary; there was so much to do. In contrast, a rock album is wrought—especially for bands that are selling successfully. For example, the Beatles recorded *Sgt. Pepper's Lonely Hearts Club Band* over a four-month period, from late 1966 until 1967.[104] Songs were reworked or replaced; overdubs and studio effects enhanced the performances. The cast album for *Little Shop* would be recorded more like a rock album—not because of the rock-inflected score but because of David Geffen. "David was most interested in the album," co-producer Mackintosh explained.[105] Geffen was a music person first, claiming many successes in his career as a music manager and then a producer. Yet he did not see the recording as an end in itself: "I view cast albums as a way of promoting the show and would never do an album of a show that I didn't produce." As the partnership agreement stipulates, Geffen Records "shall have the right to produce, manufacture and distribute an original cast album."[106]

Ashman prepared to record his musical, just as he had prepared to direct it: rigorously. Goddard Lieberson, the Columbia executive who mastered the art of the cast album through recordings of *Gypsy* and other shows, argued that a record and a piece of theatre are two different media: "I would have to explain patiently to the librettist and the composer and the lyricist that you could listen to a song on a record forty times, but to hear some banal, spoken introduction to the song drives you nuts after the third time."[107] Ashman required no such explanation. On a copy of the script, he marked timings and cuts in anticipation of recording the show. Each number and reprise is timed to a fraction of a second. For instance, "Da-Doo" runs one minute and 5.2 seconds; "Now (It's Just the Gas)" clocks in at "3:13:27." Further, there are cuts indicated to help the score fit on a vinyl record and to obviate the problem that Lieberson addressed. Ashman made cuts to the dialogue in "Somewhere That's Green," after the verse and before the chorus. He also added words, when needed, to clarify a story point. During the song "Don't It Go to Show Ya Never Know," Chiffon says, "You was great, Seymour!" (30). For the album, Ashman added "on the radio"; now the listener understands the context.[108]

Thus prepared, Ashman entered the studio with the cast and musicians on a day off, Monday, August 9, 1982, just two weeks after the Orpheum opening.[109] The location was A & R Recording, in Manhattan, named for Jack Arnold and Phil Ramone. In fact, Geffen selected Ramone, a rock 'n' roll producer, to record *Little Shop of Horrors*. Born Philip Rabinowitz, in South Africa, Phil Ramone recorded many musical acts, including a series of hit records for singer-songwriter Billy Joel. That first day of recording was typical for a show album: the band and singers performed the score as they would in the theatre. Paul

Mills Holmes called it "standard-operating procedure." It was a long day; the singers worked from ten in the morning until eleven at night.[110] It was also freezing in the studio. Steve Gelfand, the bassist who joined the Orpheum production, complained to the producer multiple times; however, Ramone would not raise the temperature.[111] Either the recording equipment liked it cold, or Phil Ramone did.

In the chilly studio, Ramone did not follow show order for the numbers, and he was ready for "Somewhere That's Green" at twelve noon.[112] Music director Bob Billig played piano for most of the tracks, but Menken played a few, including this one.[113] Ellen Greene, who was unafraid to voice her opinions during the rehearsal process, was true to form in the recording process. She preferred to record her solo later in the day and asked Holmes to intercede with the legendary producer. "Ellen sort of treated me like a manager," Holmes remarked. He explained to her, "This is the way they scheduled it." Billig recalled that "Ellen was not in great voice"; she chose to take an "alternate note" in the song "Skid Row (Downtown)." On the line "Where relationships are no-go," she sang a lower note on "go," Billig said, "because she didn't have the D."[114] The last song recorded on that long day was "Git It" (aka "Feed Me").[115]

If this were a Broadway cast album, then the cast album would be done. The producer would mix the tracks; the record would be pressed and released. But Geffen and Ramone imagined a longer process, and Geffen was willing to pay. "It was a multi-week recording," Wilkof remembered.[116] The urchins returned to the studio two days later, on August 11. More recording time was scheduled over the next two Mondays, August 16 and August 23.[117] Wilkof was called in many times, and he noted that he recorded "Suddenly, Seymour" alone in the studio, not with Ellen Greene. He also remembered recording more than one version of "Git It."[118] Further, as on a rock album, Ramone used overdubs to enhance the Orpheum band; the four musicians were joined by Hammond organ and by guitar, played by David Brown, lead guitarist for Billy Joel in the 1970s and early 1980s. Robby Merkin began to fear for his credit. *Little Shop* could launch his career as a theatre orchestrator, and now he felt that Ramone's process was encroaching on his work. Ramone knew just what to say: "Of course, you're gonna get the credit. You're the orchestrator. This is overdubbing; this is recording; this is a whole other thing."[119]

During those long days of recording, Franc Luz, who was the show's Equity deputy, found himself reminding the authors of the union-required meal breaks. Ashman and Menken wanted to keep going: get the next take, move to the next song. So Luz confronted Ashman, who did not want to hear about anything as mundane as food. "Have you ever done a cast album before?" Ashman demanded. "This is big. And you're worried about your *meal*?"

"Well, Howard, I'm flagging. I wanna have half an hour to clear my head and have a meal, and I'll come back. And it's the rules."

"The rules? This is a cast album!"[120]

Luz felt that his background among the Irish and Italian working classes of Massachusetts made him more assertive, less cowed by management, more attuned to workers' rights. He also clashed with the director when it came time to record the prologue.[121] At the WPA, the prologue was spoken by Ron Taylor, into his microphone.[122] When the show moved to the Orpheum, the part was reallocated to Luz, since he played Orin "and everyone else" (5). In the studio, Ashman directed Luz's performance, but the actor was not able to deliver the lines the way Ashman wanted. Then Luz proposed an idea: "Why don't you do it?" Ashman resisted, at first. Menken played piano on a few of the tracks; now Ashman could perform on the album as well. "It's kind of your little cameo," Luz suggested.[123] Late one night, Ashman recorded the opening words of the show:

> On the twenty-first day of the month of September, in an early year of a decade not too long before our own, the human race suddenly encountered a deadly threat to its very existence. And this terrifying enemy surfaced—as such enemies often do—in the seemingly most innocent and unlikely of places. (13)

Around two o'clock in the morning, an excited Ashman called Albert Poland with an update: "It's going brilliantly." From the studio, Ashman played his recording of the prologue over the telephone. "Well, I have to be honest with you," Poland responded. "I really don't like it." He preferred Franc Luz.[124]

At last, the album was complete. Geffen installed high-end audio equipment in the Orpheum Theatre, and a listening party took place after the performance on September 7, 1982.[125] As Grappo recalled, "People were just elated." A note of dissent came from Paul Mills Holmes. "I remember being just a little disappointed," he said. "It didn't feel like the show." He missed "the raw, downtown feel" of the theatrical experience.[126] Before the album was released, Ashman and Menken asked Kurt Vonnegut to write liner notes; however, Vonnegut's lawyer, Donald Farber, insisted on a payment.[127] The record sleeve does include liner notes, attributed to no one. One line reads, "This album is dedicated to Lehman Engel." The famed conductor and musical-theatre teacher did manage to see *Little Shop* at the WPA; he reversed his earlier judgment and saw the merits of the Ashman-Menken musical. Engel died on August 29, 1982. He left a legacy of musical-theatre craftsmanship: writing stories through songs and songs that tell stories.[128]

He did not live to see *Cats* on Broadway. The British import, with music by Andrew Lloyd Webber and lyrics by T. S. Eliot (based on his 1939 collection *Old Possum's Book of Practical Cats*), opened at the Winter Garden, a Shubert house, on October 7, 1982. While it shared a set of producers with *Little Shop* (Geffen, Mackintosh, and the Shuberts), *Cats*, as a dance show and a spectacle, is the antithesis of Ashman's downtown musical ideal, perfected at the WPA Theatre. After *Cats* opened, Bernie Jacobs invited Albert Poland to the Shubert offices, where the general manager caught a glimpse of an accounting statement for the new musical's first operating week and its profits: $186,000. Poland thought, "I am doomed. This is being shown to me for a reason."[129] For an Off-Broadway play, Poland was happy to see profits of three to five thousand dollars a week; in October, *Little Shop* earned six to eight thousand dollars.[130] "Bernie kept trying to raise the prices, and I kept telling him he was gonna destroy Off-Broadway," Poland explained. Eventually, the Shuberts did raise the ticket prices for the Orpheum production, and profits increased to around twenty thousand dollars a week.[131]

There was another way to maximize profits: move the show. Stephen Wells clarified the businessman's point of view: "Why keep it down at the Orpheum if we could move it up to one of our Broadway theatres and make more money?"[132] *Little Shop* would not be the first musical to make such a journey; over the previous decades, *The Golden Apple*, *Once upon a Mattress*, *Godspell*, *A Chorus Line*, and *The Best Little Whorehouse in Texas*, among others, moved from Off-Broadway. While the environments and legal parameters of Broadway,

Off-Broadway, and Off-Off-Broadway are distinct, critic Elizabeth L. Wollman finds that they are "interconnected entities."[133] Indeed, Off- and Off-Off-Broadway could serve as a proving ground for commercial material. Because of the "Unilateral Move Clause," the producing team could not transfer *Little Shop of Horrors* without the authors' consent. In December 1982, Clive Barnes referred to *Little Shop* as a "Broadway-bound musical."[134] Ashman was at least willing to entertain the notion. One afternoon, with the plant puppeteer Anthony Asbury, Ashman traveled uptown by taxi, from Greenwich Village to midtown Manhattan; they stopped at 239 West 45th Street and entered the Music Box Theatre. "Why are we here?" Asbury inquired. "They've just offered me this theatre," Ashman responded. "I don't think I'm gonna take it." Holmes recalled that Ashman preferred a slightly smaller Shubert house in the same block, the Booth.[135] *Little Shop of Horrors*, a downtown hit, could move uptown and become a Broadway musical.

But "Howard's vision was always a more intimate piece of theatre," argued Sarah Ashman Gillespie. Assistant director Connie Grappo also visited some of the smaller Broadway venues. "Howard was the one who always *knew* this belonged Off-Broadway," she said, because "he knew what made it work."[136] One issue was that of scale. "You need the conceit that the plant was taking over the universe," Wells speculated. "If you have a small space, the conceit works." Sound designer Otts Munderloh emphasized the importance of the Orpheum to the musical's success. "The show must be better than the theatre," he said. "If you go to a dingy, Off-Broadway house and the show is great, then you have a hit." Sheila Kay Davis believed that the answer was obvious: "Let's face it: it's a *Little Shop*."[137] In a radio interview, Ashman reflected on the possibilities of Broadway: "Those big theatres are scary. They're hard." Moreover, "You need *Dreamgirls* to fill that kind of house." He concluded, "What I would *not* like to do is try to torture one of my innocent, unpretentious little musicals into Broadway scale."[138] Unspoken here was Ashman's concern that he would not be accepted by the musical-theatre community uptown. "Howard didn't think the show had a Broadway sensibility," Ashman Gillespie offered.[139]

And yet: if *Little Shop* became a Broadway show, then it could compete with *Cats* in the Tony Awards for the 1982–83 season. The Ashman-Menken musical would be a strong contender for Best Musical, Best Book, and Best Original Score. Ashman resisted the chance to win a Tony Award, and *Little Shop* remained at the Orpheum. He told Grappo, "Trust me. This is where it belongs."[140]

In 1983, *Little Shop* did win awards from the Drama Desk, the Drama Critics Circle, and the Outer Critics Circle. The musical was a success—first at the WPA and now at the Orpheum—a success that eluded Ashman and Menken's earlier collaborations. But it remained to be seen whether the new show would work anywhere else. The producing team decided it was time to discover how *Little Shop* would play outside the narrow confines of lower Manhattan.

CHAPTER FIVE

It Conquered the World: New York to London and Beyond

Theatre is that which is reproducible: it can be performed here, there, anywhere—on a Broadway stage, in a high school auditorium, at a summer camp, in a pie shop. Furthermore, cast members are replaceable. Some die; some move on. If only one person in human history could ever play Prince Hamlet, then it's possible that no one would have seen him since the reign of Elizabeth I. Even Hamlet is replaceable. For *Little Shop of Horrors* to survive over time and in different places, it needed to be reproducible.

At the WPA Theatre, there were no understudies; all nine performers showed up for all twenty-four performances. But an open-ended, commercial run required understudies to go on when cast members were unavailable, ill, or trapped in the subway. An understudy is like a sequel to a book or a film: it's the same—but different. But as one company member indicated, "The whole purpose and intention always stayed the same."[1] The first understudy to join *Little Shop of Horrors* was dancer Katherine Meloche, a veteran of *Grease* who also worked for Bob Fosse: she was hired to be the dance captain and to cover the role of Audrey.[2] During rehearsals prior to the Orpheum opening, she worked with Edie Cowan to learn the "intention behind each step."[3] Thereafter, Meloche would teach the dances to future urchins. Because the choreography was never notated, Meloche scribbled her own notations. For the role of

Audrey, Howard Ashman told her, "I don't want you to be Ellen"; instead, he invited Meloche to discover her own interpretation. Greene, nevertheless, was "possessive of Audrey" and said to her understudy, "I probably won't ever be out." Yet Greene had the opportunity to see Meloche perform as Audrey, when Greene arrived early at the theatre one afternoon and happened upon an understudy rehearsal. She was alarmed to see herself on stage—that is, Meloche in the Audrey wig and Audrey costume—a doppelgänger, a moment of the uncanny. Greene gasped and ran out of the theatre. Later, Meloche apologized to the star of the show, who realized that understudies were part of the process. Calmer now, she said, "I just wish I had known."[4]

To understudy both Seymour and Orin, the Little Shop Company hired lanky, kinetic Brad Moranz, who took over the Groucho Marx role in *A Day in Hollywood/A Night in the Ukraine*, which played on Broadway from 1980 to 1981. For his *Little Shop* audition, he prepared both parts. For Seymour, he donned "nerdy glasses" and a baseball cap. Then he performed a quick change in the aisle of the Orpheum: he splashed the contents of a water bottle onto his hair and "slicked it back as James Deanish as [he] could." Adding mirrored sunglasses and a motorcycle jacket, he auditioned for the dentist. Ashman was impressed: "You wanna try singing the voice of the plant?" As Moranz explained, "At that time I could sound like Ron Taylor—I mean, it wasn't great, but it was pretty darn close."[5] So the young actor was engaged to cover three men in the show, a decision that Paul Mills Holmes attributed to general manager Albert Poland at "his most financially prudent." Hidden from view, Moranz was a plausible substitute for the voice of Audrey II; but during the curtain call, he was embarrassed when "this scrawny white guy comes out." (He would not be the last white guy to understudy the voice of the plant, which Holmes thought "didn't make any sense."[6]) Covering three performers also entailed some risk: if two miss a given show, then what? Franc Luz and Ron Taylor both missed a holiday matinee on December 29, 1982; Taylor was shooting the film *Trading Places*, for director John Landis.[7] Moranz covered the dentist, and stage manager Holmes was obliged to take the microphone and sing as Audrey II. "You wouldn't hire me to do it," he admitted.[8]

Deborah Sharpe-Taylor also covered three roles: Crystal, Ronnette, and Chiffon. Because she was married to Taylor, she was familiar with the show. At a cast party at the end of the WPA run, she sang and entertained; Ashman noticed her vocal range and decided that she could understudy the urchins. Without a formal audition, she "got a contract." Each week she would practice a different character. Despite the potential for confusion, she felt that "they were very clearly separated in my brain." Now, like any understudy, she simply had to wait. "Divas don't give up that easy," she said of urchins Warren, Davis, and Jones.[9] On October 24, 1982, Jones missed her first performance since rejoining the company, and Sharpe-Taylor played Chiffon.[10]

The first cast member to quit the Orpheum production was Hy Anzell, who had replaced Michael Vale in the role of Mushnik. As early as August 1982, the stage manager noted that Anzell committed errors onstage.[11] Donna Rose Fletcher, now the follow-spot operator, found that "he was very inconsistent in his performance." Furthermore, his hygiene had not improved: "nobody wanted to be around him." Holmes said that Anzell "got messy and was gonna do what he wanted to do." Fletcher added, "In the back pocket was Fyvush, who was fabulous."[12] Fyvush Finkel, a veteran of the Yiddish stage, covered the role. "He just had that twinkle in his eye," offered Holmes. Finkel's take on the character was different from that of his predecessors: "I try to endear myself to the audience. That's very important!"[13] Marty Robinson disagreed with this approach and argued that Mushnik was "kind of mercenary." In any case, Hy Anzell gave his two-week notice in February 1983, and Finkel took over the role.[14]

At last, it was time to launch a second company of *Little Shop of Horrors*. Poland and Bernie Jacobs considered a production on the east coast, maybe in Boston; David Geffen preferred his coast, Los Angeles. Geffen won. Poland liked the Roxy Theatre, on Sunset Boulevard, where *The Rocky Horror Show* had played (after London and before New York), but Ashman did not appreciate its nightclub-like ambience: "I don't want glasses tinkling during my show."[15] The producers settled on the Westwood Playhouse, near the University of California, Los Angeles. The setting, in the student-centric village of Westwood, was far from Second Avenue, in New York, which many mistook for Skid Row. The front of the building was a retailer in modern design, Contempo Westwood Center. "You had to go through the furniture store to get to the theatre," Connie Grappo complained. Holmes added, "The lobby was in fact the furniture store."[16]

In order to reproduce *Little Shop*, Marty Robinson needed another set of plants. "I did not want to get into the puppet-making business," he clarified. Robinson already had two jobs: working on *Sesame Street* by day and performing in *Little Shop* by night. With a contract to offer, he approached his other employer, Jim Henson, who felt that *Little Shop of Horrors* should remain Robinson's project. So the assignment went to MCL Designs, a company run by Susan Moore, who built new plants to Robinson's specifications.[17] But it was not only the plant that needed to be reproduced: just as Wilkof, Greene, and Anzell required understudies, so did Marty Robinson. He asked fellow puppeteer Anthony Asbury to join the Orpheum cast. A native of Arlington, Texas, Asbury worked with Robinson on *The Haggadah*, Julie Taymor's show at the Public.[18] Robinson also needed help building new finale branches, so he hired another puppeteer, Lynn Hippen, who hailed from Kentucky. After the Orpheum opening, he said to her, "I think this show is gonna be a hit. You should stick around." Hippen remained on salary as "laundress to the stars"; her job was to wash everyone's costumes while also maintaining the puppets and keeping them in good repair. When Ashman asked Marty Robinson to travel to Los Angeles, Asbury became the new puppeteer and Hippen his understudy.[19]

Los Angeles would be the vital test of *Little Shop*'s wider appeal; therefore, Ashman wanted key ingredients from the original production. For LA, he kept the choreographer, music director, set designer, lighting designer, and costume designer. At the same time, the director refused to decimate his flagship, at the Orpheum, still running strong in early 1983. Wilkof, Greene, and Robinson would travel to LA; other cast members would stay behind in New York. Once again, Franc Luz asserted himself. His longstanding dream was to move to LA—not as another out-of-work actor, with a headshot, a résumé, and a restaurant job—he wanted to move to LA on his terms, in a hit play. However, Ashman refused to include him in the new cast. "You and Ellen and Lee are the core of the show; you're the spine of the show," Ashman explained to Luz. "I need to keep *you* here." But the actor would not back down; he threatened to quit the Orpheum cast. Ashman called his bluff: "You'll quit the biggest hit show? Most actors are never in a show like this in their entire lifetime. You're gonna quit this show because you're not going to LA?"

"Yes."

"I don't believe you."[20]

On Tuesday, January 25, 1983, Franc Luz submitted his two-week notice. Auditions were already underway for Los Angeles, but now the Little Shop Company would need *two* Orin Scrivellos (east coast and west).[21] By the following week, Ashman relented: "Ok, you're going to LA, but you have pissed *everybody* off." Because Luz played Orin and nine other characters, he was difficult to replace. The producers could find only one acceptable surrogate, who would join the New York company. Luz would go to LA.[22]

Four members of the original WPA cast—Wilkof, Greene, Luz, and Robinson—gave their final New York performances on Friday, March 18. One day later, a new generation made its début: Brad Moranz as Seymour, Robert Frisch as Orin, Anthony Asbury as the plant puppeteer.[23] However, Katherine Meloche did not earn a promotion; she stayed on as understudy. Instead, Ashman decided to cast Faith Prince, who had been offered the role at the WPA but could not commit. Now, a year later, she won the chance to play Audrey. A fellow actor found Greene's performance "more sexual"; Faith Prince was "sweeter," and "her jokes are precise." Costume designer Sally Lesser remembered the transition: "We thought we could reimagine her look because she was a very different performer. And she didn't want to wear what Ellen was wearing."[24] Because Prince was a redhead, the crew tried a different wig, not platinum blonde. Holmes, in charge of the Audrey wigs, found a suitable red wig on 47th Street, which Prince donned for her first performances, but music director Bob Billig discovered that "it did not work."[25] Holmes agreed: "Red is a different funny" because "redheads are usually sidekicks, unless you're Lucille Ball." For the next performances, on Sunday, the stage manager's report noted, "Miss Prince wearing blonde wig instead of red. Very successful."[26] Audrey would remain a blonde.

While Prince took over in New York, other cast and crew members traveled west. Many stayed at the Highland Gardens Hotel, on Franklin Avenue, in Hollywood. Robinson and Greene lived there together, and he noted that "it was the place where Janis Joplin had died of an overdose."[27] Touring companies of *Dreamgirls* and *Forbidden Broadway* were also ensconced in the landmark building—an eastern invasion into the LA theatre scene. Holmes, for one, enjoyed his California lifestyle: "you sit by the pool, and you do cocaine, and then you go do your show."[28] Driving to work from Marina Del Rey, Franc Luz could see the Pacific Ocean; by contrast, his New York commute was on the subway, headed downtown. "Let's not lose what this show really is," he urged.[29]

Despite the changed location, the staging remained the same, a "clone" as crew members called it.[30] New performers joined the LA company, including Michael James Leslie, the first African American since Ron Taylor to perform the plant. His trajectory to the stage was unusual: a graduate of Cornell Law School, he practiced law for six months but disliked it. He stumbled into an audition for the 1977 Broadway revival of *Hair* and found a new career as an actor. Yet his voice was different from Ron Taylor's—by no means was he a clone. "I'm not a blues singer," Leslie confessed. He asked to pick up the tempo on "Git It," and Menken agreed.[31] Another newcomer was Jesse White, playing Mr. Mushnik. Like predecessor Michael Vale, he was a character actor best recognized for his work on television; White played the Maytag repairman in a series of commercials from the 1960s to the 1980s. Like Faith Prince, he wanted to distinguish himself from earlier actors in the same role. Rather than wear Mushnik's faded suit, he preferred "a grubby T-shirt" with trousers to match. He threw the rejected suit across the room and told Sally Lesser, now costuming the west-coast premiere, "I refuse to wear it!" Her response: "Let me go get Howard. See what he says."[32] Jesse White wore the suit. In addition to Leslie and White, three new urchins joined the cast: Marion Ramsey, Louise Robinson, and B. J. Jefferson. However, the producers wanted Lesser to make the urchins sexier: "Can you shorten the skirt? Can the tops be a little tighter?" She said that "it was always kind of a battle" to maintain Ashman's original vision of the characters.[33] Although his intention was to replicate the Orpheum production, he was still open to innovation. One urchin improvised a line for the scene in which they give directions to Audrey's abusive boyfriend: "Ooooh, took his dollar!" (40).[34] The line went into the script.

Rehearsals began at Debbie Reynolds Studios, in the San Fernando Valley, owned and operated by the former M-G-M starlet and mother of Carrie Fisher. However, in Los Angeles, Ellen Greene experienced vocal problems, and she was at risk of developing nodes—a threat to a singer's career. "Ellen was on total vocal rest," but Holmes feared that her understudy, Connie Danese, was not ready to go on.³⁵ So Faith Prince flew to Los Angeles to temporarily cover for Greene.³⁶ At last, Prince got to play Audrey opposite Lee Wilkof's Seymour, as she might have done at the WPA. The first preview was on April 19, and Greene was sufficiently recovered by opening night, April 27, 1983.

The LA production generated another kind of reunion—between past and present, between *The Little Shop of Horrors*, directed by Corman, and its musical adaptation. Three cast members from the 1960 film attended the show at the Westwood Playhouse: Jonathan Haze (Seymour), Jackie Joseph (Audrey), and Mel Welles (Mushnik). When the two Audreys met, Greene appeared humble in the presence of her cinematic forebear: "I wouldn't be here if it wasn't for you." Joseph replied, "Yeah, you're right." They both laughed.³⁷ To commemorate the opening, Ashman gave presents to his cast: "individualized ID bracelets" in "keeping with the period." One went to Connie Grappo, his

Figure 8 *Two Seymours and two Audreys. Jonathan Haze and Jackie Joseph, who played Seymour and Audrey in the 1960 film, met their successors, Lee Wilkof and Ellen Greene, at the Westwood Playhouse, on April 27, 1983. (From left to right): Haze, Wilkof, Joseph, Greene. Note the portrait of Mr. Mushnik (Jesse White) on the wall.*

assistant director at the WPA, the Orpheum, and now the Westwood. On Grappo's bracelet he engraved the words "HEIR APPARENT"; she observed that his message "gives you a sense of how he felt about his own role."[38] A month later, on May 27, Wilkof, Greene, and other cast members performed on *The Tonight Show Starring Johnny Carson*—an indication that *Little Shop* had traveled from the cultish fringe to the cultural mainstream.[39]

Reviews in Los Angeles were positive; in a perceptive review, Drew Casper, in the *Hollywood Reporter*, claimed that "Ashman knows very well that parody loves what it sends up." However, the *Los Angeles Times* was more tepid, observing "the cool style of the 1980s" but also "shallow and rather mirthless laughs."[40] With a larger theatre (around five hundred seats), the production was earning over $70,000 a week that summer.[41] The LA company managed a seven-month run, and the producers readied a third company, in London, where Greene would reprise the role of Audrey. When she left LA to prepare for her conquest of Britain, Faith Prince permanently replaced Greene, starting in August 1983.[42] This time, however, Lee Wilkof was not invited to the next incarnation of the show. "My biggest disappointment was I didn't get to do London," he said. "Ellen was considered the star." Grappo explained what happened next: "Lee quit." To replace Wilkof, the producers turned to his friend Brent Spiner, who had seen the WPA production. Spiner, like Wilkof, planned to audition for the dentist, and he sang "Heartbreak Hotel," by Elvis Presley. Instead, Ashman offered him the role of Seymour in Los Angeles; "needless to say, I jumped at the opportunity," Spiner said. He rehearsed in New York, under the direction of Grappo; then he flew to LA and went on after one rehearsal.[43] Compared to Wilkof, Spiner was taller, with an "air about him of sophistication," as if he were "a botanist with a PhD."[44]

By the time the LA company closed, on November 27, Ashman had already directed the show in London. Cameron Mackintosh, based in the UK, took charge of this premiere. But the theatrical environment was different: "we didn't have Off-Broadway," he explained, so the show was mounted in the West End, at the Comedy Theatre, built in 1881. In this traditional, proscenium playhouse, with more than seven hundred seats, *Little Shop* "needed to be designed up," the producer believed.[45] Again, several alumni from New York lent their talents: Connie Grappo, Edie Cowan, Bob Billig. Hawk's set was now supervised by Tim Goodchild, and David Hersey created the lighting. Cowan noted that Hersey illuminated Audrey II with a red light, but Ashman disapproved: "the plant creates the magic, not the lights."[46] Anthony Asbury recalled that each new production "had to be true to the original. Howard was always an absolute stickler for that."[47]

Three Americans joined the London company: Asbury, Michael James Leslie, and Ellen Greene.[48] (British members of the cast employed American accents.) Because the *Sesame Street* schedule conflicted with the London opening, in October 1983, Marty Robinson could not commit to performing the puppets, so Asbury traveled to England.[49] Michael Leslie flew from Los Angeles to London, to reprise the voice of the plant. For lodgings, the UK company offered him a dumpy flat in Brixton, where many West Indian immigrants lived. Leslie discovered trash on the sidewalks and a slum-like atmosphere—yet another Skid Row. Soon the actor complained to company manager Robert West, who countered, "My darling, we thought you'd like to be amongst your own."

"I do. And this is not it."[50]

Until a new flat was secured, Leslie spent a few days with Ashman, near Sloane Square, not far from Harrods. Leslie found his director to be the perfect host: "he would get up in the morning, and my breakfast would be ready."[51]

Sally Lesser was not among those invited to the UK, but Greene insisted, "I'm not going to London without Sally clothes."[52] So Mackintosh offered Lesser "a flat fee" for the use of her costumes. But she clarified that Audrey's wardrobe in London was not based on the original designs; Greene "literally wore the same clothes. It was not a rebuild. It was: 'Put the stuff in the suitcase. I'm taking it.'" That is to say, Greene wore the same outfits in New York, Los Angeles, and London. However, Lesser felt that the clothes "looked tired after a while."[53]

Rehearsals were scheduled to begin on Monday, September 5, at Urdang Studios.[54] From the start, there was something of a culture clash between Ashman and his British production team. Assistant director Connie Grappo witnessed the mounting misunderstanding. "They're just so lovely," she said of her British colleagues, "on the surface." Michael Leslie agreed: "They're very civil."[55] A typical call sheet, for Saturday, September 10, is more formal than its US counterpart.

"MR. JAMES" and "MR. TOWB" were called at 10:00 am—that is, Barry James, as Seymour, and Harry Towb, as Mushnik. They were to work with "MISS COWAN" and "MR. BILLIG." An important reminder appears near the bottom of the page: "Please note COFFEE and TEA BREAKS WILL BE GIVEN at intervals thru the day."[56] Back in New York, Franc Luz had to fight for his union-guaranteed meal break during a long day of recording. In the London rehearsals, Grappo learned the truism that America and Britain are divided by a common language. "If they said they *preferred* something, that meant you had to *do* it," Grappo discovered, whereas Americans hear the word *preference* as one possible option. "So Howard kept making that error." Eventually, someone was obliged to explain that "I would like" means "You must do." This British brand of indirection was hard for Ashman to grasp. Oftentimes, he thought that he had choices when in fact he was given instructions. "One might consider" was a favorite phrase. "Yeah, if you're an idiot," thought Grappo. "If you don't know what you're doing, you might consider that!"[57]

A theatre program, which sold for fifty pence, offered the reverse translation: American phrases and pop-cultural references that may be obscure were defined for British audiences. Readers learn that "The Wolfman," mentioned by Crystal in Act One, is the "[a]ffectionate name for Wolfman Jack, archetypal American DJ," and "Donna Reed" signifies the "perfect Mum."[58] "A little nooky" is what the English would call "[a] tumble in the hayloft"; "Sominex" is a sleeping pill; and zits are spots. Three of the glossed entries clarify the song "Mushnik and Son," and nine of them refer to "Somewhere That's Green" and the dialogue scene just before.[59] In fact, a capsule review in the comic journal *Punch* suggested that the allusions in the latter song should have been made British.[60]

By the time *Little Shop* began previews, Ellen Greene suffered yet again from vocal issues. In a disappearing voice, she warned Mackintosh, "I think I've lost her"—meaning the character of Audrey.[61] Claire Moore, the understudy, covered for Greene during a few shows and was the subject of a glowing column in the London *Times* about a week later:

> Understudies are pretty remarkable people though; constantly ready to mobilize and seldom required to do so, simmering, par-boiled, with only a

few hours' warning to produce a cordon bleu performance. In the event, the show was a rare pleasure, and the understudy, tottering about on four-inch heels, sang like an angel and was greeted with roars of delight. What a comfort for the splendid Miss Greene to know that she has Claire Moore in the wings ....[62]

However, other reviews were less enthusiastic. High praise appeared in *The Observer*: "the wedding of Mr Ashman's words to Alan Menken's gleamingly exact song parodies exemplifies what the musical theatre is for."[63] But others found *Little Shop* inferior to homegrown favorite *The Rocky Horror Show*, which premiered in London in 1973.[64] The most scathing notice appeared in *The Guardian*, a day after the official opening (October 12, 1983). This reviewer calls *Little Shop* "a prime example of the witless celebration of the fifth-rate." Further, "The jokes, such as they are, are terrible." Even Menken's melodies fall under the critical knife: "forgotten even before they are even finished." The review concludes with a final blow: "it is a short, thin, empty evening."[65] On the other hand, Greene won adulation in the London press. "I have a rare and radiant new heroine to introduce," begins Jack Tinker in the *Daily Mail*. Indeed, he calls her "the funniest lady currently on the London stage."[66]

American members of the cast felt that the show was not received as well in the UK. Puppeteer Anthony Asbury commented, "They'd laugh, but they didn't know why they were laughing."[67] Less than two months into the run, Mackintosh was concerned enough to refashion the economic model to keep *Little Shop* on the boards: the so-called "New Arrangement," by which royalty participants would receive their payments from only 50 percent of earnings above "fixed weekly costs." The remaining sums would be deferred until the show recouped its cost, estimated at this point to be £323,094. Mackintosh hoped that the New Arrangement would lead to "a profitable, long-running enterprise."[68]

That same month, he revealed to his co-producers that their show would win the *Evening Standard* Award for Best Musical; the official announcement would be made in January 1984. He also wrote that "John Cleese of 'Monty Python' fame is about to do a free radio campaign for the show as he likes it so much."[69] Despite these blandishments, *Little Shop* in London "didn't become a smash hit," according to Mackintosh. "It wasn't absolutely boffo like it was in the Orpheum." He noted that the musical was "much more expensive to run per seat in London." After almost two years and 813 performances, *Little Shop* at the Comedy Theatre closed its doors.⁷⁰

In 1983, *Little Shop of Horrors* played in New York, Los Angeles, and London simultaneously. The Orpheum production alone grossed more than three million dollars in its first full calendar year.⁷¹ But Ashman also suffered a personal loss, when his former partner Stuart White, one of the founding members of the revamped WPA, died of HIV/AIDS. Ashman and White had not been together for years, but they stayed in touch. And this was only the beginning of the devastating impact of this disease on the creative community. In the program available at the Comedy Theatre, Ashman wrote that he "would like to dedicate this production of *Little Shop* to his friend and colleague R. Stuart White (1949–1983)."⁷²

Ashman directed the musical one more time, for the first national tour, in 1984. The LA Ronnette and Chiffon, Louise Robinson and B. J. Jefferson, joined the tour (Suzzanne Douglas rounded out the trio), and Michael James Leslie again voiced the plant. The Off-Broadway producing team handed the reins to a new set of producers, led by Mitch Leigh, the impresario and composer who enjoyed a hit with *Man of La Mancha* and then a surfeit of flops. "This was a first-class tour," said Joseph Church, its music director; however, Holmes complained that "the venues were so big," thus overwhelming "our sweet little show."⁷³ Church agreed that the tour was "misproduced" and mounted in "giant theatres." For example, Shea's Buffalo, with three thousand seats and "beautiful gargoyles and ornate boxes," was the wrong setting for *Little Shop of Horrors*.⁷⁴

One newcomer to the cast was Eydie Alyson. She auditioned in 1983, when *Little Shop* needed Audreys: one in New York, one in Los Angeles. In her audition, she sang "Wherever You Are (I Love You)," from the 1968 musical *Promises, Promises*. Ashman asked her to sing it again—this time as Audrey. Later, he told Ellen Greene, "I found this girl who could be your little sister." Alyson was invited to join the LA company and to understudy Faith Prince, who would soon take over the role from Greene. Ashman recommended that Alyson travel to LA early so that she could observe Greene in her signature role: "I think it would really help you to watch her for the week." Later, when Prince missed a few performances, her understudy got the chance to play

Audrey. Playing Seymour was none other than Lee Wilkof, who created the character at the WPA, the Orpheum, and in the cast album.[75] In the second act, Eydie Alyson heard the following: "Lift up your head / Wash off your mascara" (68). She said, "I literally started crying because I realized: oh, my God, I really am here, in this moment, playing Audrey with Lee Wilkof, and the voice—the voice that I have heard a million, trillion times—is now singing at me." She remained Prince's understudy until the LA production closed and then auditioned for the national tour in January 1984. She was cast as the touring Audrey.[76]

During rehearsals in New York, Alyson and her co-stars, Ken Ward as Seymour and Ken Land as Orin, learned the staging while Ashman and Menken decided to revise their musical once again. Understudy Brad Moranz recalled that the director would watch the show "night after night," always looking to tinker.[77] It might seem unusual to rewrite a hit show after it played in New York, Los Angeles, and London, but Menken explained, "it's not *that* unusual." The authors focused on the song "Mushnik and Son" because "Howard wanted to improve it."[78] The new version is an expansion, an excavation of the earlier song, which was performed from 1982 to 1984 and preserved on the original cast recording, sung by Hy Anzell and Lee Wilkof.

In Act One, Mushnik fears that Seymour (and his miraculous plant) will leave the florist shop that is suddenly successful. In desperation, the old man offers to adopt Seymour, who is "an orphan, / A child of the street," according to the song "Skid Row" (19). "Mushnik and Son" is a ditty, almost a throwaway, composed in C minor to evoke Mushnik's Eastern-European, Jewish heritage. However, as Wilkof pointed out, "There's references that people did not know what the fuck they were saying."[79] For example:

> Like Andy Hardy and the judge
> Like Zeus and Mercury
> Like Dumas fils and pere[80]

Andy Hardy is a hyperactive character played by Mickey Rooney in a series of M-G-M films, beginning with *A Family Affair*, from 1937. But the next two lines break a rule of theatrical lyric-writing: they are difficult to catch on first hearing. A poet can explore ambiguities and homophones on the page, but a commercial musical wants the patrons to understand. A theatre audience might hear the following:

> Like Susan Mercury
> Like duma fees in pair

Questions arise. Who is Susan Mercury, and what does she have to do with fathers and sons? Further, the uninitiated could miss Ashman's reference to French novelist Alexandre Dumas *père*, author of *The Three Musketeers*, and his novel-writing son, known as *fils*. One could also argue that Mr. Mushnik and his clerk, with their lack of educational opportunities, would not refer to nineteenth-century French authors. Even worse, the lyric seems to contain an error: "Like Honey-Fitz and take your pick!"[81] John F. Fitzgerald, known affectionately as Honey Fitz, did father three sons, but he was remembered as the father of Rose Fitzgerald Kennedy, mother to the US president. The song had to change. About a week into rehearsal, Ashman and Menken developed their new version, with music director Joseph Church sitting at the piano. He transcribed the music and lyrics onto sheets of music paper, which he entitled "MUSHNIK INSERT."[82] Through this rewrite, "Mushnik and Son" grew more substantial and less obscure.

The corrected version was first performed when the national tour opened at the Palace Theatre in Cleveland, Ohio, on March 14. Next stop, Baltimore—a sweet homecoming for native son Howard Ashman. The show opened at the Morris A. Mechanic Theatre on Wednesday, April 11, and on "Friday, the 13th" at 10:30 pm, Ashman summoned a handful of guests to a party. "Dress: cheap and cheerful," the invitation recommended. For the occasion, Ashman rented the Charles restaurant; on a wall he projected Roger Corman's 1960 film.[83] Eydie Alyson attended the party, where she met filmmaker John Waters and Ashman's mother, Shirley.[84] Reviews on the road were enthusiastic, and the company felt confident. Joanna Connors, in the Cleveland *Plain Dealer*, praised the first performance by quoting the show's advertising copy: "Totally hilarious? No. Not strong enough." Her review continues, "The monstrously hilarious 'Little Shop of Horrors' spoofs just about everything—horror flicks, Broadway musicals, girl groups, Greek choruses, the Motown sound, bad-girl-with-the-heart-of-gold stories, schlemiel-with-the-soul-of-a-lion stories, dumb blonde jokes, urban jungle films, sci-fi tales, romances."[85] Less overjoyed was the *Washington Post* reviewer, Lloyd Grove: "The show sometimes slides into the tried-and-tried-again," and it holds "glib disdain for the middle class." Even so, the reviewer admired the "clever lyrics" and the "agreeable music, composed along the nostalgic lines of Sha Na Na."[86]

Yet wherever *Little Shop* traveled, it was haunted by a feline specter, *Cats*, the British import, which began its own national tour in December 1983. In Washington, DC, while *Little Shop* played at the Warner Theatre, *Cats* lingered further down Pennsylvania Avenue, at the National. "Everyone's going to *Cats*, but nobody's going to *Little Shop*," lamented Joseph Church. The same phenomenon happened again in Boston: after *Cats* reigned at the Shubert, *Little Shop* struggled at the Colonial. "They hated us," Alyson said of the Boston audiences. "They were *Cats* crazy."[87] As business dwindled, one stop on the tour was cancelled, and the cast and crew went on a forced hiatus.[88] The tour resumed and eventually concluded at the Warfield, another large theatre (over two thousand seats), in San Francisco. One venue that did not get to book the *Little Shop* tour was the Harlequin Dinner Playhouse, in Santa Ana, California. In August 1984, its producer wrote to the agent Esther Sherman to request the rights to the man-eating musical and mentioned, without irony, the "traditional buffet."[89]

But if *Cats* could stretch its paws into international terrain, then *Little Shop* could do likewise. From 1983 to 1984, the Ashman-Menken musical débuted in Norway, Denmark, Israel, Japan, South Africa, Sweden, and Australia. Many of these productions were licensing deals, in which the Little Shop Company granted the rights to a certain territory to a local producer for a negotiated fee. Even so, *Little Shop* alumni participated in some of these openings. One person who did not was Howard Ashman. Preparing for London in the summer of 1983, he said, "This has been two years of my life, and it's allowed me to buy a word processor and not worry about the groceries, but enough is enough."[90]

First out of the gate was *Terrorsjappa*, "En ny musical," according to its cover page; the Norwegian translation was by Geir Håvard Uthaug. Musical numbers include "Gro for Meg," "Den Grønne Gren," and "Mushnik og sønn."[91] The show played at the Rogaland Teater, in Stavanger, Norway. In October 1983, after the London opening, Ashman traveled to Norway to experience his work in a new

Figure 9 *International shop of horrors. The souvenir program for* La botiga dels horrors, *which opened in Barcelona, Spain, in 1987.*

language.⁹² Dramaturge Michael Evans wrote a letter to Sherman to convey news of the show's success, and he translated a rave review: "It really seems to be something of a coup that the Rogaland Theater has gotten the European premiere of 'Little Shop of Horrors.'" The review then offers a pithy summary of *Little Shop*'s genetic makeup: "This is musical Theater of the Absurd; this is Kafka on the set of West Side Story; this is Ionesco done up has [*sic*] a B-film from the fifties."⁹³

Other European territories followed. In 1984, Denmark enjoyed *Blomstergys i den lille horror shop*, and Sweden saw the début of *En fasansfull affär*. For the English-language premieres, Ashman and his producers exerted more control. Edie Cowan stated, "Howard wanted the magic of that original production, with all the raw edges showing, to be there," and Anthony Asbury agreed that there was a certain consistency: "It was like a cheeseburger anywhere in the world. It's always gonna be a cheeseburger."⁹⁴ Since Ashman no longer wanted to direct the piece, he turned to his "HEIR APPARENT," in the words of the bracelet he gave her in Los Angeles: Constance Grappo. "Howard wanted the show maintained in a certain way, but Howard moved on," she explained. As the assistant director, she was a natural choice: "I didn't just know how the show worked; I knew the reasons behind every choice."⁹⁵

On August 18, 1984, the South African production opened at the André Huguenet Theatre. However, as an artist with a social conscience, Connie Grappo was concerned about the political situation; she was "uncomfortable because apartheid was still in existence." International artists were boycotting the country to compel a change in policy. Grappo did not want to go. So Sherman connected her with another William Morris client, the South African playwright Athol Fugard, who expressed to Grappo that *Little Shop* "should come to South Africa, that it has a message that should be done there." Grappo felt that she had his "blessing" and proceeded to fly to Johannesburg. By coincidence, Fugard traveled on the same flight. A non-drinker, he handed Grappo his little bottles of complimentary liquor. The playwright added, "You may need this."⁹⁶

After assisting Ashman in multiple productions, Grappo took the directorial reins. "I looked like I was about sixteen," she admitted, adding that she was five-foot-two and 105 pounds. But now she had to command a cast and crew in a foreign country: her "baptism by fire," as she called it. She arrived in South Africa during the waning period of apartheid, and she was pleased to work with "an interracial cast"—a breakthrough at the time for a commercial playhouse. The Market Theatre, where Fugard's plays were often performed, had previously employed interracial casts because it was zoned differently. For *Little Shop*, the co-producer, Pieter Toerien, "insisted that we have Black urchins." Stella Khumalo, Connie Chiume, and Mandisa Dlanga lived in Soweto, which was a ghetto at the edge of Johannesburg. "They didn't even have telephones," Grappo recalled. "There was a number you would call, and then somebody would take a message, get it to them." Yet Grappo found her three urchins to be "ultra-professional": "it took them like four hours to get to work in the morning. They were always early." After the first rehearsal, the music director said to Grappo, "I didn't have to teach them anything. They already knew all their harmonies."[97]

The cast was hired before Grappo reached South Africa, and she felt that her Seymour, Eddie Eckstein, was too old for the part: "He would've been a *great* Mushnik."[98] And yet the musical worked once again. A review in the *Sunday Times* stated, "Seldom can a show in Johannesburg have elicited such a delightful response from its audience." The reviewer, Adrian Monteath, enjoyed all the performers but submitted the urchins for special praise; in terms of their music, he noted the influence of "the Shangri-Las, the Drifters, the Supremes and the Ronettes." Grappo, in her *Little Shop* directorial début, also won kudos.[99] She went on to direct the show in Australia and Canada.

But Grappo had no interest in working in non-English languages, so Ashman selected stage manager Paul Mills Holmes to oversee productions in Israel and Japan, both in 1984. In Tel Aviv, he could communicate with his cast, who spoke some English (although he could not understand the Hebrew translation). Holmes noted that "the initial ticket-buyers were all older folks," who did not respond well to *Little Shop*. "But the younger set loved it."[100] In a piece of unfortunate timing, the production overlapped with Holocaust Remembrance Day, observed in Israel that year at the end of April. The image of a monstrous entity that devours the world seemed less than delightful to Israeli Jews (even as a metaphor). Holmes also noted that Israel was still a young nation: "they don't have a cinematic history that is equal to ours," with its tradition of B movies and exploitation films. But in Japan, Godzilla, Gamera, and Rodan are national icons, so *Little Shop* played better. Holmes directed the Tokyo premiere, with the help of an American-educated translator.[101]

After the initial burst of international *Little Shops*, the Paris opening took longer because it required two translators and the intervention of a lawsuit. The French producers, Claude Martinez and Paul Lederman, hired Boris Bergman to translate Ashman's book and lyrics. This time, however, Ashman supervised the rendering of his work, because he was a Francophile and had studied French in high school with a beloved teacher, Robert Rifkin.[102] Further, as Ashman's partner, Bill Lauch, explained, "I think because he was so enamored of French theatre, he wanted the French translation and this particular production of *Little Shop* to be real top notch."[103] The producers sent Bergman's translation, *La petite boutique de l'horreur*, to Esther Sherman in August 1984. She told them that Ashman responded well and that the effort could be improved through a "working session."[104] Ashman kept a version of the Bergman typescript, with handwritten corrections and emendations. By December, however, Sherman wrote to the producers to explain that her client "does not approve the French translation as prepared by Boris Bergman."[105] In February 1985, the rejected translator sought legal remedy through the Tribunal de grand instance de Paris, in the lawsuit *Boris Bergman v. Productions Paul Lederman et Claude Martinez*.[106]

Meanwhile, another writer, Alain Marcel, attempted the same task. His translation, *La petite boutique des horreurs*, includes a dedication, "à Howard"—a reasonable insurance policy given that his predecessor was fired.[107] A number of song titles and lyrics changed in the process. For example, Bergman rendered "Somewhere That's Green" as "Quelque part où tout est vert," a literal translation, significantly longer than Menken's four-note melody for the song's hook.[108] A subsequent draft offered "Un coin de verdure" (a corner of greenery), which is more concise.[109] Marcel finally settled on "Au coeur du vert" (in the heart of green), an image that approximates Ashman's original.[110]

To improve his translation and the eventual production, Marcel traveled to the United States in April 1985. He worked with Ashman on the translation to get "the cultural nuances right" because "Donna Reed doesn't mean anything to the French culture."[111] The aim was to find references from France in the

1950s and 1960s that could serve as the equivalents. Marcel also attended the show at the Orpheum Theatre, twice. On Saturday, April 13, he sat in the house during the early performance. Then, for the late show, he watched again, now from backstage, to learn the mechanics.[112]

Further, Marcel was aided by two representatives of the New York production. By 1986, Connie Grappo and Paul Mills Holmes graduated to other projects, so Ashman selected two members of the Orpheum crew: Donna Rose Fletcher and Lynn Hippen. Both are examples of how the Little Shop Company promoted from within. Robby Merkin progressed from the triple-keyboard part to conductor; Pete Calandra followed the same path; and Hippen moved from her job as laundress to plant understudy to puppeteer when Anthony Asbury joined the London cast. As Fletcher observed, Ashman liked "institutional memory." At the Orpheum, she rose from follow-spot operator to assistant stage manager and then to stage manager, in 1985, when Holmes left the show.[113] By this point, she knew *Little Shop of Horrors* as well as anyone.

Fletcher and Hippen took leave of the Orpheum to live in Paris and to supervise the production and its puppets. Again, a knowledge of the language was not a prerequisite: "I spoke no French whatsoever," Fletcher said. "But after two months, I was giving notes in French." She found that she could understand "the language of the show"; for example, *poubelle* means trash can. Rather than learning tourist French, she mastered *Little Shop* French.[114] Hippen worked with the local puppeteer, who was unenthusiastic, a chain smoker, and not in sufficient shape to handle the acrobatic performance the show required. Listening to her concerns, the producers hired a replacement, who was "feisty," "health-conscious," and "willing to do the work."[115] In June 1986, the show opened at the Théâtre Déjazet, described as "an ancient music hall in an out-of-the-way quarter."[116] Later in the year, the Ashman-Menken musical was popular enough to move to a grander location, Théâtre de la Porte Saint-Martin. The color souvenir booklet displays the grand façade of the old opera house in two phases: first with a tiny plant near the entrance; then with Audrey II bursting out of the doors and invading the wider world—a visual analogue of the show's progression.[117]

While *Little Shop* conquered audiences from Paris to Tokyo to Melbourne, there were those who were less than enthusiastic about what Ashman and Menken had wrought. A dental hygienist in Lansdale, Pennsylvania, wrote a letter to Ashman, care of the Shubert Theatre in Philadelphia, where *Little Shop* played on tour. "I must take exception to the use of the 'Dentist' in such a sadistic, medieval torture role," wrote Patricia A. Bechtel. "As a member of this profession for fifteen years, I must take offense at the way our profession is portrayed in your show." She hoped that in future projects, Ashman would "draw on new sources of humor."[118]

Another person who took exception to *Little Shop of Horrors* was Charles Griffith, screenwriter of the film on which the musical was based. He first heard about the potential musical in 1980, when Kyle Renick had written to Corman about the rights. Back in 1959, Griffith earned only $1,800 for his work on the film. Now Corman was making money from the musical version all around the world; Griffith was excluded from the deal. "I got a lawyer," he said.[119] In October 1982, he retained Carl Seldin Koerner and commenced a lawsuit.[120] Unfortunately, no one could find Griffith's contract for *The Little Shop* screenplay. Throughout his career, Corman produced films fast and cheap; record keeping was not a priority. So it was not clear who actually owned the underlying rights.[121] In the end, the parties settled, and the neglected writer would thereafter earn 25 percent of Corman's take—at least 0.25 percent of the weekly gross of a hit musical. Griffith later quipped that "it has kept me going since 1983."[122] Living in Los Angeles, he attended the show at the Westwood Playhouse and "was enthusiastic about it."[123] Thereafter, the credits for the musical were adjusted to include the creator of Seymour; Audrey; and Audrey Junior, the original man-eating plant.

Meanwhile, the flagship production at the Orpheum Theatre continued to entertain audiences, Tuesdays through Sundays, without fail. Original cast members moved on. In the spring of 1985, Jennifer Leigh Warren and Leilani Jones booked Broadway musicals, and both women attended the Tony Awards ceremony that spring. Warren appeared in *Big River*, based on Mark Twain's *Adventures of Huckleberry Finn*, which won the award for Best Musical. Jones starred in *Grind*, for which she won as Best Featured Actress in a Musical, but her show folded after seventy-nine performances. Ron Taylor and Sheila Kay Davis quit *Little Shop* even earlier, although both found their way back to Second Avenue. Taylor starred in a Broadway musical based on *The Three Musketeers*, the novel by Dumas *père*, earlier that same season, in November

1984. However, *The Three Musketeers* survived for only nine performances. By February 1985, Taylor was ready to replace *his* replacement as the voice of the plant.[124] Davis left the show in August 1984 (Ellen Greene watched her final performance). By 1986, Davis was out of work and back in New York City. Albert Poland, with a general manager's unfailing instinct, called her when the Orpheum needed an urchin. She was reluctant to return—seemingly a backward step—but he told her, "The way this business works is that you need to take work when it's offered to you."[125] Lee Wilkof also returned to the Orpheum but only as a vacation cover. He lived in New York and sometimes would make himself available as Seymour for one week. As a result, he played opposite quite a few Audreys and rehearsed with a young Donna Murphy; "she was my favorite," he said.[126] He was also obliged to learn the new version of "Mushnik and Son," which was incorporated into the production in April 1984.[127]

Of course, many New York audiences never saw these original performers. In the role of Audrey, many saw Marsha Skaggs (née Waterbury), who took over the part in 1983 after Faith Prince moved to the LA production for a second time. Fletcher thought that the newcomer "was like original Ellen"; in fact, "this was the Audrey that Howard had directed Ellen to be."[128] Skaggs connected with the character: "I really wanted to tell her story." Further, she asked herself, "When am I ever going to get to be in a bad '50s movie? Never." As a performer, Skaggs was intuitive, less mannered, less stylized. Holmes put her in the show while Ashman was in London. The director eventually saw the new Audrey, although "I never really got any notes," she said.[129]

A highlight for Skaggs and other cast members was a performance with the publicity-hungry mayor of New York City, Edward I. Koch. The 63rd Annual Inner Circle show took place on Saturday, March 9, 1985, in a ballroom at the New York Hilton, on Sixth Avenue and Fifty-third Street, with 1,800 people in attendance: "a black-tie audience of the political and corporate who's who," according to the *New York Post*.[130] The event, organized by reporters, gave the press a chance to mock their natural opponent, his Honor, the Mayor, through songs and sketches. Part of the tradition was the mayor's rebuttal, also in the form of a sketch-like performance. In 1985, the mayor's office selected *Little Shop of Horrors* as the vehicle for Koch's rebuttal. Typically, the City Hall staff would create the production, but Ashman, being Ashman, said, "I'll do it for ya!"[131] So he directed a cast that included the Orpheum actors, Mayor Ed Koch, John Houseman, and the well-known sex therapist Dr. Ruth Westheimer. Rehearsals took place at the Orpheum over the preceding week. Robby Merkin, now music director of the show and the rebuttal, found the mayor "nice and humble"; while the others rehearsed, he sat and quietly waited his turn.[132]

Speechwriter Clark Whelton wrote the script, entitled "City Hall of Horrors," with lyrics by Howard Ashman. An expert parodist, he now parodies his own writing. In the song "Down on Park Row," named for the mayor's business address, Ed Koch and the urchins sing new lyrics that reproduce the intricate rhyme scheme of "Skid Row":

Downtown
Where they legislate
You go downtown
Where the press ain't great
You go downtown
Where the wheels of state revolve slow
Down on Park Row[133]

There is a modest plot, in which Seymour is "dumb enough" to run against Koch in the upcoming election. Audrey II also joins the race and eats the incumbent. Houseman, as the pompous narrator, explains, "The plant defeats its opponents the old-fashioned way. It *eats* them." So Koch gets fed into the jaws of the ravenous plant. However, Audrey II regurgitates the politician, who reappears for his punchline: "Does this mean I'm hard to swallow?"[134] The *Daily News* and the *New York Post* ran amused stories about the performance, although the *New Yorker* complained that the mayor's little entertainment "did not mention the issue of the black vote."[135] Afterwards, Koch sent grateful notes to the *Little Shop* team and invited everyone to dinner at Gracie Mansion.[136]

Stage manager Paul Mills Holmes claimed that the musical "changed all of our lives."[137] There was a family-like atmosphere at the Orpheum Theatre, with frequent potluck dinners on Sundays, between shows. Lifelong friendships were forged—and there were material benefits as well. Marty Robinson, through the intervention of Ashman and Esther Sherman, earned enough to purchase a house in Connecticut.[138] Ashman himself moved out of the shared apartment where he wrote the musical and found a duplex in the West Village. In February 1984, he met Bill Lauch, an architect, who became his life partner. Lauch remembered that Ashman was occupied with the national tour, among other responsibilities; it was an "exciting and vibrant" time.[139] That same month, Connie Grappo married Lee Wilkof. They held a celebration at the Ukrainian National Home, on Second Avenue, just one block north of the theatre. After performing in *Little Shop*, current cast members arrived at the party and heard Wilkof sing the Sam Cooke favorite "You Send Me" to his bride.[140]

The monster musical on which they all labored reached a milestone when it achieved the permanence of print, a hardcover from Nelson Doubleday. In 1985, the authors assigned the stock-and-amateur rights to Samuel French, Inc., which made the book and lyrics available in paperback, with Byrd's artwork on the cover. Readers of the script on the page may notice how Ashman embeds the show in the musical-theatre tradition to which he thought it belonged; there are references to *West Side Story* and *Fiddler on the Roof*, Walt Disney's *Snow White and the Seven Dwarfs* and "an M.G.M. touch."[141] Anyone could now produce *Little Shop of Horrors*—a school, a university, a church, a social organization—anyone willing to pay the fee to Samuel French. However, Ashman was concerned about the show's viability. He discussed the matter with Marty Robinson: "I want this production to be eminently producible. I don't want anyone to look at this property and say, 'Ooh, plants. Let's do something else. Let's do *Oklahoma!*'"[142] So Robinson generated a series of drawings and explanations to help theatre companies operate their very own Audrey IIs.

In a way, the Samuel French agreement resembles the role of Patrick Martin, the marketing guru from World Botanical Enterprises who appears at the end of the play. "It's a very simple licensing deal," he says. "Why, with the right advertising, this could be bigger than hula hoops" (91). Now the little musical that began at the WPA Theatre could play in any town, city, or nation. But there was one more field for *Little Shop* to conquer, and that was the place where it all began: the cinema screen.

Chapter Six

Audrey III: Cinematic Dreams and Disillusionment

In November 1982, Howard Ashman began work on a screenplay entitled *Little Shop of Horrors*. It would be an adaptation of an adaptation—a film version of the stage musical based on the original 1960 movie—and the third iteration of the story of Seymour and his diabolical plant. Ashman typed a few prose treatments of the film, ranging from seventeen to twenty pages in length. A cover page states, "The following is a sort of pre-outline outline."[1] Already he was thinking in cinematic terms; "VO" (for voice-over), "credits," and camera moves are indicated.[2] A new character, the radio host from Seymour's broadcast, joins the company. Yet it is striking that just four months after the opening at the Orpheum Theatre, Ashman was willing to rethink the shape of *Little Shop*. Seven musical numbers are cut: "Don't It Go to Show Ya Never Know," "Closed for Renovation," "Mushnik and Son," "Now (It's Just the Gas)," "Call Back in the Morning," "The Meek Shall Inherit," and "Sominex."[3]

Of course, a few favorites remain, including "Somewhere That's Green." In what may be the first outline, Ashman explores the visual equivalent to Audrey's fantasy:

> As she describes her dreamlife, it appears before us in true fifties-musical-comedy-dream-sequence fashion. We see an Ozzie and Harriet bungalow in shimmering pink and turquois technicolor, in which little Seymour Juniors

(who look just like their Dad) watch Shari Lewis and eat Cheerios on metal snack tables, while Housewife Audrey vacuums and dusts prettily in pop-beads and shirtwaist, and outside, Daddy Seymour sprinkles the emerald Zoysia grass. Neighbors in Capri pants drop by for Mah Jong. All is generally right with the world.[4]

The outlines also present two additional musical moments. The first is something of a restoration, an idea retrieved from the earliest outlines that Ashman wrote for the stage musical. He wanted a "Hello, Dolly!" number, and he and Menken had written such a song, entitled "Audrey II." Catchy in the extreme, it was repurposed on the occasion of the Orpheum production's one-hundredth performance (October 22, 1982).[5] Now, a month later, Ashman inserted a similar moment into the film treatment: "NEW MUSICAL NUMBER (The 'Hello Dolly' sequence)." A note explains, "Number parodies the conventional 'Dolly' or 'Mame' number, in which a chorus gathers to sing the hyperbolic praises of a geriatric leading lady. In this case, the lady is none other than AUDREY II."[6] Another outline includes a penciled annotation suggesting that the song could feature a "guest star like David Bowie or Tim Curry or Duran Duran."[7] Besides the big production number, one other new musical idea is imagined at this point: "A rap song, sung by the plant as SEYMOUR begins a series of attempts on the Plant's life and person." In the unnamed number, Audrey II "compar[es] itself to Godzilla, King Kong, and the rest of moviedom's Greatest Monsters" and claims to be "the Baddest of them all."[8]

Less than a year later, Ashman began to draft the screenplay in earnest. By this time, he had directed the musical again, in Los Angeles and London. In August 1983, he told a newspaper reporter about his plans for after the London premiere: "I'm going to clear my desk, unplug the phone and work on adapting the script for the screen."[9] On his calendar that November, he wrote the words "major work on screenplay." By Thanksgiving, he had drafted the first twenty-five pages. By December 19, he was able to note, "Complete draft of L. S. of H." Three days later, he forwarded the script to producer David Geffen, then in Paris. On Christmas Day, Geffen telephoned to say that he loved the script.[10]

It begins with a "chilling, 'Phantom of the Opera' organ chord." Then "A VOICE NOT UNLIKE GOD's (or Charlton Heston's)" delivers the prologue.

Despite the prologue's temporal ambiguity, the first draft seems to take place in 1962. A radio announcer mentions President John F. Kennedy, and the radio later plays the Crystals song "Uptown," which indirectly inspired "Skid Row (Downtown)." "Skid Row" itself is now expanded to include "WINOS, DERELICTS, BAG LADIES, and the rest of the earth's UNWASHED SCUM." The "Somewhere That's Green" fantasy remains, with the addition of a dance break: "The mood is now pure Leslie Caron"—that is, the young dancer who appeared in the 1950s M-G-M musicals *An American in Paris* and *Gigi*. Again, quite a few numbers are absent, making way for new songs. One is "Thundercrash," to be sung by the urchins, "in an exaggerated 'Donna Summer meets Irene Cara' style." Like the references to rap and Duran Duran in the outlines, this moment suggests a musical slippage—away from the late '50s/ early '60s style that Ashman and Menken mastered in their stage version. Near the end, the plant's final number is further delineated and now called "Bad" (before Michael Jackson claimed to be "Bad," in 1987). The screenplay concludes with an apocalyptic ending worthy of a 1950s B movie when the military battles Audrey II, now "tall as a medium-sized skyscraper."[11]

An annotated photocopy of this same draft indicates second thoughts. "Thundercrash" seems to be out, replaced by "Closed for Renovation," from the stage show. "The Meek Shall Inherit" is also restored.[12] In these early drafts, Ashman revived a few ideas from the Corman film as well. Many recall *The Little Shop of Horrors* for Jack Nicholson's appearance as a masochistic dental patient, Wilbur Force. Ashman's first draft includes just such a character, with a new name, Arthur Denton.[13] Subsequent drafts restore the hardboiled police officers from Corman's film, who seem lifted from the TV series *Dragnet*. Two such officers interview Audrey, and a marginal note says, "Dragnet thing might work here."[14] Through all these drafts, Ashman reimagined *Little Shop* through the lens of American popular culture, with allusions to Gene Kelly, Elvis Presley, Broadway director Jerome Robbins, the film *Invasion of the Body Snatchers* (from 1956), and the 1957 Fred Astaire musical *Funny Face*. As Kyle Renick said, "Our references are all based on other media."[15]

The public began to notice the film-in-development and recognize its potential as a major motion picture. In March 1983, the *New York Post* revealed that "David Geffen is reportedly interested in filming the hit Off-Broadway musical *Little Shop of Horrors*."[16] It was a natural transition from co-producer of the stage play to producer of the film, since Geffen had served as vice chair of Warner Bros. in the mid-1970s. In 1982, he produced his first feature, *Personal Best*, which he parlayed into an overall deal at Warner Bros.[17] *Risky Business*, his next film, stars Tom Cruise as an enterprising high school student who opens a brothel in his suburban home. But the *Little Shop* movie attracted a bigger player: Steven Spielberg, the hit-making director of *Jaws*, *Raiders of the Lost Ark*, and *E.T. the Extra-Terrestrial*. Spielberg saw the musical in August 1982, and rumor held that he would direct the picture, with Madonna in the role of Audrey.[18] By April 1983, *Daily Variety* announced that the film would be shot in 3-D—a revival of that 1950s gimmick once used to lure audiences back to the cinema and away from the television. The article said that Martin Scorsese, the New York–based filmmaker who had recently completed *Raging Bull* and *The King of Comedy*, would direct the *Little Shop* adaptation, with a modest budget of three million dollars. Spielberg would serve as a producer.[19]

In August 1983, Ashman wrote to his former boss, Harriet McDougal, the editor at Tempo Books, about the film's progress. "I'm afraid I'm 'the kid' in this whole thing," he confessed. He had met Spielberg once in person, and they had chatted once on the phone: "He sort of manages 'Hey, how's it goin'?' and that's about it." Scorsese seemed more interested, but "the only person who takes the LITTLE SHOP movie seriously right now is David Geffen."[20] That month, Ashman traveled to Los Angeles and signed a contract to assign the movie rights to *Little Shop of Horrors*.[21] Warner Bros. paid $500,000; part of that sum would go to the Orpheum producers (the WPA Theatre, the Shuberts, Mackintosh, and Geffen himself).[22] Now the proposed budget was eight to ten million dollars.[23] However, Scorsese chose to direct another comedy set in a nightmarish version of downtown, *After Hours*, released by the Geffen Company and Warner Bros. in 1985.

By March 1984, a new *Little Shop* director emerged: John Landis.[24] It was an inspired choice: he had mastered comedy, the movie musical, and the horror film. His first studio feature, *National Lampoon's Animal House*, starring John Belushi and some relative unknowns, surprised almost everyone when it became one of the biggest hits of 1978. Two years later, Landis directed an epic musical-comedy, *The Blues Brothers*, based on characters created by Belushi and Dan Aykroyd on *Saturday Night Live*; musical performers included Cab Calloway, Ray Charles, and Aretha Franklin. A year after that, Landis made *An American Werewolf in London*, a grisly horror movie that updated the werewolf legend. Surely, this director could handle the *Little Shop* blend of comedy, music, and horror. He attended the musical, with Ashman, on March 4, 1984, and Landis and his wife later dined with Ashman and his partner, Bill Lauch.[25] The plan was to produce the film for around ten million dollars and shoot at Estudios Churubusco, in Mexico City. At the Russian Tea Room, in New York, Landis met with Ellen Greene and Marty Robinson, still a couple after two years. The director offered them the roles of Audrey I and II, respectively; they would all make the film together.[26]

Fate intervened. A few days before *Little Shop of Horrors* opened at the Orpheum, a real-life horror occurred on the set of *Twilight Zone: The Movie*, where Landis directed one of four segments in the anthology feature. A helicopter explosion took the lives of three performers, including Vic Morrow. By 1984, as Robinson explained, Landis was "embroiled" in legal issues.[27] He would eventually face both civil and criminal liability; it seems that the studio or Geffen no longer wanted Landis for the movie musical. The director wrote an affectionate letter to Ashman on June 29, 1984: "I will unfortunately not be directing the film version of 'LITTLE SHOP OF HORRORS.'" He continued, "I remain a fan of yours," and mentioned the possibility of future collaboration.[28]

Now that Spielberg, Scorsese, and Landis would not direct the *Little Shop* adaptation, there was a job opening in Hollywood. A list appeared with the names of potential directors—a who's who of early 1980s filmmakers. At the top of the list are two alumni of "the Roger Corman school" of film: Ron Howard and Jonathan Demme. Both directed low-budget fare for Corman before graduating to studio pictures. John Hughes, the director of *Sixteen Candles*, which opened in May 1984, appears on the list, as well as Geffen's director on *Risky Business*, Paul Brickman. Among the "Interesting possibilities" are Hal Ashby, Robert Zemeckis, and horror master Larry Cohen. Near the end appear a few long shots: Jim Henson is suggested, alongside the comment "I can see it now: Kermit as Seymour, Miss Piggy as Audrey." For the sake of sentiment or a punchline, Roger Corman shows up dead last; credits include *The Little Shop of Horrors*. One name that did not make the list is Frank Oz.[29]

Born in England, in 1944, Frank Oznowicz joined Jim Henson's Muppets at the age of nineteen. On *Sesame Street*, the two puppeteers performed one of the great double acts in children's television, Ernie and Bert, with Henson as dreamy, childlike Ernie, and Frank Oz as fussy, unibrowed Bert. They recreated the dynamic on *The Muppet Show*, with Henson as Kermit the Frog and Oz as the unfunny comedian Fozzie Bear—a name that seems to derive from the initials F. Oz. Henson's protégé also performed the beloved character Miss Piggy, whose tempestuous persona inspired Ashman's conception for *Little Shop* ("the plant was to be Miss Piggy").[30] Some critics noted the connection, including Diana Maychick, who found that Audrey II "resembles a drug-crazed Miss Piggy."[31] But Frank Oz was more than a Muppeteer; he became Henson's collaborator and creative partner. Together they co-directed the ambitious fantasy film *The Dark Crystal* (Ashman saw it on December 20, 1982).[32] Then Oz earned a solo directing credit on *The Muppets Take Manhattan*, released by Tri-Star in July 1984. Oz distinguished himself without Henson by performing the puppet character Yoda in *The Empire Strikes Back*, the 1980 sequel to *Star Wars*. In November 1984, a newspaper ventured that Oz would direct *Little Shop*, and Ashman typed "Frank Oz Draft" on the latest screenplay.[33] Production was to begin in 1985 with a release date in the summer of 1986.

By directing the screen adaptation of *Little Shop*, Frank Oz caught the zeitgeist of the 1980s with the show's mashup of genres: it's a romantic comedy and a monster movie and a musical. Generic purity was out; hybrid was in. *Alien*, from 1979, combines science fiction and horror; *Outland*, made two years later, blends science fiction and the western; *Blade Runner*, from 1982, is a sci-fi flick and a film noir. During the heyday of the Hollywood studio system, in the 1930s and 1940s, genre was an essential part of the filmmaking practice: the melodrama, the gangster picture, the backstage musical. Genre displays a "commitment to pre-existing forms"; audiences and producers appreciate the predictability—you know what you are going to get.[34] On the other hand, genre mashups offer a way to refresh and reinvigorate older forms. By the 1980s, Hollywood filmmakers, like some kind of mad botanist, proceeded to crossbreed genres, to break down categories: *Ghostbusters*, *Beetlejuice*, *Who Framed Roger Rabbit*.

One of the most potent combinations is comedy and horror. The pairing descends from the tradition of gallows humor, also known as sick humor or dark comedy. Typical example—a man awaits the guillotine and tells the executioner, "Just a trim, please." Dark comedy laughs at that which is not funny: death, disease, dismemberment, suicide, homicide, cannibal apocalypse. Ashman, so dedicated to the form of the musical, also "liked splatter movies," according to Nancy Parent. After *Little Shop* opened, he worked with her husband, Michael Serrian, on another potential Off-Broadway show, entitled *Splatter!* Ashman then realized that his new project was too close to *Little Shop*.[35] Nevertheless, there is a structural similarity between musicals and the slasher film: both work toward a climax every five or ten minutes, either a musical number or the next decapitation. The comedy-horror film formalizes the link. In the words of Ian Frazier, "Horror and comedy entangle themselves with each other in these great American works of satire until our laughter and recoiling become almost the same."[36] True, he was thinking about Mark Twain and Vladimir Nabokov, but laughter and recoiling defined the viewer experiences of *Gremlins* and *A Nightmare on Elm Street*, both released in 1984.[37] *Little Shop* participates in the trend, with its fusion of high and low, the comic and the tragic—a tuneful confection of hope and horror.

To create a movie that could hold its own against *Gremlins* and Freddy Krueger, Ashman and Menken decided to write new songs. One might wonder: why mess with a hit? Why write another tune? Alan Menken knew the answer: "Oscars, Oscars." He explained that "you have to write a new song." "Suddenly, Seymour" may be a delight, but according to the Academy of Motion Picture Arts and Sciences, it is not a song written for the screen. Even a mediocre *Little Shop* number added to the score would qualify for an Academy Award nomination. "There's too much publicity value," Menken said.[38] A nominated song would appear on the Academy Awards broadcast, seen all around the world. So Ashman and Menken wrote as many as seven potential new numbers for the screen. Five were slotted into the story: "Thundercrash," "Some Fun Now," "Bad," "Bad Like Me," "Mean Green Mother from Outer Space"; two were proposed for the end credits: "Your Day Begins Tonight" and "Crystal, Ronette, and Chiffon."[39] (By the time he developed the movie version, Ashman conformed the spelling of the character Ronette to match her namesake musical group.[40])

"Thundercrash" was meant to replace "Don't It Go to Show Ya Never Know" and "Closed for Renovation" (the word *thundercrash* appears in the former).

The new song would offer a burst of energy after "Somewhere That's Green."[41] Menken also recalled that "we wanted a number that was gonna be just for the girls."[42] "Some Fun Now" then replaced "Thundercrash." An early draft contains a compact, somewhat awkward verse:

> Seymour, the shnook,
> His life was the worst
> Oh what a bore dirt poor is
> Now take a look
> His luck has reversed[43]

Unsatisfied, the writers created a hybrid song—something old and something new—appropriate for a generic mashup like *Little Shop of Horrors*. Ashman wrote to Frank Oz to explain the innovation: "Frank—Finally! Here's a SOME FUN NOW version I can live with, musically & lyrically. It has a different intro verse, lifted sort of from the YOU NEVER KNOW song in the stage show."[44] Now the song begins:

> Poor Seymour pushed a broom
> Nothin' in his news but gloom and doom
> Then he lit a fuse and give him room
> He started an explosion, holy cow!
> That thing went bang kerboom
> And he's havin' some fun now!

This variant on "Ya Never Know" leads perfectly into the bouncy new refrain:

> Some fun now!
> Pop quiz:
> What's he havin'?
> Some fun now!
> Sho' is![45]

To produce this and other musical numbers, the studio hired a genuine piece of the 1960s: Robert (Bob) Gaudio, a member of the Four Seasons who wrote and produced some of their most popular songs. He attended *Little Shop* at the Orpheum and discussed arrangements with orchestrator Robby Merkin.

Gaudio wanted a closing-credits song to be performed by Freddie Mercury (this never happened), and he agreed that the plant needed a final number.[46] Ashman and Menken attempted this moment three times: first "Bad," then "Bad Like Me." The screenplay dated September 27, 1985 includes the third and final attempt, "Mean Green Mother from Outer Space."[47] Ashman recorded the vocal for a demo with a band; such demos would be sent to Los Angeles for approval. Merkin recalled this performance in the recording studio: lyric sheet in hand, Ashman "gesturing and yelling." "You would have thought he was the goddamn plant," Merkin said. "You would have thought his arms were tentacles. He was so alive."[48]

Ashman attended a pre-production meeting in January 1985, with David Geffen; his production head, Eric Eisner; and director Frank Oz. Oz wanted to shoot the film in England, where he had worked on *The Muppet Show*, *The Empire Strikes Back*, and *The Dark Crystal*. He knew the sound stages; he knew the technicians. As Merkin remarked, "Everybody has their safety issues."[49] At the time, the dollar was strong compared to the British pound, so shooting in the UK would save money. During this meeting, Geffen wondered if their film might need a happy ending. Couldn't Seymour triumph and get the girl? Ashman pointed out that Seymour kills people; the film would be on "morally shaky ground." Geffen argued by anecdote. *Risky Business* had a downbeat ending, in which Joel, the young protagonist, lost everything: the chance to attend Princeton University, the money generated by his whorehouse, and co-star Rebecca De Mornay. Recruited test audiences were asked to look at the film and offer their judgments: they didn't like it. As Geffen realized, "The nerds in the audience needed to win something." With a new, upbeat ending, the film tested better, and *Risky Business* proved popular when it opened in 1983. Oz and Ashman insisted that the *Little Shop* film stay true to the stage production and its finale: the plant conquers the world, so don't feed the plants.[50]

It is intriguing that Geffen mentioned "nerds" because *Little Shop*, in its various forms, resembles another 1980s trend, indicated by *Revenge of the Nerds*, a lowbrow comedy that became a hit in the summer of 1984 and spawned many sequels. The *Peninsula Times Tribune* identified Corman's *The Little Shop of Horrors* as "one of the earliest (and most sinister) variations on the Revenge of the Nerd theme."[51] *WarGames*, from 1983, also foregrounds the power of the nerd: Matthew Broderick, as a video-game enthusiast and computer hobbyist, hacks the national defense system and nearly starts a nuclear war. Nerds are clever and potentially dangerous. Of course, there are traditional narratives that tell the story of the smallest or the youngest who outwits the giants and the ogres—everything from David and Goliath to *The Hobbit*, published in 1937. But the Revenge of the Nerd motif updates the narrative with a layer of technology and scientific ingenuity. Although somewhat clueless, Seymour is one such character, an amateur botanist. By 1985, as Lee Wilkof indicated, "The nerd of the moment was Rick Moranis."[52] The Toronto-born comedian starred in the comedy show *Second City Television* (known as *SCTV*), which began airing in 1976 as Canada's answer to *Saturday Night Live*. In *Ghostbusters*, released in the same summer as *Revenge of the Nerds*, Moranis plays the prototypical nerd, an accountant with a crush on his neighbor. Geffen imagined him as Seymour, and Moranis won the part.

Casting continued through 1985. A few women with movie-musical credentials were considered as possible Audreys: Barbra Streisand, who appeared in the 1969 film version of *Hello, Dolly!*, and Liza Minnelli, who starred in the 1972 film version of *Cabaret*.[53] Another possibility was pop singer Cyndi Lauper; her début album, *She's So Unusual*, launched a few hits after its release in 1983. A problem arose when "she wanted to write the score herself."[54] Bill Lauch noted that "Howard loved Cyndi Lauper"; nevertheless, "he felt that the role belonged to Ellen."[55] Despite two film appearances, Ellen Greene was not a movie star. But Geffen and Oz agreed to produce a screen test, in April 1985, to learn how she would appear in the role on film. Robinson, her boyfriend, saw the test: "it was stunning," he said. "Done deal."[56] By August, the movie cast included Moranis, Greene, Steve Martin as Orin, and Vincent Gardenia as Mushnik.[57] In place of the series of musical cameos envisioned in the outlines (Duran Duran and the rest), the film would include cameos from comedic stars of the day, known from *SCTV* or *Saturday Night Live*: Christopher Guest, John Candy, and Bill Murray in the role of Arthur Denton, the masochist.[58]

Apart from Greene, no other member of the original WPA cast joined the film-in-progress, although it seems that the urchins met with Franz Oz. Jennifer Leigh Warren auditioned: "It's so strange to go in for something that you've been doing for years—to audition for it." The original Ronnette, Sheila Kay Davis, explained that no one thought to negotiate in advance for the right to appear in a potential film adaptation: "This was a tiny, Off-Broadway show in a dump, you know. We didn't think it was gonna make millions and millions upon millions." She, too, met with Oz, but she felt that he did not want to use the original cast from the play.[59] According to Equity rules, members of that original company would earn a penalty payment if not included in a feature-film version. Leilani Jones, who missed the Orpheum opening, remembered a modest payment for originating the role of Chiffon. So the film would proceed without Lee Wilkof, Franc Luz, and the original urchins; in the words of Davis, "it was a separation of church and state."[60]

Broadway stars were often denied the chance to appear in the films that preserve their stage musicals—ask Mary Martin, Ethel Merman, and Chita Rivera. More surprising in the case of *Little Shop* was the fact that Ashman and Menken removed themselves from the process. "Film is really a director's medium," Ashman explained. "I decided early on that I wouldn't be involved." His sister, Sarah, added that he knew the way it worked: "basically, you're the writer, and it's taken away from you."[61] Ashman participated in pre-production, and he saw the storyboards prepared by artist Mike Ploog, formerly of Marvel Comics. As the *Little Shop* film headed into production, in the autumn of 1985, Ashman would be occupied with his own project: a Broadway-bound musical, composed by Marvin Hamlisch and based on the 1975 satirical film *Smile*. Readings and workshops took place in September, October, and November.[62] So Ashman and Menken decided that Robby Merkin would serve as their representative on the *Little Shop* film. "I'm supposed to fight for everything they wanted," Merkin said. By coincidence, he had written for *Sesame Street* and already knew Frank Oz. For the movie, Merkin orchestrated the songs and lived in London during the shooting process to assist Oz and serve as musical "liaison."[63] Yet the authors who created *Little Shop of Horrors* stayed away. "Visited the set once," Menken recalled. "That was it."[64]

What did he see? Like the plant at the heart of the story, *Little Shop* grew: from a low-budget Roger Corman film shot over a few days to an Equity Showcase held at the not-for-profit WPA Theatre to a commercial run at an Off-Broadway house. Now *Little Shop* grew again, into a multimillion-dollar cinematic spectacle, designed to be a summer blockbuster. The film shot at Pinewood Studios, in Buckinghamshire, a quick jaunt from London. In fact, the filmmakers worked on the largest sound stage anywhere—the same used for many James Bond films (the stage was known as 007).[65] The Corman film and the show at the WPA expressed youthful vitality, a sense of play—the stakes are low, so let's try something! Corman would hire unknowns and give them a chance (and pay them very little). *Little Shop* at the WPA also created opportunities: it was the first show designed by Marty Robinson and Sally Lesser, the first starring role for Lee Wilkof, and Jennifer Leigh Warren's New York début. In contrast, Oz hired seasoned professionals. Director of photography Robert Paynter shot many films, including *An American Werewolf in London* and *Trading Places*, both for John Landis, and *The Muppets Take Manhattan*, for Frank Oz; production designer Roy Walker won an Academy Award for his recreation of the eighteenth century in Stanley Kubrick's 1975 film *Barry Lyndon*; costume designer Marit Allen was well known for her fashion and cinematic designs.

And then there was the plant. Robinson hoped to work on the film, so he pitched his concept for a cinematic version to Frank Oz, with a three-dimensional model and many drawings. Later, Oz called to say that it would not work out. The production was growing, and it was moving to the UK, where Robinson had few contacts: "Frankly, it was beyond me at that point—the technology required."[66] The designer that Oz had in mind was Lyle Conway, an American-born animatronics expert who made a career in the UK. He worked on *The Muppet Show*, *The Dark Crystal*, and a special-effects laden *Wizard of Oz* sequel entitled *Return to Oz*, which sank at the box office in 1985. His *Little Shop* designs drew inspiration from Paul Blaisdell, who created monsters for 1950s B pictures such as *Invasion of the Saucer Men* and *It Conquered the World*.[67] Conway also noticed the "realistic quality" of Roy Walker's set designs and felt that the plants needed to be realistic and not cartoonish.[68]

He joined the production in March 1985. Unlike Robinson's plants for the theatre, which appeared in four stages of growth, Conway's creations proceeded in seven stages, from the baby pod to the behemoth that sings "Mean Green Mother from Outer Space."[69] "The challenge," he said, "was to take something twelve and a half feet tall, weighing slightly more than one ton and make it rap and boogie with a life of its own."[70] Robinson admired Conway's Audrey II: "It's the last great rubber monster." In fact, the *Little Shop* effects department did not employ stop-motion animation—the technique mastered by Willis O'Brien, in the 1933 film *King Kong*, and his disciple Ray Harryhausen. Further, the movie plants were not electric; they were mechanical, "cables and levers," as Robinson observed.[71] The performance of the plants happened right there on the stage, with technicians standing off to the side or hiding underneath, each operating something like a 1980s video-game joystick, connected to a long cord. Each and every movement—the curl of a lip, the bend of a vine—was controlled by a human operator, like a worker in a Ford automobile factory performing a single, monotonous task.[72]

Lip sync proved to be a challenge for the two larger plants, which sing "Git It" (aka "Feed Me") and "Mean Green Mother." Frank Oz, as a Muppeteer, expected the synchronization to be perfect.[73] But it was difficult to get latex operated by cables to move at tempo. "We wound up undercranking everything," Conway admitted.[74] The trick is one of the oldest in the cinematic vocabulary, dating to the period when motion-picture cameras were cranked by hand. If the film moves through the camera at twenty-four frames per second, then to undercrank means to turn the camera at a slower rate, maybe eighteen or nineteen frames per second. When projected at the usual speed, any action performed would then appear to be very fast—a comedic effect used by Charlie Chaplin and Benny Hill. (Overcranking is the opposite: to increase the frame rate so that action appears *slower*.) To synchronize the plant's movements to the pre-recorded audio track, the film usually ran at sixteen frames per second (fps)—a third slower.[75] Likewise, the recording would be played at the slower rate; then the technicians could craft the lip movements for every vowel and consonant. When played back at sound speed (24 fps), the song's tempo would resume and the movements would match. When the plant sang with a human performer in the same shot (Rick Moranis or Ellen Greene), the actor had to slow down as well— to walk and talk *ve-ry slowwwwwly*.[76] Many shots were generated this way, with Moranis moving at a snail's pace. As Robby Merkin said, "He's a patient man."[77]

The voice of the plant was provided by singer Levi Stubbs, of the Four Tops. Since his acting experience was minimal, he spoke on the phone with Merkin;

this served as a kind of audition. Merkin asked him to perform as if he were "in different situations." They agreed to try the 1965 song "In the Midnight Hour," by Wilson Pickett. Merkin offered a series of directions: "Sing 'The Midnight Hour' as though you're six inches tall." "Sing 'The Midnight Hour' as though you're about to eat somebody." "Sing 'The Midnight Hour' like you're walking through New York, knocking over high rises."[78] Stubbs then traveled to London to record all his spoken dialogue and music. His job completed, he did not have to show up for the actual filming. The plant crew worked with the singer's disembodied voice on a tape, hour upon hour.[79]

A member of that crew was one of the few to participate in the stage show and its film adaptation: Anthony Asbury. After performing the plant at the Comedy Theatre, Asbury remained in London. He joined the puppet film *Labyrinth* (produced in 1985), which was Jim Henson's follow-up to *The Dark Crystal*, and met Frank Oz. One day Oz said, "I want to talk to you about this other project"; Asbury knew it was the *Little Shop* film.[80] Around the same time, Asbury was offered the Marvel Comics special-effects movie *Howard the Duck*; he chose Howard Ashman instead.[81] Brian Henson, son of Jim, performed the "Git It" plant, and Asbury crawled inside the largest one, which required five weeks just to film "Mean Green Mother."[82] For the more complex shots, as many as fifty technicians worked at once. There was a tank or a pit underneath the heavy plant where most everyone operated cables; they watched the action overhead on small, black-and-white television monitors. Conway compared these workers to Morlocks, the subterranean dwellers in *The Time Machine*, the 1895 novel by H. G. Wells. It was dank and smelly down there in the pit, with dozens of bodies perspiring for hours each day to make movie magic appear on screen.[83]

While Conway and his crew built and rehearsed the various plants, Frank Oz commenced principal photography in October 1985.[84] He was aware that singing-and-dancing movie-musicals were not in vogue: there had not been a bonafide hit since *Grease*, in 1978. Three years later, MTV began to air, and the popularity of the music video changed approaches to film editing and introduced a new brand of youth-oriented dance musicals driven by pop soundtracks, such as *Flashdance*, in 1983. At the same time, Oz wanted to preserve his theatrical source, which proved successful in so many places:

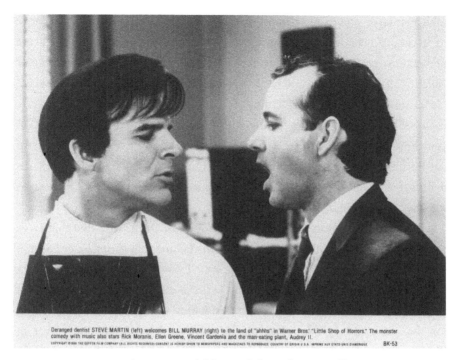

Figure 10 *Doctor and patient. A lobby card from the 1986 film. Steve Martin as Orin Scrivello and Bill Murray as Arthur Denton (based on the character played by Jack Nicholson in 1960).*

"I didn't want to balloon it into a musical 'War and Peace' or a big, splashy '40s extravaganza."[85] Yet he was acutely aware of the delicate balance that Ashman's direction of *Little Shop* maintained, between the heartfelt and the absurd. "Frank knew to stay pretty true," Asbury suggested. "This is Gospel according to Howard." The film's director hit upon a formula that he thought could work: "What I am trying to achieve is heightened reality."[86] Pursuing the real, his film crew built an entire Skid Row on the 007 stage, with a functioning elevated train and garbage "imported from New York." Further, Oz's perfectionism required his actors and his plant technicians to perform multiple takes for every shot. Asbury explained that "Frank will make you shoot a scene over and over and over again. He made me shoot one like 103 times. We all wanted to stab him in the eye."[87]

Steve Martin, in the role of the dentist, also pursued a kind of comic perfection. In the recording studio, the actor held himself to an "incredibly high standard," according to Robby Merkin. Martin would ask for another take of "Dentist!" if he felt that his pitch was not right on a single note. The same dedication appeared when Martin worked on set. Whenever the director yelled, "Cut, we'll take five, and we'll do it again," Martin remained and rehearsed his actions. He was always looking for an audience; he might ask a crew member sweeping the stage to stop and observe a bit of comic business. "Do you think it's funny this way?" the actor would ask.[88] Oz gave credit to Martin for inventing some highlights during the filming of the song "Dentist!" To demonstrate "pain" and "inhumane," Orin punches a dental assistant and rips the head from a child's doll.[89]

Of course, perfection is expensive. The *New York Times* reported that *Little Shop* would cost 17.5 million dollars; Geffen claimed that shooting in London would save the studio four million dollars.[90] By way of comparison, Stanley Kubrick's *Full Metal Jacket*, shot in the UK around the same time, also cost seventeen million. Kubrick said that in England, "you get more on the screen for the same money"; he was able to recreate South Vietnam.[91] Over at Pinewood, the Frank Oz film went over budget and fell behind schedule. Asbury understood why: "Anytime you involve puppets or children, things are gonna take a hell of a lot longer than you imagine."[92] The line producer hired to supervise the London shoot was fired and replaced.[93] Production was supposed to conclude in March 1986, but Oz needed more time. The studio granted eight additional weeks of principal photography—a significant expense.[94]

Ashman remained in the US, although he stayed in touch with Oz by phone and fax. When Ellen Greene proved typically hard to handle, Ashman was summoned to intervene on the filmmakers' behalf and get her back on track. "Ellen was Ellen," Merkin concluded.[95] As the film progressed, Ashman got to see edited versions of scenes. At one point, Geffen flew to New York and telephoned Ashman around 10:30 at night. "I just got in, and I've got the reels for the opening," the producer began. "You've got to come up and watch it." Ashman was reluctant. "My boyfriend's here," he replied. "We're in bed, watching TV!" Unaccustomed to the answer "no," Geffen insisted that they travel uptown and see the footage immediately. So Ashman and Lauch tumbled out of bed and took a taxi from the West Village to the Upper East Side. In Geffen's modernist apartment, they screened a videotape, a rough cut of the song "Little Shop of Horrors." "I think that opening number just works so beautifully," Lauch said.⁹⁶ Crystal, Ronette, and Chiffon move through space effortlessly; they explore the built environment of the Skid Row set; and they pass through closed doors and observe Mushnik and Seymour. Rain descends from the heavens above, but the girls do not get wet.

At last, the film was assembled in 1986; but before it could reach the malls and multiplexes of America, it required the approval of a test audience. Just as Geffen had used test screenings to refine his earlier production *Risky Business*, he and Warner Bros. screened a cut of *Little Shop* for a targeted audience of teenagers. In San Jose, California, the screening went very well—"until the plant ate Audrey," Frank Oz remembered. "It was like a deep freeze." He knew at once what was wrong with this picture: "we had these two leads, and we killed them. And the audience hated us for it." As Anthony Asbury remarked, "They couldn't stand that the devil won."⁹⁷

The test audience saw the original ending. It was the finale, "Don't Feed the Plants," visualized in horrifying detail. The plants did what they came here to do: eat and destroy everything. Richard Conway (no relation to Lyle), an Englishman and a special-effects master, built a series of miniature cities that the plants could then demolish. Lyle Conway's crew prepared two medium-sized plants (three and a half feet tall) that would romp through the miniature sets, as if appearing in *Godzilla the Musical*. Again, no stop-motion animation was used; the system was hydraulic, with plant movements controlled by computer. In contrast to Lyle Conway, who shot his gigantic plants by undercranking, the other Conway employed the opposite technique: overcranking. By filming his miniatures at an extremely high speed (120 or 360 frames per second), he could achieve a look of weight and gravity. The plants, moving very quickly on the set, would be shot at 120 fps; they would then look convincing when the footage was played back at the normal speed. Richard Conway spent almost a year preparing and shooting this finale, a vintage B-movie ending with better production value.⁹⁸ Oz called it "the best model work I've seen." But it was five million dollars wasted, now on the cutting-room floor.⁹⁹

Like the test audience, Ashman saw the original cut, and he showed the videotape to friends, including Paul Mills Holmes. "The biggest thing that he knew was gonna have to change was the ending of the movie," Holmes recalled. "It was so scary and so violent and not in the *Little Shop* way." Lauch agreed that the film's climax was troubling: "when everybody dies at the end, it's just more traumatic to the viewer." On stage, he said, "it just feels more playful."[100] One important distinction is that in the theatre, actors appear for a curtain call at the end: you know that they survived. It was all just make-believe.[101]

Ashman, as screenwriter, was obliged to corrupt the musical on which he had labored for so long. Lauch felt that the process was a brutal one: "it was disheartening to think that they were sort of making judgments about how this film should be crafted based on an audience of thirteen- to seventeen-year-olds."[102] Connie Grappo, Ashman's former assistant, told him to fight, but he countered, "I don't have a choice." By selling the movie rights, he surrendered the decision-making power. Lauch explained what happened next: "in order to just protect what he had already created, he figured he would do what was necessary to give them the kind of ending they wanted."[103]

In September 1986, the crew re-assembled for a two-week shoot, costing around two million dollars.[104] The director returned, along with Rick Moranis, Ellen Greene, and Anthony Asbury, who would climb into the largest plant once again, supported by an army of technicians. In the original ending, Paul Dooley played marketing ace Patrick Martin, in a rooftop scene in which the businessman pitches Seymour the idea of Audrey II as a consumer product. In the reshoots, Dooley would be replaced, and Ashman saw an opportunity: "I think this 'one last' cameo gives the scene a comic lift." For the revised scene, he wrote, "And barging into the alley and the shot comes Rodney Dangerfield as PATRICK MARTIN."[105] In the event, the role was played by James Belushi, younger brother to the late John Belushi. Seymour rejects the money-making opportunity, and this time he rescues his beloved Audrey from the jaws of the plant. He electrocutes the thing from another world—Audrey II is vanquished! Then the happy ending: boy and girl join together, and they retire to what appears to be the set of Audrey's fantasy, where they live out their days somewhere that's green.

The movie was completed by the end of the year, and members of the Orpheum production attended a screening on December 15. Donna Rose Fletcher, now the stage manager, thought, "This is so weird. It's not our show;

it's not our show."[106] Differences between the stage play and the film range from the obvious (happy ending) to the subtle: the date on which the action begins is now September 23, not September 21.[107] A few musical numbers are lengthened, and "The Meek Shall Inherit" appears but is truncated. Ashman and Menken extended the opening number with a new musical section ("Oh, here it comes, baby / Tell the bums, baby") and an additional bridge. The longer version gives the filmmakers enough time for all the names in the opening credits.

Audiences appreciated the film. A premiere took place on December 16 at the Motion Picture Academy, in Los Angeles. Ashman heard about the event from a colleague in LA: "The audience applauded after each musical number," she wrote, "something I have never seen before in a movie screening." The *Hollywood Reporter* also noted the "bursts of applause" but cautioned that the Academy audience was older than "the ticket-buying public."[108] Newspaper reviews appeared when the film opened nationwide, on December 19, 1986. Janet Maslin, in the *New York Times*, found "just the right mixture of playfulness, tunefulness and blood lust." Despite hours of excruciating effort that went into making the film, Roger Ebert enjoyed "the offhand charm of something that was concocted over the weekend." Identifying the essence of *Little Shop*, he mentioned "a basic sweetness and innocence."[109] The LA trade papers offered conflicting opinions, with *Variety* calling the movie "funny but uninvolving" and the *Hollywood Reporter* discovering "a Christmas gift for all ages."[110]

Released in time for the holidays, the film underperformed, relative to its cost. In the opening weekend box office, *Little Shop* landed in fourth place, behind *The Golden Child*, starring Eddie Murphy; *Star Trek IV: The Voyage Home*; and *Three Amigos*, with *Little Shop*'s own Steve Martin. On the other hand, the musical outperformed a competing monster movie, *King Kong Lives*.[111] In February 1987, Ashman and Menken earned an Academy Award nomination for best song.[112] Levi Stubbs and backup dancers performed "Mean Green Mother" at the Oscars broadcast. Bernadette Peters presented the statuette, but *Little Shop* lost to "Take My Breath Away," from *Top Gun*.[113]

For fans of *Little Shop* on screen, there were consumer products, including the well-produced soundtrack and a series of trading cards from Topps. A paperback book tie-in, by Robert and Louise Egan, offered a selection of

Figure 11 *The 1986 graphic novel from DC Comics. Audrey's daydream, as adapted by Michael Fleisher, with art by Gene Colan and Dave Hunt and lettering by John Costanza.*

black-and-white stills appended by bits of text. A more informative paperback, entitled *The Little Shop of Horrors Book*, missed the film's release date and did not appear until 1988.[114] One curious offering was the graphic-novel adaptation from DC Comics (owned by the studio's parent company, Warner Communications). Adapted by Michael Fleisher, this is *Little Shop of Horrors* without the songs, either because of copyright or because musical numbers don't play well in a graphic medium. The artists avoid caricaturing Moranis, Greene, and their co-stars. Drawn in a muscular DC style, bespectacled Seymour looks like a Clark Kent who never becomes Superman. Audrey appears younger than her screen equivalent, and Orin Scrivello is now a long-haired blond, more a hippie than Steve Martin's raven-haired descendant of Elvis. As a musical without songs, the graphic novel sometimes paraphrases the lyrics. Instead of singing "Grow for Me," Seymour talks to his plant, "I've given you sunlight and plant food! I've tried grow-lights and mineral supplements!" When Orin first arrives on his motorcycle, a thought bubble presents his inner monologue: "Even when I was a little kid, I used to get off on doin' real nasty things—like poisonin' guppies and shootin' puppies with a B.B. gun!" Most surprising is the inclusion of a song that never made it into the play or the film: the "Hello, Dolly!" number that Ashman had long contemplated. A few lyrics appear for Audrey II's television début.[115]

As the film adaptation progressed from screenplay to general release, *Little Shop of Horrors* continued to play at the Orpheum Theatre, in New York. By 1986, this production alone had grossed fourteen million dollars.[116] Albert Poland was optimistic about the impact that the forthcoming Warner Bros. film would have on business downtown: "I think the release of the movie can only help us." As he later reported, "the grosses shot up."[117] Audiences who knew about the Hollywood version wanted to discover the source.

At the Orpheum, most of the original and subsequent cast members had moved on to other shows or other endeavors, but Katherine Meloche remained. Hired in 1982 as dance captain and Audrey understudy, Meloche in fact played the role many times. She was given the chance to audition to become the permanent replacement but lost out to a series of other women—always a bridesmaid, never an Audrey. One day Meloche said to Ashman, "You know, you're gonna hire me eventually." He answered, "Oh, your time is coming." It happened in July 1986, as the production turned four years old. Ashman encountered Meloche once again: "I want you to take over the role of Audrey."

"Why, is the show closing?"

"No, no, as a matter of fact, it's doing quite well."[118]

Other changes took place in 1987, the show's final year. Donna Drake, assistant stage manager, was ready to leave the production. Therefore, Donna Rose Fletcher, the stage manager, needed a new assistant. At the same time, Paul Mills Holmes, who had left the show in 1985, was out of work and looking for his next gig after stage managing *Les Liaisons Dangereuses*. By this point *Little Shop* was selling half-price tickets; Fletcher believed that the end must be near. So she devised an elegant solution. Rather than train a brand-new assistant, she would resume that track herself and ask Holmes to return as stage manager. She pitched the idea to Ashman, who was not enthusiastic. In essence, she was telling him that his show was about to close. He was not ready to hear this. He said to Fletcher, "It's not what I want. But if that's what you want, I'll support you."[119]

Around the same time, there was a discussion that Ellen Greene might return to boost ticket sales, "which would have been a nightmare," quipped Poland. He feared that if she arrived "as the savior," she would be even more difficult to handle. After the play suffered "a month of operating losses," he telephoned the designers and asked them to waive their royalties to help the bottom line.[120] Otts Munderloh, the sound designer, earned a flat weekly rate of seventy-five dollars. When asked to forgo this fee, he replied, "If you're telling me that my piddling seventy-five dollars a week is going to mean the difference between closing the show and keeping it open, then I have to say to you, 'Close the show.'"[121] Once the general manager realized that he had no more options, he called Howard Ashman to share the bad news. "No! You're closing it too soon!" Ashman cried.[122]

On October 15, 1987, Albert Poland wrote a letter to the Little Shop Company: "our business here at 'Little Shop of Horrors' has begun to wind down." He mentioned a closing date of January 3, 1988; *Little Shop* would play through the holidays.[123] Four days after this announcement, the US stock market plummeted, one of the greatest single-day losses in history. About a week later, Poland issued another announcement: "'Little Shop of Horrors' will play its final performance at the Orpheum Theatre on Sunday, November 1, 1987 at 5:00 PM."[124] Peter Mumford, another stage manager who had worked on the show, was shocked by the news. He wrote a supportive letter to Fletcher and Holmes: "It never occured [sic] to me that an institution such as Little Shop would ever come to an end." Further, he mentioned the stock market's impact on the New York theatre business in general. Long-running hit *La Cage aux Folles* would soon close, as would a revival of *Dreamgirls*.[125]

The final performance of *Little Shop* at the Orpheum took place on November 1.[126] On stage: Stuart Zagnit as Seymour, Katherine Meloche as Audrey, Walter Hudson as Orin (and others), Fyvush Finkel as Mushnik. The three urchins were Mary Denise Bentley (Crystal), Gayle Samuels (Ronnette), and Chelli Jackson (Chiffon). Audrey II was operated by William Szymanski, who learned the part from Robinson. And the voice of the plant was Ron Taylor, the one and only survivor of the WPA company.[127] Ellen Greene was in the house that night. At the end, she approached Fletcher, who was closing the shop after the audience had departed. Greene asked, "Can I just be the last one out of the theatre?" Fletcher let her have this moment. She re-opened the doors, and Greene walked down the aisle, ascended the stage, and sat on the trash can, where she had performed "Somewhere That's Green" so many times. Then she returned to the lobby, exited the building, and headed uptown.[128]

A party was held at La Spaghetteria, at 178 Second Avenue, the restaurant that replaced Tempus Fugit at the same location; both were favorite hangouts. That same night, Ashman and Lauch hosted another party for their circle of intimates.[129] As Lauch observed, "It was kind of like the end of a very happy era."[130] *Little Shop of Horrors* had closed. *Little Shop* would live on.

Chapter Seven

We'll Have Tomorrow: The Curious Afterlives of a Man-Eating Musical

The first person to capitalize on the Off-Broadway success of *Little Shop of Horrors* was Roger Corman. Renewed interest in his 1960 film earned it additional bookings in revival cinemas, and Corman negotiated a deal for himself when Warner Bros. acquired the film rights to the musical.[1] He described a "cash payment plus a percentage of the movie's profits," but according to Hollywood accounting, the Frank Oz picture lost money.[2] (Corman's films almost invariably showed a profit.) Further, the mid-1980s saw a boom in the home-video market after the introduction of videocassette players. *The Little Shop of Horrors* appeared on video; but because Corman neglected to copyright the film, other companies were able to exploit this property with pirated videos drawn from old 16mm prints. Corman's attorneys tried to suppress the competitors; in the meantime, he decided to join them. To vanquish the pirates, he would remaster the film and release a pristine home-video edition of the 1960 classic.[3]

California native Steve Barnett attended UCLA and decided to enter the film business. In 1985, he landed a job with Roger Corman's latest company. Barnett worked in post-production, and he was tasked with *The Little Shop* home-video release. Deluxe Laboratories found the original negative; however, Barnett needed the original audio tracks for the best possible transfer. The sound would have lived on 35mm magnetic tape, with three tracks: dialogue, music, and sound effects. Gene Corman, Roger's brother, remembered that the audio work was done at Ryder Sound, in Hollywood. On the front desk were "three gigantic rolodexes," Barnett recalled. This was Ryder Sound's database. But he could not find an entry for *The Little Shop of Horrors*. Exploring the building's dusty basement, Barnett combed through old, ragged boxes containing reels of 35mm sound. One set of boxes held up frail pieces of masking tape, which bore the original title, "The Passionate People Eater." Thrilled that he found the missing elements, Barnett declared, "I saved *Little Shop of Horrors!*" These materials were used to make a crisp home-video transfer, in glorious black and white.[4]

Screenwriter Charles Griffith also hoped to benefit from the newfound interest in the bizarre little movie that he spawned long ago. He planned a sequel, to be called *Son of the Little Shop of Horrors*, which he would write and direct. Despite the fact that many of the characters are dead by the end of the original film, Griffith imagined them alive and thriving. Audrey is now married to Mr. Mushnik (a different reading from the Ashman-Menken musical), and Seymour grows another plant. Unfortunately, the project was never realized.[5]

Instead, *Little Shop* appeared in the form of a Saturday-morning cartoon, produced by Haim Saban and Marvel; Corman served as "Creative Consultant." Just as Howard Ashman drew inspiration from the Muppets, this animated show borrows from *Jim Henson's Muppet Babies*, a 1984 CBS cartoon that derived from a sequence in Frank Oz's *The Muppets Take Manhattan*. How do you revive a franchise? Make everyone younger: now Seymour and Audrey are thirteen years old. In the cartoon, Audrey is the daughter of Mushnik, still running the florist shop; Seymour works there after school. Although adapted from Corman's film and not the stage play, *Little Shop* the series is kind of a musical. There are songs, and the plant, here named Audrey Junior, likes to rap (as does Audrey II in Ashman's outline for the 1986 film). The pilot, "Bad Seed," launches the concept: young Seymour discovers a baby pod, which utters, "Yo, feed me." In the happier realm of children's television, this plant is not a killer. After devouring a pepperoni pizza, Junior grows. Further, the animated Seymour aspires to be like his forebears Lee Wilkof and Rick Moranis; when first introduced, the character says, "I've spent thirteen years trying to become a nerd." *Little Shop*, which premiered on September 7, 1991, lasted only one season.

But the producer of *Slumber Party Massacre II* and *III* was not a man to let a good idea die. As the animated *Little Shop* appeared on TV, Corman developed a live-action series based on the same property. Cable television's USA Network wanted to develop a slate of scripted shows, especially "pre-sold properties." For example, *Swamp Thing*, based on a character from DC Comics, began airing on USA in 1990. So Corman agreed to produce a *Little Shop* TV show for the network, which hired Lee Goldberg and William Rabkin to create the series and write the pilot. Their most recent credit was *She-Wolf of London*, a syndicated series based on another old movie, from 1946. The two writers met Corman in his office, where all the furniture dated from 1973 because "he didn't want to spend a dime."[6] Hovering behind the desk was a framed poster of the Ingmar Bergman film *Cries and Whispers*, which Corman's company distributed in 1972.[7] "I was expecting to work for a car salesman," Goldberg commented, but he found the producer to be charming and literate.[8]

Writing partner Bill Rabkin proposed that the TV show could be "a throwback to 1960s gimmick comedies," like *Mister Ed*, the 1961 series about a talking horse, and *Bewitched*, from 1964, in which a man marries a witch.[9] *Little Shop* would be a half-hour filmed comedy, shot at Corman's production facility in Venice, California. The writers settled on five principal characters: Seymour Krelboin (note the name), Audrey, Mushnik, Audrey Junior, and a new character named Dallas Breen (a sleazy journalist).[10] Because of Corman's cost-cutting philosophy, the show would *not* be set in the 1960s; instead, it seems to be contemporary Los Angeles. Now there are references to Madonna, Dr. Hannibal Lecter, and *Terminator 2: Judgment Day* (released in the summer of 1991).[11] Goldberg and Rabkin wrote the pilot in late 1991 and submitted the second (and final) draft in February 1992. In the script, Seymour works in the eponymous shop and adores coworker Audrey. The plant enters a flower competition and wins a cash prize, but sentimental Audrey gives the money to charity. Along the way, secondary characters get eaten.

The USA Network occupied an imposing office tower in Century City, California, where television executive Medora Heilbron seemed indecisive; the development process dragged on for over a year. Corman, on the other hand, mastered the art of producing films quickly. As a result, he was "extraordinarily frustrated" by the glacial pace.[12] Finally, he burst out, "I made seventeen movies in the time it's taken just to get the story approved on this pilot!"[13] Further, Heilbron, placed in charge of the show's development, did not understand comedy. Goldberg said, "She wanted to have the jokes underlined and italicized and asterisked."[14] She suggested that they reprint the script with different kinds of comedy indicated, so she would not miss a single joke. For Corman, this was the end. Exasperated after this meeting with Heilbron, he rode the elevator down with his two writers: "Is this how television works?"[15] The live-action series joined *Son of the Little Shop of Horrors* in the category of what might have been.

In the autumn of 1991, as Goldberg and Rabkin worked on the pilot, Walt Disney Pictures released its next animated feature, *Beauty and the Beast*, with music by Alan Menken and lyrics by Howard Ashman, who was also executive producer. Surprisingly, after the global success of *Little Shop*, they did not create another stage musical together. Producer David Geffen encouraged his friend Jeffrey Katzenberg to work with Howard Ashman. Katzenberg then ran Walt Disney Studios, and in 1986 he invited Ashman to write and produce live-action and animated films. Ashman ultimately decided that he preferred animation, and he asked Alan Menken to join the new effort. They collaborated on the animated feature *The Little Mermaid*, released in 1989, and wrote songs for *Aladdin*, which appeared in 1992. These three films rejuvenated the American animated film, earned a fortune for the Walt Disney Company, and created the soundtrack for a generation.[16] However, Ashman did not live to see the cycle's completion. He died of complications related to HIV/AIDS, in March 1991, at the age of forty. A memorial took place on May 6, the anniversary of the opening of *Little Shop* at the WPA Theatre, and the location was the Orpheum, where the musical played for over five years. Many friends and collaborators spoke or performed favorite Ashman songs. Lee Wilkof and Ellen Greene reunited on stage to sing "We'll Have Tomorrow," the beautiful ballad cut from the show.[17]

Once again, *Little Shop of Horrors* carried on. By the 1990s, revivals became a big business—an American counterpart to the British spectacles that dominated Broadway stages in the wake of *Cats*.[18] Through gentrification, Times Square, once derelict (like an uptown Skid Row), grew safer for tourists looking for an innocent good time. Revivals of familiar titles were used to fill

Broadway houses and capture tourist dollars. In 1994, the Encores! series began to revive musicals that might not warrant a full-scale reproduction—second-tier shows or forgotten flops. In 1996, Encores! revived a genuine hit, *Chicago*, which first opened in 1975. Moving to a series of commercial theatres, *Chicago* became Broadway's longest-running revival, outrunning its original production by a few decades. In 1999, Gregory Boyd, artistic director of Houston's Alley Theatre, wanted to remount *Little Shop*, so he hired members of the WPA creative team: Edward (Hawk) Gianfrancesco, Sally Lesser, and Martin P. Robinson. To refresh his revival, Boyd selected Marguerite Derricks to create new choreography. She was well known for her work on a Gap TV commercial as well as feature films, including *Austin Powers: International Man of Mystery*, from 1997. Hawk and Lesser found that the new production vulgarized a musical that they both loved. "It wasn't gonna go to Broadway," Lesser concluded.[19]

Another set of producers approached Alan Menken and the Ashman estate (Sarah Ashman Gillespie and Bill Lauch) for permission to produce *Little Shop* on Broadway. Of course, Ashman always believed that the show did not belong on the Great White Way, but maybe it was time to try. As an insurance policy, the rights holders demanded that the producers hire Ashman's former assistant, Constance Grappo, who had directed Ashman's version of the show multiple times. But the producing team, led by Marc Routh and Richard Frankel, wanted to use Jerry Zaks, the Tony-winning director who had staged a beloved revival of *Guys and Dolls* in 1992.[20] The stars were none other than Nathan Lane and Faith Prince—two actors who *might have* created the roles of Seymour and Audrey at the WPA had things turned out otherwise (a counterfactual *Little Shop*).[21] In order to proceed, the producing team hired Grappo, and they also called on Marty Robinson, who created a set of next-generation plants, given his improved skills and the generous budget of a Broadway musical. The plan was to rehearse the show in New York and then hold a pre-Broadway tryout in Coral Gables, Florida, west of Miami. The venue was the Actors' Playhouse at the Miracle Theatre—an optimistic name. Menken found it to be "a glorified community theatre." As he remembered, "Essentially we were doing it to test out the plant. Supposedly." But he felt the producers were "auditioning the person"—that is, Connie Grappo.[22]

She gathered a talented cast. Hunter Foster, star of the recent Off-Broadway and then Broadway hit *Urinetown*, took on the role of Seymour. Alice Ripley was Audrey; Reg Rogers played Orin and miscellaneous parts. In the role of Mr. Mushnik, Grappo cast her husband, Lee Wilkof, who had created the role of Seymour twenty-one years earlier. Now he graduated to Mushnik, and he could stand where Michael Vale and Hy Anzell had stood and interact with a younger man playing a version of himself. Foster noted that Wilkof "was so supportive of my Seymour and was not territorial." Occasionally, Foster would ask him for advice: "He was just a wealth of knowledge."[23]

Marty Robinson redesigned his plants, and this time, the Jim Henson Company agreed to make the monsters. The show's producers included the Henson name in the billing because "they thought that would put butts in seats." At the WPA and the Orpheum, Robinson operated the plants himself; now he was part of a four-person team, working on a rotation system.[24] The fourth and largest plant required two puppeteers—one inside, one operating a boom to make the creature rise and fall. Gathering his crew, Robinson sent an email to Anthony Asbury: "Hey, do you want to do a Broadway musical?" After moving to England to work on *Little Shop* on stage and screen, Asbury stayed in London. "I felt like E.T.," he said. "The ship that brought me there finally came to take me home." Asbury returned to the US to join the Florida puppeteers.[25] For the voice of Audrey II, the producers hired Billy Porter. Robinson called him "brilliant," but the actor had maybe too much fun. Sometimes he would improvise a line, like "Help me, Lord! Help me!" As Robinson explained, "Those are five syllables I did not catch."[26]

Previews began on May 7, 2003, with an opening night scheduled for May 16. The producers announced that the show would move to the Virginia Theatre, with previews in July and a Broadway opening on August 14. The Virginia, at 245 West Fifty-second Street, was run by Jujamcyn, the theatre owner that lost the chance to host *Little Shop* in 1982 when it went to the Shuberts. According to Wilkof, the understanding between Grappo and her producers was that they would allow her the space to work in Florida; he felt that they broke their promise when they showed up for the first preview.[27] Menken agreed that "it was a bit of a bait and switch." Audiences in Coral Gables were unenthusiastic, and "it wasn't really entirely clicking," Menken said.[28] When a Broadway-bound musical is not working, then something has to change. "Somebody saw Jerry Zaks in the audience," Robinson recalled. "And then the rumors started flying."[29] Zaks could have served as a "show doctor," a task he had performed in the past, but the producing team had other ideas. Connie Grappo soon left the production, and *Variety* announced that it would close out of town.[30]

Little Shop, like a B-movie monster, did not die. Replacing Grappo, the producers hired Zaks to direct the musical, with a new rehearsal process beginning on July 21, 2003. Jujamcyn held open the Virginia Theatre, and previews would begin in August. The show, budgeted at eight million dollars, added $2.1 million for the cost for its makeover.[31] Most everyone from Florida was fired. Menken called it "a bloodbath" and "one of the most painful things I've been through in my life."[32] The survivors included Hunter Foster, choreographer Kathleen Marshall, scenic designer Scott Pask, Marty Robinson and his puppets. Menken's music department also remained intact: conductor Henry Aronson and orchestrator Danny Troob.

A new cast was built around Foster's Seymour: Kerry Butler as Audrey, Douglas Sills as Orin Scrivello. Rob Bartlett appeared as Mushnik, replacing Wilkof, who departed in solidarity with his wife. A few alumni of *Little Shop* also joined the Broadway company. Michael James Leslie agreed to understudy the new voice of the plant (Michael-Leon Wooley), and bassist Steve Gelfand joined the musicians in the pit. But he missed the familial atmosphere of the Orpheum, where he played the show for many years. "We had very little contact with the cast," Gelfand said of the Broadway company.[33] Now everything was departmentalized, professional.

During the first preview, on August 29, 2003, Foster noted that "it felt like we were doing a rock concert."[34] The audience loved the show. However, when the revival opened, on Thursday, October 2, reviews were mixed. The most important review was Ben Brantley's, in the *New York Times*. It is not *terrible*, but it is not what producers of a ten-million-dollar musical want to read with their morning coffee. Brantley argues that "the show's edges have been sanded" and that "a bit more vulgarity might be welcome." He compares the show's look to the Haunted Mansion, an attraction at Disneyland and Walt Disney World—presumably not a compliment. Ultimately, the review finds the production inauthentic; Foster and Butler are "clean-cut winners" and not "smudged, bruised losers."[35] Among the readers of the *Times* that morning was Lee Wilkof. "I've only levitated once in my life," he said. "I know I danced on air." He defended this feeling of *schadenfreude*, relishing the pain the producing team must have felt: "they hurt my wife very deeply."[36] Still, the show managed to run, selling around 70 percent in a theatre with 1,210 seats.[37] In 2004, to boost ticket sales, the producers replaced Hunter Foster, and they cast Joey Fatone, of the boy band NSYNC (aka 'N Sync).

At the same time, Kerry Butler was leaving the show. Robinson argued that the producers should hire Ellen Greene to return as Audrey and thus revive the revival. "See the legend!" he proposed. By this point, his romantic relationship with Greene was over (it did not survive the 1980s), but he thought it was a good business plan: Ellen Greene as Audrey on Broadway.[38] It didn't happen. Two months after the début of Fatone, the Broadway version of *Little Shop* closed, on August 22, 2004.

Eleven years later, Greene had the chance to reprise her signature role—thirty-three summers after she created Audrey on stage. In the film *Sunset Boulevard*, silent-screen diva Norma Desmond insists that she is not planning a comeback: "I hate that word. It's a return." In 2015, Greene returned. After completing her work on *Little Shop*, from the WPA Theatre to the James Bond soundstage, she told a reporter, "I have tried to find *something* else like it, but there *isn't* anything like it."[39] She continued to work in film and television, with a starring role in the TV comedy *Pushing Daisies*, which premiered in 2007. But she never played another role like *that*. In 2013, Encores! launched a sister series for Off-Broadway musicals, called Encores! Off-Center. The model was the same: after a slapdash rehearsal process, a musical would play in concert form a few times at City Center, on West Fifty-fifth Street, in midtown Manhattan. Composer Jeanine Tesori became artistic director of the new series, and she pitched the idea of *Little Shop* starring Ellen Greene to Michael Mayer, who had directed a revue of Ashman's work, entitled *Hundreds of Hats*, in 1995. "Isn't she just a little old for it?" Mayer queried. Tesori countered that the project would be a "celebration." Unfortunately, a scheduling conflict prevented his participation, so Dick Scanlan directed instead.[40]

Costume designer Sally Lesser received an email from Greene: "Oh, my sweet Sally, you wonderful woman, I miss your beaming smile!"[41] Lesser thought, "Oh, God, what does she want?" They had not spoken in thirty years. Greene explained that she intended to wear the original dress and nightgown from the WPA production; she wanted to give Lesser appropriate credit in the theatre program. Lesser could not believe that Greene still owned these outfits, which she wore on stage when Ronald Reagan was president. Now she would wear them again, during the presidency of Barack Obama. Finally, Greene's return took place on the first two days of July 2015. Lesser attended the concert with fellow alumni Wilkof and Grappo. When Greene made her entrance, "it just stopped everything. People went crazy."[42] Marty Robinson went to the show with Anthony Asbury, who thought that "Ellen was exactly the same." Ashman's surviving partner, Bill Lauch, attended twice, and he described the "warmest and most welcoming audiences I've ever seen."[43]

The reviews were glorious. Ben Brantley stated that the City Center roof "was blown right off." On Greene's performance, he wrote that "she still unconditionally holds the patent on Audrey." Many reviewers noticed the age difference between Greene and her Seymour, Jake Gyllenhaal, who was approximately one-and-a-half years old when *Little Shop* first opened. Yet "the 30-year gap between the stars melts away. Things like that happen in musicals," claimed another reviewer, in the *Daily News*.[44] Because there was no budget for the equivalent to Marty Robinson's puppets or Lyle Conway's complex creations, Audrey II was embodied on stage by two actors, first a child, then an adult. For the song "Git It," Eddie Cooper wore a sleek suit with a green tie as he swivelled in a rotating chair. In his lap, he held a nasty-looking plant. By Act Two, he wrapped himself in a Santa Claus robe of emerald green. As the *Hollywood Reporter* observed, "It's a simple, low-tech solution that yielded a lot of laughs." The industry website *Deadline* concluded that the evening "felt like Homecoming, Sunday church in Harlem and the Governor's Ball all rolled into two joyfully cathartic hours."[45]

Like the iconic plant after it tastes human blood, Ellen Greene wanted more. Among friends and former associates, she was mysterious about her plans: "I'm working on something, but I can't tell you about it."[46] After City Center, she reconnected with Frank Oz and planned to remount her revival in a hybrid production that would incorporate elements of the 1986 film (in particular, scenes of the plant). Of course, Greene, now in her sixties, would star as Audrey:

"I wanted to do this for the people who'd never seen me on stage." Her idea was to launch the new version of *Little Shop* as a commercial production—maybe in London, where she also received adoring notices. However, the Ashman estate said no because they were in discussions with another producer.[47]

Busy with her own plans, Greene chose not to participate in a reunion concert held at Feinstein's/54 Below in 2016. The location was the basement of the legendary disco Studio 54, which operated from 1977 until 1986, hosting Andy Warhol and other New York icons for nights of revelry, drug use, and general misbehavior. Greene herself partied there and was photographed with singer-songwriter Peter Allen.[48] Later, the building became a legitimate theatre and the basement a cabaret, owned by some of the producers of the *Little Shop* Broadway revival, in collaboration with Michael Feinstein, a lover of vintage American music and musicals.

Little Shop's original orchestrator, Robby Merkin, conceived of the concert with director Stephen Nachamie, who began his career as a teenage assistant at the Orpheum while *Little Shop* was still running. Two concerts (early evening and late) were performed with minimal staging on June 27, 2016. Three members of the WPA Showcase appeared: Jennifer Leigh Warren, Sheila Kay Davis, and Marty Robinson (operating his puppets). They were joined by many subsequent performers—understudies, replacements, members of the Broadway company, and players from the Orpheum band. At the first rehearsal, when the singers practiced "Skid Row (Downtown)," Andrew Hill Newman, who took over the role of Seymour in 1985, "broke down in tears," according to Merkin. "It was so emotional." Late in the rehearsal process, Alan Menken joined the company.[49] On stage, he sat at the piano and performed a medley of cut songs, from the ebullient "Audrey II" to the masochistic solo, "The Worse He Treats Me (The More He Loves Me)." As alumni reunited to prepare the concerts, Steve Gelfand described "a warm, wonderful feeling." Many of the participants worked on many other shows, but the *Little Shop* family felt a peculiar bond. "All these years later," Robby Merkin said, "it means that much."[50]

In addition to revivals and reunions, *Little Shop of Horrors* inspired a series of musicals that sought the formula for success through a combination of toe-tapping tunes and the *outré*. In 1982, the *New Yorker* remarked that *Little*

Shop could be "a model show for Off Broadway," and Thomas S. Hischak, in his thorough history of Off-Broadway musicals, notes that the Ashman-Menken hit "created a new genre"—namely, "the camp pulp musical."[51] Often a B movie (or a B-movie-type scenario) would supply the unprepossessing storyline on the assumption that the worst ideas are always best. Since the 1990s, New York audiences have tasted the pleasures of *Eating Raoul*, *Zombies from the Beyond*, *Zombie Prom*, *Bat Boy: The Musical*, *Reefer Madness*, *Evil Dead: The Musical*, and *The Toxic Avenger*—to name a few.

Bat Boy, which opened Off-Broadway in 2001, is not based on a film but rather a series of articles in the *Weekly World News*, a supermarket tabloid with a tenuous hold on the truth. The title character, originally played by Deven May, is part man, part bat. Kerry Butler, two years before her *Little Shop* début, created the role of Bat Boy's love interest. One member of the producing team was Nancy Nagel Gibbs, who had served as company manager at the Orpheum. She said, "I tried to produce *Bat Boy* using the *Little Shop* model."[52] *Reefer Madness*, like *Little Shop,* derives from a rediscovered movie: the 1936 low-budget, independent feature meant to frighten young people away from drugs. By the 1960s, audiences found the incompetent film hilarious, just as Ashman delighted in *The Little Shop* on television—a trash treasure, in the phrase suggested by *Time* magazine's Richard Corliss. *The Toxic Avenger*, another low-budget movie, from 1984, begins with a Seymour-like nebbish who transforms into a mutant superhero (these things happen). By 2009, the film inspired another stage play. Hischak remarks that "twenty-seven years after *Little Shop of Horrors*, Off Broadway was still trying to recreate the critical and commercial success of that show by turning yet another cheaply made cult horror film into a hit musical."[53] Even the WPA Theatre tried to recapture some of the magic. In the spring of 1992, a decade after *Little Shop* premiered, the WPA reunited Menken and Greene for *Weird Romance*, a pair of science-fiction one-act musicals, with lyrics by David Spencer. However, the new musical closed without an Off-Broadway transfer.[54]

More successful was Britain's answer to *Little Shop*: *Return to the Forbidden Planet*, which opened in the West End in 1989. It is a *Little Shop of Horrors* without the songwriting talents of Ashman and Menken. Author Bob Carlton reverse engineered the formula by mixing three essential elements: a B-movie plot, the music of the 1950s and 1960s, and a literary source. In the case of *The Little Shop*, it was *Doctor Faustus*, Christopher Marlowe's retelling of the Faust legend. Carlton turned to Marlowe's esteemed contemporary, William Shakespeare, and his late play *The Tempest*. Further, Carlton borrowed or stole from an intermediating text, the 1956 M-G-M movie *Forbidden Planet*, which is *The Tempest* in outer space. In his musical, an intergalactic crew lands on a planet inhabited by the marooned Dr. Prospero, who lives with daughter Miranda and a chatty robot named Ariel. Further, the spoken dialogue is copied or parodied from the words of Shakespeare. For example, Prospero misquotes Hamlet by claiming, "There are more things in Heaven and Earth / Than are dreamt of in my laboratory."[55] For songs, Carlton incorporated a series of hits from the *Little Shop* era. A voyage through an asteroid field requires the cast to sing "Great Balls of Fire," the emphatic Jerry Lee Lewis number from 1957. Miranda wonders, "Why must I be a teenager in love?"—another 1950s hit.[56] In other words, this is a jukebox musical, the term employed for shows that repurpose familiar songs, organized into a revue or retrofitted into a plot. After the success of *Little Shop*, a number of shows exploited the music of the same period: *Beehive, Leader of the Pack, Forever Plaid*. In 1995, Jerry Zaks directed a jukebox musical celebrating the same era and featuring the songs of Leiber and Stoller, entitled *Smokey Joe's Cafe*, which played for years at the Virginia Theatre.

Little Shop's influence on the Broadway musical is less obvious, yet Charles Isherwood declared that "its most successful spawn" was the musical *Hairspray*, which opened on Broadway in the summer of 2002. Producer and author Jack Viertel agrees that *Hairspray* "owes more than a little to *Little Shop of Horrors*."[57] John Waters wrote and directed the source film, his first studio feature and a modest hit in 1988. Of course, he had been directing films for years, the most notorious of which was *Pink Flamingos*, released in 1972 as an exercise in bad taste. Waters, like Ashman, was a native of Baltimore. Ashman adored Waters's outrageous films and often watched them on video; they also met, through mutual friends.[58] *Hairspray*—the film and the musical—is set in 1962, and it is a love letter to the music (and hairstyles) of the period. *Little Shop* occupies the same historical moment, even though the date is imprecise. Both works employ nostalgia and locate a beating heart in material that could have been exploitative. In *Hairspray*, the protagonist, Tracy Turnblad, joins in the opening number, "Good Morning Baltimore," which serves as a kind of "Skid Row" introduction to the world of the story and a young girl's dreams.

Success, in postmodern culture, is marked by successors—imitations, cheap knockoffs, sequels and prequels, parodies on television or the Internet. *Jaws* can be considered successful because it made a lot of money for Universal in 1975 but also because it gave us *Piranha*, directed by Joe Dante, and *Piranha II: The Spawning*, directed by James Cameron. Cameron's next film, *The Terminator*, from 1984, led to *RoboCop* and *Robot Jox*. When the feature film *Transformers* appeared on cinema screens, in 2007, *Transmorphers* appeared on home video. Further, to be parodied in this culture is not a misfortune but a compliment. If "Weird Al" Yankovic reimagines a song, it is probably a popular hit. Often, postmodern audiences perceive an original through the lens of parody or imitation—the order is reversed. We recognize Hungarian Rhapsody No. 2 from a cartoon starring Bugs Bunny or Tom and Jerry; we chuckle at a space monolith and only later get around to watching *2001: A Space Odyssey*. Indeed, success, in this culture, is no longer reckoned by praise in a printed newspaper; it is a knowing reference on *The Simpsons* or a mashup on YouTube.

By these measures, *Little Shop of Horrors* became a success. *Family Guy*, which began airing on FOX in 1999, parodied the musical at least three times. One episode, from 2005, recreates "Somewhere That's Green" as filmed by Frank Oz, with a creepy neighbor in the Audrey role. In a 2008 episode, Stewie remarks, "Let's ask Rick Moranis and the backup singers from *Little Shop of Horrors*." The show then delves into a quick rendition of "Da-Doo," with an animated Seymour and three urchins, who all appear out of nowhere. In 2013, the *Family Guy* audience learned of Peter's experience in his high school production of *Little Shop*. Dressed as an oversized plant in the role of Audrey II, he makes an unwelcome entrance during "Suddenly, Seymour" because, he admits, "I pooped in the pod again!"

But it was not only the professionals who mined *Little Shop of Horrors*; inspired amateurs created fan art or shared videos of their mashups and reenactments. This effort relates to fanfiction and cosplay—that is, participatory culture. Media scholar Henry Jenkins explains that "fans raid mass culture, claiming its materials for their own."⁵⁹ In a way, the distinction between author and audience blurs. Audiences are no longer passive consumers; now they are collaborators, co-creators. A search on YouTube discovers many *Little Shop* videos, usually inspired by the 1986 film: animation exercises, live-action reenactments, and music videos. "Dentist!" proved an Internet favorite. One parody was created by a class of dental hygienists in training, at a community college in North Carolina. The students wrote and recorded new lyrics to Menken's tune, and they sang, "Choose dental hygiene / You'll be a success!"⁶⁰

A compelling series of home reenactments was shared by a user named R2ninjaturtle (itself a pop-culture mashup). She and her collaborators demonstrate a vivid awareness of and affection for the Frank Oz film. In their version of "Feed Me" (aka "Git It"), posted in 2014, a young woman appears in Rick Moranis drag; she even resembles 1980s Moranis with her oversized glasses and pouty lower lip. Another young woman plays Audrey I and II (a fascinating bit of doubling). In a green T-shirt and green tights, she essays the hungry plant. With Levi Stubbs's voice emanating from this slender blonde, the startling effect is like that of Dennis Potter's experiments with lip sync, in his television series *Pennies from Heaven* and *The Singing Detective*. Over the next few years, R2ninjaturtle and her collaborators proceeded to film five more songs and won thousands of views.⁶¹

That young people embrace *Little Shop of Horrors* may be considered an unintended consequence. The musical produced at the WPA was not meant for children, given the midnight shows and the proximity to a brothel. Although the play transferred to the Orpheum intact, something changed. In December 1982, the *New York Times*, in an article entitled "A Christmas Bounty for Youngsters," recommended *Little Shop* "for older children and adults." Promoting the musical, Ashman mentioned that "we don't use the F word."⁶² In 1983, *Los Angeles* magazine found the musical "surprisingly suitable for the whole family." With bitterness intended, a British newspaper described "a juvenile cult show that no self-respecting child can afford to miss."⁶³ By 1985, general manager Albert Poland tracked a change in the Orpheum audience: "it's gone from being a cult show to being a family show," he told a reporter.⁶⁴ Part of what happened was that children's entertainment grew up and gained sophistication. A new movie rating appeared, PG-13, which allowed the same young audience to experience more gruesome effects, more violence, and more adult situations. (Now they've been warned.) The impetus came from parental complaints about earlier films, including *Gremlins*, that comedy-horror hybrid. When Warner Bros. released *Little Shop of Horrors*, it bore the new rating, PG-13.

For *Little Shop* to retain its hold on the imagination, it needed to stay relevant and inclusive. In the 1990s, modes of non-traditional or "colorblind" casting offered ways to rethink and rejuvenate the musical-theatre canon. Rodgers and Hammerstein's *Carousel* was revived in London with a nonwhite Mr. Snow; when the show moved to New York, in 1994, audiences met a nonwhite Carrie Pipperidge, portrayed by Audra Ann McDonald, in a star-making role. Productions of *Little Shop* over the years have been cast based on local talent pools. The urchins in the first Scandinavian productions were white. In Japan, everyone was Japanese. American high schools produced *Little Shop* using their own populations, in ways that may have deviated from Ashman's original casting assignments.

In 2019, a revelatory production of *Little Shop* opened at the Pasadena Playhouse, in Southern California. Although Menken's music retained its early 1960s flavor, the narrative seemed to drift closer to the present. One reviewer thought that the show might be set in the 1990s, indicated by the "Salt 'N Pepa meets Seattle grunge outfits." But the actors onstage drew the most attention. As the review on *Deadline* states, "The casting goes full *Hamilton* with its inclusive casting in roles that are typically portrayed by white actors."[65] George Salazar, the child of an Ecuadorian father and a Filipino mother, played a convincing and vulnerable Seymour Krelborn. In the role of Audrey, the theatre cast Mj Rodriguez, a transgender actor who broke barriers in the TV show *Pose*, which began in 2018 and won Rodriguez an Emmy Award. The *Los Angeles Times* admired the production and claimed that "this is a modern take." In particular, casting Rodriguez as Audrey "mak[es] us see her shattered pieces in a new light."[66] The character has always been something of a broken leaf, but this performance maps the intersection of racial identity, the character's economic hardship, and a dubious past. According to one critic, "Her story echoes the story of countless Black and trans women."[67] In "Suddenly, Seymour," a song about transformation, the lyrics gain new resonance, especially "The girl that's inside me" and the "sweet understanding" that the characters in this production desperately need.

By coincidence, on September 17, 2019, as the show opened in Pasadena, another *Little Shop* began previews in New York City. Diep Tran, in *American Theatre*, observed that six other professional revivals of the musical were scheduled for the same season.[68] The New York production would be the first commercial, Off-Broadway revival since the 1980s. Indeed, this version would be doubly nostalgic: looking back on America in the early 1960s but also New York in the early 1980s, when the musical premiered. One of the producers, Tom Kirdahy, knew at a young age that he was gay; he decided to move to New York City and attend New York University. In 1981, he worked at NYU's medical center and admitted patients with a "mysterious disease." During the 1980s, as HIV/AIDS ravaged the creative community, Kirdahy discovered *Little Shop of Horrors* at the Orpheum; he saw the show many times and "was never disappointed." Later working as a lawyer, he gave free legal advice to people with HIV and segued into producing for the theatre. Another producer, Robert Ahrens, pitched him the idea of a *Little Shop* revival. "I'm in," replied Kirdahy, who became the show's lead producer.[69]

He met with Sarah Ashman Gillespie and Bill Lauch and "understood instantly that they were protecting a legacy." Kirdahy said, "I knew that it's more than just licensing out a show, that there's a responsibility that comes with caring for a work of art."[70] The Ashman estate did not want to repeat the error of 2003; this time, the show would be revived Off-Broadway. The estate had a fondness for Michael Mayer, who almost directed *Little Shop* at Encores! and then mounted *God Bless You, Mr. Rosewater* at City Center in 2016. Mayer was thrilled to stage the subsequent Ashman-Menken musical, and he planned to honor its original production: "My dedication was completely to try to get into Howard's mindset. I wanted to just try to channel him the best way I could." Nevertheless, the new team was open to new ideas. "We really considered doing an immersive production," Kirdahy explained.[71] There was a vogue for kinds of interactive theatre in non-traditional spaces, like abandoned warehouses. *Sleep No More*, a retelling of Shakespeare's *Macbeth*, moved its audience through a series of rooms in which fragments of the play were enacted. Lewis Carroll's *Alice's Adventures in Wonderland* received a similar treatment in *Then She Fell*, staged in a creepy building in Brooklyn. In April 2019, *Little Shop* enjoyed the immersive treatment, when university students staged the musical at Bool's

Flower Shop in Ithaca, New York.[72] However, the producers of the Off-Broadway revival were unable to find a satisfactory space in terms of acoustics and practical needs (like bathrooms), so they settled on the upstairs venue at the Westside Theatre, at 407 West Forty-third Street.[73] As pre-production commenced, Michael Mayer knew whom he wanted to play Seymour.

Jonathan Groff hailed from Lancaster, Pennsylvania. As a child, he watched movie musicals on television, rented from the local Blockbuster Video—including *Oklahoma!* and *Little Shop of Horrors*. He was struck by the song "Skid Row (Downtown)." "I rewound 'Skid Row' over and over and over and over again and would sing along with the movie," he said. Seymour's line "Someone show me a way to get outa here" resonated with Groff as a gay kid who wanted to be in the theatre.[74] Later, as an actor, he starred in *Spring Awakening*, a 2007 Off-Broadway and then Broadway musical that Mayer directed. Groff appeared in the Broadway company of *Hamilton* (as George III) and worked in film and television. Then Mayer invited Groff to play Seymour in this new production. "Oh, my God, really?" was the reply. Mayer argued that even though the actor was "incredibly charismatic and handsome and talented," he was "at his core" a Seymour Krelborn.[75] Now that decades had passed since *Little Shop* first opened in New York, generations of young actors who grew up on the musical could play their favorite parts, in amateur or professional productions. Groff, for one, did his homework. He watched the 1960 film and "listened nonstop to the original Off-Broadway cast recording." He did not return to the 1986 movie until rehearsals were underway, but revisiting the film, he found that "Rick Moranis was beautifully simple, was so beautifully true."[76]

For the role of Audrey, "we knew we wanted to surprise," Kirdahy said. Michael Mayer described Tammy Blanchard as "a gal from New Jersey," with a working-class background.[77] Her mother was a housekeeper; her father was a Vietnam veteran and an alcoholic. Blanchard explained her introduction to musicals: "I fell in love with Judy Garland and *The Wizard of Oz*." At the age of ten, Blanchard sang "Over the Rainbow" at a school assembly; years later, she got to play young Judy Garland in a 2001 TV miniseries. Like Jonathan Groff, Blanchard encountered *Little Shop* on the small screen. She recalled watching a video of "Suddenly, Seymour" on YouTube and thought, "Man! If I could ever play that role!" Weeks later, she got the phone call.[78] Because she had not appeared on Broadway in a few years, she agreed to sing for the director and his music director, Will Van Dyke. She sang a bit of "Suddenly, Seymour" and all of "Somewhere That's Green." Mayer admitted, "She just broke our hearts that day."[79] Indeed, Blanchard felt a strong connection to the character she was about to play: "I had experienced a rocky relationship that got a little too intense for me, and I had to leave." Further, she confessed, "I didn't think I was worth anything for a long time, and I knew that pain of feeling like someone as good as Seymour would never even look at me."[80] The sweet understanding articulated by "Suddenly, Seymour" would prove healing for this Audrey as well.

Rehearsals began at Sunlight Studios, in a room with no windows.[81] Alan Menken addressed the gathered cast, ready to work on the musical he wrote so long ago: "I don't want you to treat it like some sacred text. That being said, please sing all the correct notes and all the exact words."[82] Van Dyke created new orchestrations because, in Mayer's view, "the '80s synth stuff from the original dated it a little bit and made it actually sound a little '80s, as opposed to '50s." A synthesizer would be used, but only in moments that correspond to the otherworldly plant.[83] Yet in surprising ways, the new production emulated the original. At the Westside Theatre, "all the boys were in one dressing room; all the girls were in the other dressing room"[84]—an unintentional recreation of the layout of both the WPA and the Orpheum. With 270 seats and a top ticket price of $299, the revival cost approximately three million dollars.[85] From the start, audiences adored the show. Bill Lauch attended the first preview, on September 17, 2019, and he told Mayer, "Howard would have been absolutely thrilled with 'Mushnik and Son' because he always felt like that never worked."[86] The song was restaged for the Orpheum and rewritten for the 1984 national tour. Now, with an extended dance break, Mushnik courts the younger man in a tango, a peculiar choice for a would-be father and son. Other members of the original production also came to see the revival. Lauch invited Kyle Renick and Albert Poland to the opening night, Thursday, October 17.

Once again, *Little Shop of Horrors* won enthusiastic reviews. "The musical comedy our climate-denying age requires," claimed *The Guardian*. David Rooney, in the *Hollywood Reporter*, appreciated the "scrappy little pastiche musical" that works best "in an intimate house." Ben Brantley, in the *New York*

Times, reviewed the show once again and described "the shivery elation I felt seeing 'Shop' at the East Village's Orpheum nearly four decades earlier." Further, he wrote that the new production "restores the show to its original scale and sensibility."[87] Because the producers were not able to drop objects onto paying customers, there were no falling tendrils in the finale.[88] So Mayer invented another surprise: a baby Audrey II bursts from the mouth of the giant plant—an image that recalls the chest-bursting scene in the film *Alien*.

By the early months of 2020, *Little Shop* felt strangely relevant. An article in *Elle* magazine observed that "the opening of the 1986 musical *Little Shop of Horrors* hits a lot harder in spring 2020 than it did before."[89] There was a new biological menace, in the form of the disease Covid-19; and, as the show's prologue explains, "the human race suddenly encountered a deadly threat to its very existence." Much of everyday life was interrupted, including the New York theatre business, a major source of revenue for the city and the livelihood of many inhabitants. On Wednesday, March 11, word spread that an usher in one of the city's theatres contracted the disease. At the Westside Theatre, Tammy Blanchard was putting on her wig to play Audrey. She and others discussed whether or not the show should go on. "I'm here," Blanchard insisted. "I'm doing the show!" The audience was waiting. So the company performed *Little Shop of Horrors* that night—"and it was phenomenal," she added.[90] On Thursday, Mayer rehearsed Jeremy Jordan, who was scheduled to take over the role of Seymour. Mayer gave him notes, "and then we all went home," the director said. There would be no more performances of *Little Shop* that year. Producer Tom Kirdahy remembered the 1980s and all the HIV patients that he tried to help: "Another pandemic has robbed us of so many lives."[91] In 2021, theatres reopened. Jordan at last got to play Seymour at the Westside Theatre, a role he had prepared a year and a half earlier. In 2022, Conrad Ricamora, an Asian American actor, joined the cast as Seymour—expanding yet again the show's expressive possibilities.

Six decades after Corman attempted to shoot a feature film in just two days, and four decades after Ashman and Menken adapted the nasty little tale, *Little Shop of Horrors* remained a vital piece of theatre, admired and remembered by fans everywhere. It makes sense because it's a musical about memory: Ashman *remembered* the experience of watching an outrageous black-and-white film on

Figure 12 *138 Fifth Avenue, New York, New York. The WPA Theatre occupied the second floor from 1977 until 1985, and it was here that* Little Shop of Horrors *made its début.*

a flickering television screen; the score remembers the music of the early 1960s, when Ashman and Menken were young. One of the most insightful reviews appeared after the LA opening, in 1983. The reviewer, Jack Viertel, wrote, "Somehow Roger Corman, the Ronettes, monsters from outer space, and the lure (and/or horror) of the suburbs are all wrapped up together in our memory banks."[92] This was the view of 1983, when audiences in their twenties and thirties could remember the 1960s—it was part of their lived experience. But what about subsequent generations? In the original production, the audience could smirk at the line "Lookout! Lookout! Lookout! Lookout!" in the opening number and recognize the reference to the Shangri-Las and their song "Leader of the Pack." Now it's a line from *Little Shop of Horrors*. So *Little Shop* remains a memory play. It remembers the 1960s; it remembers the 1980s. Further, *Little Shop* incorporates the memory of its reception and the later adaptations.

"It is a perfect piece of writing," according to music director Will Van Dyke. Michael Mayer argued that "the songs are uncannily good." He found a similar quality in perennial songs of the past: "It's why you never get tired of hearing 'Embraceable You' or 'White Christmas' or 'Over the Rainbow.'"[93] His Audrey, Tammy Blanchard, expressed her own views on the show's longevity: "I think that there will always be a Skid Row, and I think that there will always be precious souls that deserve and need redemption."[94] After a performance at the Westside Theatre, actor Kevin Kline, who had seen *Little Shop* in the 1980s, chatted backstage with Jonathan Groff. Decades after the Orpheum production, Kline saw the musical afresh: "Now it's *Macbeth*. This show is *Macbeth*."[95] Groff felt the truth of this observation as he performed the show night after night; he described a distinction between the audience's view and his internal experience. "The audience gets to have an incredible time," he said, but inside, "you get to be in a Shakespearean drama"—he called it an "exorcism," the catharsis that Aristotle required of tragedy, in the *Poetics*.[96]

Yet *Little Shop of Horrors* remains a curious entry in the musical-theatre pantheon, with a disreputable origin story as a quickie film produced on the tattered fringe of Hollywood. Ashman and Menken transformed their source material into something iconic: an apocalypse with a smile. When asked about the show's enduring afterlife, Cameron Mackintosh said, "It's timeless: a little work of art."[97]

Appendix A
Comparative Song List, 1981–82

FIRST DRAFT (1981)	ORPHEUM THEATRE (1982)
Little Shop of Horrors	Prologue (Little Shop of Horrors)
(Downtown) Skid Row	Skid Row (Downtown)
Da-Doo	Da-Doo
Grow for Me	Grow for Me
	Don't It Go to Show Ya Never Know
The Worse He Treats Me (The More He Loves Me)	Somewhere That's Green
	Closed for Renovation
	Dentist!
Mushnick and Son	Mushnik and Son
A Little Bit Anemic	Sudden Changes
Git It	Git It!
A Little Dental Music	Now (It's Just the Gas)
Just a Hobby	Act One Coda
	---ACT BREAK---
	Call Back in the Morning
Suddenly, Seymour	Suddenly, Seymour
Suppertime	Suppertime
The Meek Shall Inherit	The Meek Shall Inherit
The Plant Who Loves You	
We'll Have Tomorrow	
	Sominex
Suppertime (Reprise)	Suppertime (Reprise)
We'll Have Tomorrow (Reprise)	Somewhere That's Green (Reprise)
The Meek Shall Inherit (Reprise)	
All Gone	Finale (Don't Feed the Plants)

Appendix B
"Somewhere That's Green" Song Development

EARLY DRAFT	FINAL DRAFT
A matchbox of our own	A matchbox of our own
A fence of real chain-link	A fence of real chain link
A grill out on the patio,	A grill out on the patio
Dispose-all in the sink	Disposal in the sink
A washer and a dryer and	A washer and a dryer and
An ironing machine	An ironing machine
In a tract-house we will share	In a tract house that we share
Somewhere that's green.	Somewhere that's green
I'll rake and trim the grass	He rakes and trims the grass
I'll mulch and mow and weed	He loves to mow and weed
You'll cook like Betty Croker	I cook like Betty Crocker
But you'll look like Donna Reed.	And I look like Donna Reed
And plastic on the furniture	There's plastic on the furniture
Will keep it neat and clean,	To keep it neat and clean
In the Pine-Sol scented air,	In the Pine-Sol-scented air,
Somewhere that's green.	Somewhere that's green

Somewhere that's green—
A yard of clover, daffodils, and mums
Somewhere that's green—
We won't trip over derelicts and bums

To fill our leisure time,	Between our frozen dinner
Which we'll have plenty of,	And our bed-time: nine-fifteen
We'll tune in our TV set	
To see Lucy, who we love.	We snuggle watching Lucy
We'll snuggle as she clowns on our	On our big, enormous
Enormous twelve-inch screen	Twelve-inch screen
Til it's late, but we don't care	
Somewhere that's green.	

Somewhere that's green—
I'll bag your lunch to take to work each day
Somewhere that's green—
We'll actively support the scouts and P.T.A.

You're my December Bride	I'm his December Bride
I'm Father. I know best	He's father, he knows best
You'll fix a frozen dinner as	Our kids watch *Howdy Doody*
The sun sets in the west.	As the sun sets in the west
A picture out of *Better Homes*	A picture out of *Better Homes*
And Gardens magazine—	*And Gardens* magazine
Oh Seymour, take me there	
Somewhere that's green.	

A life like we have never known, Audrey—	
A quarter-acre of our own, Audrey—	
I picture dawn breaking over lawn	
Making such a sweetly suburban scene	
Far from Skid Row	Far from Skid Row
Trust me, we'll go	I dream we'll go
Somewhere	Somewhere that's . . .
That's	
Green.	Green.

Appendix C
Original Casts, 1982–86

	WPA (May 6, 1982)	ORPHEUM (July 27, 1982)
SEYMOUR	Lee Wilkof	Lee Wilkof
AUDREY	Ellen Greene	Ellen Greene
ORIN, etc.	Franc Luz	Franc Luz
MUSHNIK	Michael Vale	Hy Anzell
CRYSTAL	Jennifer Leigh Warren	Jennifer Leigh Warren
RONNETTE	Sheila Kay Davis	Sheila Kay Davis
CHIFFON	Leilani Jones	Marlene Danielle
AUDREY II	Martin P. Robinson	Martin P. Robinson
THE VOICE	Ron Taylor	Ron Taylor

	LOS ANGELES (April 27, 1983)	LONDON (October 12, 1983)
SEYMOUR	Lee Wilkof	Barry James
AUDREY	Ellen Greene	Ellen Greene
ORIN, etc.	Franc Luz	Terence Hillyer
MUSHNIK	Jesse White	Harry Towb
CRYSTAL	Marion Ramsey	Dawn Hope
RONNETTE	Louise Robinson	Shezwae Powell
CHIFFON	B. J. Jefferson	Nicola Blackman
AUDREY II	Martin P. Robinson	Anthony B. Asbury
THE VOICE	Michael Leslie	Michael Leslie

	TOUR (March 14, 1984)	FILM (December 19, 1986)
SEYMOUR	Ken Ward	Rick Moranis
AUDREY	Eydie Alyson	Ellen Greene
ORIN, etc.	Ken Land	Steve Martin[1]
MUSHNIK	Stan Rubin	Vincent Gardenia
CRYSTAL	Suzzanne Douglas	Tichina Arnold
RONNETTE[2]	Louise Robinson	Michelle Weeks
CHIFFON	B. J. Jefferson	Tisha Campbell
AUDREY II	William Szymanski	Lyle Conway[3]
THE VOICE	Michael Leslie	Levi Stubbs

Notes to Appendix C

1 In the film, Steve Martin plays Orin Scrivello but not the other characters covered by the Orin track in the play.

2 In the film, the character is named Ronette.

3 His credit reads, "Audrey II Designed and Created by." Many artists and technicians contributed to building and performing the plants.

Notes

The following abbreviations are used throughout the notes:

DRF Donna Rose Fletcher Collection, Walnut Creek, California
LOC Howard Ashman Papers, Library of Congress, Washington, DC
NYPL Kyle Renick Papers on the WPA Theatre, 1950–2018, New York Public Library for the Performing Arts, New York, New York
SA The Shubert Archive, New York, New York

Chapter 1

1 Roger Corman with Jim Jerome, *How I Made a Hundred Movies in Hollywood and Never Lost a Dime* (New York: Random House, 1990), 9, 15.

2 Quoted in Constantine Nasr, ed., *Roger Corman: Interviews* (Jackson: University Press of Mississippi, 2011), x.

3 Corman, *How I Made a Hundred Movies*, 55.

4 Beverly Gray, *Roger Corman: An Unauthorized Biography of the Godfather of Indie Filmmaking* (Los Angeles: Renaissance Books, 2000), 32; Mel Welles, quoted in John McCarty and Mark Thomas McGee, *The Little Shop of Horrors Book* (New York: St. Martin's Press, 1988), 81.

5 Nasr, *Roger Corman*, viii.

6 Quoted in Gray, *Roger Corman*, 58.

7 Welles, quoted in McCarty and McGee, *Little Shop of Horrors Book*, 78. See also Gray, *Roger Corman*, 49.

8 Corman, *How I Made a Hundred Movies*, 36.

9 Roger Corman, quoted in Nasr, *Roger Corman*, 211.

10 Versions of the legend appear in various places, including Corman, *How I Made a Hundred Movies*, 62; Chris Nashawaty, *Crab Monsters, Teenage Cavemen, and Candy Stripe Nurses: Roger Corman; King of the B Movie* (New York: Abrams, 2013), 32; Nasr, *Roger Corman*, 102.

11 Mark Thomas McGee, phone interview by author, December 16, 2020.

12 Quoted in Corman, *How I Made a Hundred Movies*, 64. There are a number of possible source-texts that Griffith may have known and remembered. The earliest, "The Flowering of the Strange Orchid," is an 1894 short story by H. G. Wells about a plant that drinks human blood. "Green Thoughts," a 1931 story by John Collier, tells of a bloodthirsty orchid that devours a cat, a man, and a woman. In a moment that anticipates Corman's finale, the plant sprouts three new flowers, shaped like a cat head and two human heads, now made of vegetable matter. In *Greener Than You Think*, a 1947 novel by Ward Moore, a kind of hyperbolic grass takes over Los Angeles, then the United States, then the world. Last, "The Reluctant Orchid" draws even closer to *The Little Shop*. In this story by Arthur C. Clarke, first published in 1956, "an inoffensive little clerk" breeds a carnivorous orchid and plots to feed a hateful relative to the monster. H. G. Wells, *The Stolen Bacillus and Other Incidents* (1895; London: Macmillan, 1904); John Collier, *Fancies and Goodnights* (Garden City, NY: Doubleday, 1952); Ward Moore, *Greener Than You Think* (New York: William Sloane, 1947); Arthur C. Clarke, *Tales from the White Hart* (New York: Ballantine Books, 1957), 104.

13 Chuck Griffith said, "I followed the structure of *Bucket* almost exactly." Quoted in Corman, *How I Made a Hundred Movies*, 64. *A Bucket of Blood* held Corman's previous record for speed, shot in five days, at a cost of $50,000. Corman, *How I Made a Hundred Movies*, 62.

14 McCarty and McGee, *Little Shop of Horrors Book*, 24; Corman, *How I Made a Hundred Movies*, 68.

15 McCarty and McGee, *Little Shop of Horrors Book*, 25, 20–1.

16 Nasr, *Roger Corman*, 137.

17 Corman, *How I Made a Hundred Movies*, 66; Mark Thomas McGee, *Roger Corman: The Best of the Cheap Acts* (Jefferson, NC: McFarland, 1988), 32, 124.

18 Corman, *How I Made a Hundred Movies*, 5; Gray, *Roger Corman*, 100.

19 Dennis Fischer, "Roger Corman's *Little Shop of Horrors*," *Cinefantastique* 17, no. 1 (January 1987): 29; McCarty and McGee, *Little Shop of Horrors Book*, 25.

20 David Colker, "Off-Broadway Play Stems from 1960s Cult-Horror Film," *Los Angeles Herald Examiner*, April 19, 1983.

21 Quoted in Corman, *How I Made a Hundred Movies*, 67.

22 The production cost of *The Little Shop of Horrors* has been variously reported. The lowest and earliest figure is $22,500. Chuck Griffith told Beverly Gray that the film cost $27,000, and Corman claimed $30,000. "'Little Shop of Horrors' Set for Art Theatres Booking," *Boxoffice* 79, no. 2 (May 1, 1961): W2; Gray, *Roger Corman*, 69; Corman, *How I Made a Hundred Movies*, 68.

23 Quoted in Corman, *How I Made a Hundred Movies*, 67.

24 Review of *The Little Shop of Horrors*, *Variety*, May 10, 1961, 6.

25 Picture Grosses, *Variety*, September 7, 1960, 18; Picture Grosses, *Variety*, September 14, 1960, 9.

26 McCarty and McGee, *Little Shop of Horrors Book*, 25.

27 "Krelboin" appears in Danny Peary, *Cult Movies: The Classics, the Sleepers, the Weird, and the Wonderful* (New York: Delacorte Press, 1981), 203; "Krelboined" appears in McCarty and McGee, *Little Shop of Horrors Book*, 22.

28 "From Trade Paper Reviews Roger Corman's 'Cheapie' Film Rates Cannes Bid," *Variety*, May 17, 1961, 17. For *Black Sunday*, see "Oscar Winners Help Boost LA Scores," *Boxoffice* 79, no. 2 (May 1, 1961): W4; Gray, *Roger Corman*, 64.

29 "'Little Shop of Horrors' Set," W2.

30 McGee, phone interview by author.

31 Welles, quoted in McCarty and McGee, *Little Shop of Horrors Book*, 84; Michael Weldon et al., *The Psychotronic Encyclopedia of Film* (New York: Ballantine Books, 1983), 425.

32 McGee, phone interview by author; Dick Miller, quoted in McCarty and McGee, *Little Shop of Horrors Book*, 97; Welles, quoted in McCarty and McGee, *Little Shop of Horrors Book*, 84.

33 Howard Ashman, interview by Ira Weitzman, *Anything Goes*, WBAI radio, 1982, audiotape, Howard Ashman Sound Recordings, LOC; Howard Ashman, "A Musical about a Man-Eating Plant?," www.howardashman.com. This piece was written for *Playbill* around 1983.

34 Ashman, interview by Weitzman; Howard Ashman, quoted in McCarty and McGee, *Little Shop of Horrors Book*, 123.

35 Sarah Ashman Gillespie, interview by author, July 15, 2011.

36 Sarah Ashman Gillespie, interview by author, January 4, 2019.

37 Ashman Gillespie, interview by author, July 15, 2011; Sarah Ashman Gillespie, email to author, January 27, 2022.

38 Jacky Sallow, phone interview by author, December 28, 2020. During high school, she spelled her name Jackie.

39 Ashman Gillespie, interview by author, January 4, 2019.

40 John Sadowsky, phone interview by author, December 11, 2020.

41 Otts Munderloh, phone interview by author, November 17, 2020.

42 Ashman Gillespie, interview by author, January 4, 2019; Sadowsky, phone interview by author.

43 Gilda Morigi, "Broadway Jottings," *American-Jewish Life*, June 29, 1984, box 4, folder 3, NYPL.

44 Quoted in Sadowsky, phone interview by author.

45 Norman Schwartz, phone interview by author, December 23, 2020.

46 *The Brat's Meow* program. Performances were scheduled for January 21 at 8:00 pm and January 22 at 2:30 pm. Book and lyrics were by Howard Ashman and John Sadowsky, music by Norman Schwartz.

47 Sallow, phone interview by author.

48 Quoted in "Srs. to Present 'The Brat's Meow,'" *Mill Wheel* 17, no. 5 (January 12, 1967): 1.

49 Sadowsky, phone interview by author.

50 Ibid.

51 Schwartz, phone interview by author.

52 Sallow, phone interview by author; Ashman, interview by Weitzman.

53 Valerie Velardi, Zoom interview by author, November 16, 2020.

54 Munderloh, phone interview by author.

55 Nancy Parent, interview by author, July 10, 2019.

56 Albert Poland, interview by author, October 7, 2019.

57 Ashman Gillespie, interview by author, July 15, 2011.

58 Edie Cowan, interview by author, October 11, 2019.

59 Parent, interview by author.

60 Harriet McDougal, phone interview by author, November 13, 2020.

61 Quoted in ibid.

62 This time frame is identified by Stacy Wolf in *A Problem Like Maria: Gender and Sexuality in the American Musical* (Ann Arbor: The University of Michigan Press, 2002), 11.

63 Jessica Sternfeld and Elizabeth L. Wollman, "After the 'Golden Age,'" in *The Oxford Handbook of the American Musical*, ed. Raymond Knapp, Mitchell Morris, and Stacy Wolf (New York: Oxford University Press, 2011), 111.

64 Thomas S. Hischak, *Off-Broadway Musicals Since 1919: From Greenwich Village Follies to The Toxic Avenger* (Lanham, MD: Scarecrow Press, 2011), 26; Wolf, *Problem Like Maria*, 26.

65 Quoted in Tim Carter, *Oklahoma! The Making of an American Musical* (New Haven: Yale University Press, 2007), 23.

66 Lewis Nichols, "'Oklahoma!' a Musical Hailed as Delightful, Based on 'Green Grow the Lilacs,' Opens Here at the St. James Theatre," *New York Times*, April 1, 1943; Richard Rodgers, *Musical Stages: An Autobiography* (New York: Random House, 1975), 227. Critics question the validity of the term "integrated"—for example, Carter, *Oklahoma!*, 173; Wolf, *Problem Like Maria*, 32.

67 Gerald Mast, *Can't Help Singin': The American Musical on Stage and Screen* (Woodstock, NY: Overlook Press, 1987), 290.

68 Ibid.

69 Lehman Engel makes a similar point: "No song for Laurey in *Oklahoma!* can be sung by Mrs. Anna in *The King and I* though both scores are by Rodgers and Hammerstein." *Words with Music* (New York: Macmillan, 1972), 122. The answer to the Cole Porter question: *Wake Up and Dream* (1929).

70 For a good discussion, see Mast, *Can't Help Singin'*, 27–9. There are countless examples of AABA songs. For reference, consider "Frosty the Snowman" (1950). Another popular form was ABAC. Examples include "Embraceable You" (1930) and "Put On a Happy Face" (1960). British musicians may call the B section the "middle eight."

71 Raymond Knapp and Mitchell Morris, "Tin Pan Alley Songs on Stage and Screen before World War II," in Knapp, Morris, and Wolf, *Oxford Handbook*, 87.

72 Wolf agrees that "musical theater was a part of mid-twentieth-century American culture." *Problem Like Maria*, 12.

73 This summary drawn from Lehman Engel, *This Bright Day: An Autobiography* (New York: Macmillan, 1974), especially chap. 1.

74 Ibid., 158, 162.

75 Ibid., 202.

76 Engel, *Words with Music*, 256–7, 260–4.

77 Ibid., 3.

78 Engel, *This Bright Day*, 278.

79 Ibid., 279.

80 Maury Yeston, phone interview by author, November 2, 2020. The BMI Workshop is depicted in the musical *A Class Act*, which opened on Broadway in 2001.

81 Engel, *Words with Music*, 306.

82 Yeston, phone interview by author. Judd Woldin wrote the music for *Raisin* (1973); Edward Kleban, lyrics for *A Chorus Line* (1975); Carol Hall, music and lyrics for *The Best Little Whorehouse in Texas* (1978); Maury Yeston, music and lyrics for *Nine* (1982). Alan Menken's Broadway début was *Beauty and the Beast* (1994), based on the 1991 Walt Disney animated feature.

83 Michael Kosarin, Zoom interview by author, July 15, 2021.

84 Yeston, phone interview by author.

85 Kenneth Jones, "He's a Guest: Composer Alan Menken Shares Thoughts at BMI Master Class," *Playbill*, December 21, 1998, www.playbill.com.

86 Yeston, phone interview by author.

87 Lehman Engel, *Their Words Are Music: The Great Theatre Lyricists and Their Lyrics* (New York: Crown Publishers, 1975), 243–4. Menken's contributions to the volume are "Voyeur's Lament" and "Trendell Terry."

88 Alan Menken, interview by author, April 13, 2010.

89 Yeston, phone interview by author; Menken, interview by author. BMI members Dennis Green and Marsha Malamet also recommended Menken as a composer. Dennis Green, phone interview by author, September 8, 2020; Marsha Malamet, phone interview by author, November 2, 2020.

90 Menken, interview by author. He also describes Ashman's appearance in the documentary *Howard*, directed by Don Hahn. It premiered in 2018 and was later made available on Disney Plus. For the cigarette brand: Paul Mills Holmes, phone interview by author, January 22, 2019.

91 Hischak, *Off-Broadway Musicals*, 1.

92 For more, see Stephen J. Bottoms, *Playing Underground: A Critical History of the 1960s Off-Off-Broadway Movement* (Ann Arbor: The University of Michigan Press, 2004).

93 Elizabeth L. Wollman, *A Critical Companion to the American Stage Musical* (London: Bloomsbury Methuen Drama, 2017), 144.

94 State of New York Filing Receipt, November 24, 1970; Minutes and By-Laws of Workshop of the Players Art Foundation, Inc., December 27, 1970, 1. Both in box 18, folder 9, NYPL.

95 Green, phone interview by author.

96 Ibid.

97 Clive Barnes, review of *Dreamstuff*, *New York Times*, April 5, 1976.

98 Green, phone interview by author; Stephen Wells, phone interview by author, October 20, 2020.

99 Edward T. Gianfrancesco (aka Hawk), phone interview by author, November 2, 2020; Stephen Wells, "The Other Side of Broadway" (unpublished manuscript, October 12, 2020), Microsoft Word file.

100 Stephen Wells, phone interview by author, November 18, 2020.

101 Green, phone interview by author; Wells, phone interview by author, October 20, 2020; Ashman, quoted in the documentary *Howard*.

102 Michael Mayer, Zoom interview by author, December 17, 2020.

103 Wells, "The Other Side of Broadway."

104 Kyle Renick, quoted in *Howard*.

105 Ashman Gillespie, interview by author, January 4, 2019.

106 Gianfrancesco (aka Hawk), phone interview by author.

107 Sheila Kay Davis, phone interview by author, October 3, 2019.

108 Gianfrancesco (aka Hawk), phone interview by author; Lee Wilkof, interview by author, January 7, 2019.

109 Gianfrancesco (aka Hawk), phone interview by author. According to a contemporary account, the WPA raised $25,000 for the 1977–78 season. Playwrights Horizons, another not-for-profit company, raised around $300,000. "Showcase: Issues and Answers," *Show Business*, November 23, 1978, 4.

110 Wells, phone interview by author, October 20, 2020.

111 While *Gorey Stories* was the first transfer, it did not succeed on Broadway: the show opened and closed on October 30, 1978, after sixteen previews. This production lost $300,000. Kyle Renick, "How I Learned to Stop Worrying and Love the Shubert Organization," *Theatre Times* 2, no. 3 (January 1983): 2.

112 Ashman Gillespie, interview by author, July 15, 2011; Holmes, phone interview by author, January 22, 2019; Ashman Gillespie, interview by author, January 4, 2019.

113 For more, see Barbara Lee Horn, *The Age of Hair: Evolution and Impact of Broadway's First Rock Musical* (Westport, CT: Greenwood Press, 1991); Denny Martin Flinn, *What They Did for Love: The Untold Story behind the Making of* A Chorus Line (New York: Bantam Books, 1989).

114 Malamet, phone interview by author.

115 Green, phone interview by author.

116 Wells, phone interview by author, October 20, 2020.

117 Green, phone interview by author.

118 Menken, interview by author.

119 Jonathan Sheffer, phone interview by author, October 26, 2020.

120 Ashman Gillespie, interview by author, July 15, 2011.

121 Ashman, quoted in Sheridan Morley, "Voracious Appetite," *The Times* (London), October 6, 1983.

122 Parent, interview by author.

123 As it happens, the Shubert Organization, with which Ashman and Menken would soon be associated, devised a similar scheme. Its many Broadway theatres are controlled by "a little-known charitable organization called Sam S. Shubert Foundation." Michael Riedel, *Razzle Dazzle: The Battle for Broadway* (2015; New York: Simon and Schuster, 2016), 57.

124 Eleanor Blau, "Making a Vonnegut Novel Sing," *New York Times*, September 24, 1979.

125 Menken, interview by author.

126 Ashman Gillespie, interview by author, July 15, 2011.

127 Kurt Vonnegut, Jr., *God Bless You, Mr. Rosewater; or, Pearls before Swine* (1965; New York: Dial Press, 2006), 44.

128 *God Bless You, Mr. Rosewater*, WPA Theatre, flyer, box 3, folder 8, NYPL.

129 Green, phone interview by author. "Dear Ophelia," "Rhode Island Tango," and "Rhode Island Tango" (Reprise) are the other songs for which Green received credit in the program.

130 Ibid. Skipping is also mentioned in Menken, interview by author; Parent, interview by author.

131 Menken, interview by author.

132 Clive Barnes, "A Clear and Sparkling 'Rosewater,'" *New York Post*, May 29, 1979.

133 Donald C. Farber, *From Option to Opening*, 3rd ed. (New York: Drama Book Specialists, 1977). Printed in various editions.

134 Blau, "Making a Vonnegut Novel Sing."

135 Ashman Gillespie, interview by author, January 4, 2019.

136 Parent, interview by author.

137 Menken, interview by author.

138 Ibid.; Renick, "How I Learned to Stop Worrying," 2.

139 Ashman Gillespie, interview by author, January 4, 2019; Parent, interview by author.

140 Quoted in Louis Botto, "Little Shop of Horrors," *Playbill: The National Magazine of the Theatre*, January 1983, 20.

Chapter 2

1 Menken, interview by author. Working separately, Ashman and Menken contributed songs to a later baseball musical, *Diamonds*, an Off-Broadway revue created by Harold Prince in 1984.

2 Ibid.

3 Alan Menken, interview by Sarah Ashman Gillespie, part two, www.howardashman.com.

4 Parent, interview by author.

5 Menken, interview by author.

6 Holmes, phone interview by author, January 22, 2019.

7 Howard Ashman, quoted in the documentary *Howard*.

8 Ashman, interview by Weitzman.

9 The name Miss Piggy derives from Miss Peggy Lee, a popular singer. British icon Twiggy appeared on *The Muppet Show*, season 1.

10 Ashman, interview by Weitzman.

11 Kyle Renick to Roger Corman, April 5, 1980, box 3, folder 22, NYPL.

12 Roger Corman to Kyle Renick, April 14, 1980, box 3, folder 22, NYPL.

13 Frank Rich, review of *Real Life Funnies*, *New York Times*, February 12, 1981.

14 Scott Shukat, letter to the editor, *Theater Week*, September 26–October 2, 1994, 4.

15 Ashman Gillespie, interview by author, January 4, 2019.

16 Parent, interview by author; Ashman, interview by Weitzman.

17 Ashman Gillespie, interview by author, January 4, 2019; Ron Gillespie, interview by author, January 4, 2019.

18 Esther Sherman, quoted in *Howard*; Sherman, quoted in Ashman, "Musical about a Man-Eating Plant?"

19 The exceptions are *Allegro* (1947) and *Me and Juliet* (1953), both originally conceived for the stage. Gerald Mast notes that these two original musicals were the least successful Rodgers and Hammerstein shows. *Can't Help Singin'*, 213.

20 Andrew Sarris, "The Myth of Old Movies: An Interpretation of Dreams," *Harper's Magazine*, September 1975, 38.

21 Walter Kerr, review of *Oh, Captain!*, *New York Herald Tribune*, February 5, 1958; Tim Rice, quoted in Mark Steyn, *Broadway Babies Say Goodnight: Musicals Then and Now* (1997; New York: Routledge, 2000), 118.

22 Ashman, interview by Weitzman.

23 Ibid.

24 He told theatre songwriters to "make a scene-by-scene synopsis of the source material." Engel, *Words with Music*, 319.

25 Howard Ashman, handwritten outline, box 13, folder 6, page 1, LOC.

26 McCarty and McGee, *Little Shop of Horrors Book*, 30.

27 Ashman, handwritten outline, box 13, folder 6, page 2, LOC.

28 Ibid. Central Avenue crosses the Los Angeles neighborhood known as Skid Row.

29 References in this paragraph are to Howard Ashman, handwritten story notes, box 13, folder 6, LOC. All capitals in original.

30 References in this paragraph are to Howard Ashman, one-page outline, box 13, folder 6, LOC. All capitals in original except for the first and last quotations in paragraph.

31 References in this paragraph are to Howard Ashman, three-page outline, box 13, folder 6, LOC. All capitals in original.

32 Ashman, interview by Weitzman.

33 Corman, *How I Made a Hundred Movies*, 66.

34 Ashman, three-page outline, box 13, folder 6, page 1, LOC.

35 Cf. McCarty and McGee, *Little Shop of Horrors Book*, 131.

36 These four characters are noted in pencil in Ashman, three-page outline, box 13, folder 6, page 1, LOC.

37 Ashman claimed a practical reason for the change: "after beating my rhyming dictionary to a pulp, insisting it come up with an accurate rhyme for 'junior,' I finally gave up and changed the monster's name to Audrey Two." Ashman, "Musical about a Man-Eating Plant?" Nonetheless, one lyric rhymes "petunia" and "juniah" (49).

38 Ashman, three-page outline, box 13, folder 6, page 1, LOC. All capitals in original.

39 Alan Menken, quoted in Botto, "Little Shop of Horrors," 20.

40 Ibid., 21. While developing the show, Ashman considered other possibilities. He told actor Franc Luz that the plant was to sound like a "bad boy of rock 'n' roll," possibly Mick Jagger. Franc Luz, interview by author, October 8, 2019. One early stage direction for the plant reads, "in an insinuating Jim Morrison tone." Howard Ashman, *Little Shop of Horrors* typescript, first draft, box 11, folder 7, page 54, LOC.

41 Ashman, interview by Weitzman.

42 Ashman, quoted in Dan Scapperotti, "The Off-Broadway Hit," *Cinefantastique* 17, no. 1 (January 1987): 22, 23.

43 Ibid., 23.

44 Ibid., 22.

45 Ashman, three-page outline, box 13, folder 6, page 3, LOC. All capitals in original.

46 Menken, interview by author.

47 Ashman, *Little Shop of Horrors* typescript, first draft, box 11, folder 7, page 1, LOC. Subsequent drafts would omit the year (1958) but keep the date.

48 Howard Ashman, handwritten lyric, box 13, folder 6, LOC.

49 Ashman, *Little Shop of Horrors* typescript, first draft, box 11, folder 7, page 82, LOC.

50 Ashman, handwritten outline, box 13, folder 6, page 2, LOC. All capitals in original.

51 Howard Ashman, "Feed Me" typescript, box 11, folder 6, LOC. A brief extract of this song appears in Menken, interview by author.

52 Howard Ashman, ["Audrey II"] typescript, box 13, folder 6, LOC.

53 Menken, quoted in Botto, "Little Shop of Horrors," 20.

54 Ashman, quoted in Botto, "Little Shop of Horrors," 20.

55 Ashman, interview by Weitzman.

56 Greil Marcus, quoted in Richard Corliss, "Dream Girls," *Time*, January 3, 1983, 80. Elizabeth L. Wollman makes the connection as well when she argues that girl groups "translated with ease the song-and-dance medium of musical theater." *The Theater Will Rock: A History of the Rock Musical, from* Hair *to* Hedwig (Ann Arbor: The University of Michigan Press, 2006), 136.

57 Tom Wolfe, "The First Tycoon of Teen," in *The Kandy-Kolored Tangerine-Flake Streamline Baby* (1965; New York: Picador, 2009). The chapter was originally published as an article in 1964.

58 The description of Spector's process derives from Mick Wall, *Tearing Down the Wall of South: The Rise and Fall of Phil Spector* (2007; New York: Vintage Books, 2008).

59 Ashman, interview by Weitzman. Decades later, Phil Spector's life became a kind of horror show when he was convicted for murder. The famed music producer died in prison, in 2021.

60 Menken, interview by author.

61 Phil Spector, quoted in Wolfe, "First Tycoon of Teen," 65.

62 Ashman, quoted in David Colker, "An Old-Fashioned Monster Musical," *Los Angeles Herald Examiner*, April 19, 1983.

63 Roger Corman said of this title, "it implied a horror film, but it also implied there was going to be humor in it." Jonathan Demme, "Roger Corman," *Interview*, April 2014, www.interview.com.

64 Howard Ashman, ["Prologue (Little Shop of Horrors)"] handwritten lyric, box 13, folder 6, LOC.

65 Howard Ashman, handwritten lyric and notes, box 13, folder 6, LOC.

66 Ashman, ["Prologue (Little Shop of Horrors)"] handwritten lyric, box 13, folder 6, LOC.

67 Howard Ashman and Alan Menken, *Little Shop of Horrors* (1982; New York: Samuel French, 1985), 14. Subsequent references to this edition will be made parenthetically within the text.

68 Ashman, interview by Weitzman.

69 Ibid. Petula Clark recorded the hit song "Downtown" in 1964, slightly later than the period of *Little Shop*.

70 Howard Ashman, ["Skid Row (Downtown)"] typescript, box 13, folder 6, LOC.

71 Ibid.

72 Ashman, *Little Shop of Horrors* typescript, first draft, box 11, folder 7, page 7, LOC.

73 Howard Ashman, *Little Shop of Horrors* typescript, box 12, folder 1, page 7, LOC.

74 Ashman called it "a love song to a plant." Ashman, interview by Weitzman.

75 Howard Ashman, ["Grow for Me"] handwritten lyric and notes, box 13, folder 6, LOC.

76 Ashman, ["Grow for Me"] handwritten lyric, box 13, folder 6, LOC.

77 Ashman, interview by Weitzman.

78 Jackie Joseph, quoted in McCarty and McGee, *Little Shop of Horrors Book*, 70.

79 Scapperotti, "Off-Broadway Hit," 22.

80 Ashman, *Little Shop of Horrors* typescript, first draft, box 11, folder 7, page 21, LOC.

81 Ashman Gillespie, email to author, January 27, 2022. "Everything Howard did was wonderful," she said. Ashman Gillespie, interview by author, July 15, 2011.

82 Ashman, quoted in Colker, "Old-Fashioned Monster Musical." In a way, the Shangri-Las created miniature musicals, by combining dialogue and song. In "Leader of the Pack" (1964), one Shangri-La asks another, "By the way, where'd you meet him?" The answer is sung: "I met him at the candy store." This line also suggests *The Candy Shop*, a musical that Ashman wrote as a teenager.

83 Ashman, *Little Shop of Horrors* typescript, first draft, box 11, folder 7, page 1, LOC.

84 Ibid., 13.

85 An early stage direction for the opening number reads, "Music is suddenly perky and Sha-Na-Na." Ashman, *Little Shop of Horrors* typescript, first draft, box 11, folder 7, page 1, LOC. This stage direction recognizes that the musical is retro, a revival of past forms—not the thing itself.

86 "The nostalgia mode has become a permanent fixture of our cultural economy." J. Hoberman, *Vulgar Modernism: Writing on Movies and Other Media* (Philadelphia: Temple University Press, 1991), 268. For more on nostalgia in the 1970s, see Philip Jenkins, *Decade of Nightmares: The End of the Sixties and the Making of Eighties America* (Oxford: Oxford University Press, 2006).

87 J. Wynn Rousuck, "Howard Ashman's Greenery Knocks 'Em Dead on Stage," *Baltimore Sun*, April 8, 1984. The same trio is also mentioned in the *Los Angeles Times* and *The Times* of London. Dan Sullivan, "Spoofs for, and by, the Totally Hip," *Los Angeles Times*, June 19, 1983; Morley, "Voracious Appetite."

88 For more on nostalgia and acceleration, see Elizabeth E. Guffey, *Retro: The Culture of Revival* (London: Reaktion Books, 2006).

89 John M. Clum, *Something for the Boys: Musical Theater and Gay Culture* (New York: St. Martin's Press, 1999), 157.

90 Ashman, quoted in *Howard*.

91 Quoted in Colker, "Old-Fashioned Monster Musical." Elsewhere, Ashman says that "it's a much more conventional musical with a strong plot and all the old Rodgers-and-Hammerstein devices." Quoted in Morley, "Voracious Appetite."

92 Ashman, interview by Weitzman.

93 Kyle Renick, quoted in Botto, "Little Shop of Horrors," 20.

94 Demme, "Roger Corman."

95 McGee, phone interview by author; Gray, *Roger Corman*, 65.

96 Beverly Gray, phone interview by author, February 23, 2021; McGee, phone interview by author.

97 Dick Miller, quoted in Gray, *Roger Corman*, 66.

98 John W. Schouweiler to Martin Bauer, September 3, 1982, SA. This letter refers to the earlier agreement.

99 Kyle Renick to Barbara D. Boyle, November 23, 1981, box 3, folder 22, NYPL.

100 *Little Shop of Horrors* Estimated Weekly Running Expenses, June 14, 1982, box 13, folder 8, LOC. This document was prepared for the Off-Broadway run. One percent was allocated to "Rights," meaning underlying rights to the property. After recoupment, this would increase to 1.5 percent.

101 Scapperotti, "Off-Broadway Hit," 22.

102 Ashman, quoted in Botto, "Little Shop of Horrors," 20.

103 The subsequent references to this performance are all from *Little Shop of Horrors* BMI session, audiotape, Howard Ashman Sound Recordings, LOC.

104 Ibid. Another member of the workshop, Maury Yeston, who did not attend this performance, explained the audience's reaction: "They didn't see the show. They didn't know what was going on." Further, he mentioned the "shock of the new," since *Little Shop* was unlike other musicals. Yeston, phone interview by author.

105 Ashman Gillespie, interview by author, January 4, 2019.

106 Scapperotti, "Off-Broadway Hit," 23.

107 He owned 1970s compilation records of all three groups: The Crystals, *Sing Their Greatest Hits!*; The Ronettes, *Sing Their Greatest Hits!*; The Chiffons, *Everything You Always Wanted to Hear by the Chiffons but Couldn't Get*. I thank Bill Lauch for making this collection available to me.

108 Menken, quoted in Botto, "Little Shop of Horrors," 20.

109 Ashman, quoted in Colker, "Old-Fashioned Monster Musical."

110 Scapperotti, "Off-Broadway Hit," 22, 23.

111 Howard Ashman, ["Somewhere That's Green"] typescript, box 13, folder 6, LOC. For a comparison of drafts, see Appendix B.

112 Ashman, quoted in Scott Fosdick, "Scream Play," *Baltimore News American*, April 8, 1984.

113 Quoted in Colker, "Old-Fashioned Monster Musical."

114 The musical attempted other references to *I Love Lucy*: an early version of "All Gone" begins, "On the day that it started / All our sources agree / Everybody loved Lucy / She was the queen of T.V." Howard Ashman, ["All Gone"] typescript, box 13, folder 6, LOC.

115 Jack Viertel finds that "Ashman and Menken update 'Wouldn't It Be Loverly.'" *The Secret Life of the American Musical: How Broadway Shows Are Built* (2016; New York: Sarah Crichton Books/Farrar, Straus and Giroux, 2017), 62.

116 Ashman, quoted in Colker, "Old-Fashioned Monster Musical."

117 Clum indicates the importance of this sentiment for the gay community by quoting one of his own plays: "We've earned the right to be suburban and boring." *Something for the Boys*, 26.

Chapter 3

1 Martin P. Robinson, interview by author, January 5, 2019.

2 Ibid.

3 Ibid.

4 Kyle Renick quoted in Botto, "Little Shop of Horrors," 21.

5 Robinson, interview by author.

6 Ibid.

7 Ibid.; Menken, interview by author. Additional details in Lawrence Christon, "A Stage Prop Puts Bite on 'Shop,'" *Los Angeles Times*, June 2, 1983.

8 Martin P. Robinson, quoted in Barbara Crossette, "Making a Plant Grow: A Hidden Art on Stage," *New York Times*, October 8, 1982.

9 Robinson, interview by author; Lynn Hippen, phone interview by author, December 14, 2020.

10 Robinson, interview by author.

11 Howard Ashman, quoted in Menken, interview by author.

12 Grover Dale to whom it may concern, February 7, 1982, box 13, folder 10, LOC.

13 Menken, interview by author.

14 Quoted in Robert Feldberg, "Uprooting a Budding Musical," *Sunday Record*, July 25, 1982, box 5, folder 1, NYPL.

15 Menken, interview by author.

16 Grover Dale to Howard Ashman, January 16, 1982, box 13, folder 10, LOC.

17 Ibid.

18 Ibid.

19 Dale, February 7, 1982, box 13, folder 10, LOC.

20 Quoted in Otis L. Guernsey, Jr., ed., *Broadway Song and Story: Playwrights/Lyricists/Composers Discuss Their Hits* (New York: Dodd, Mead, 1985), 417.

21 Luz, interview by author.

22 Robert Billig, interview by author, July 23, 2019.

23 Robby Merkin, interview by author, July 8, 2019. Years later, a Carole King musical opened Off-Broadway, entitled *Beautiful* (2014).

24 Ibid.

25 Ibid.

26 Ibid.

27 Ibid.

28 Quoted in Constance Grappo, interview by author, January 7, 2019.

29 Ibid.

30 Menken, interview by author.

31 Cowan, interview by author, October 11, 2019.

32 Ibid.

33 Ibid.

34 Howard Ashman, "Dentist!" typescript, box 13, folder 6, LOC. A schedule notes that on April 20, 1982, sixteen days before the first performance, the "NEW DENTIST" number went into the show. *Little Shop of Horrors* rehearsal/performance schedule, March–May 1982, box 11, folder 6, LOC. A demo recording of the earlier number appears on the 2003 Broadway cast album, under the title "I Found a Hobby."

35 Agreement between Workshop of the Players Art Foundation, Inc., and Alan Menken and Howard Ashman, February 26, 1982, box 3, folder 22, NYPL.

36 Ashman, three-page outline, box 13, folder 6, page 1, LOC.

37 Menken, interview by author.

38 Holmes, phone interview by author, January 22, 2019; Menken, interview by author.

39 Darlene Kaplan, phone interview by author, November 27, 2020.

40 Cowan, interview by author; Billig, interview by author.

41 Jennifer Leigh Warren, phone interview by author, January 26, 2020; Billig, interview by author.

42 Davis, phone interview by author.

43 Leilani Jones, phone interview by author, July 22, 2019. She sang "The Shoop Shoop Song" (aka "It's in His Kiss"), a 1963 hit.

44 Robinson, interview by author.

45 Deborah Sharpe-Taylor, phone interview by author, December 16, 2020.

46 Robinson, interview by author.

47 Kaplan, phone interview by author.

48 Grappo, interview by author; Merkin, interview by author.

49 Luz, interview by author.

50 Kaplan, phone interview by author.

51 Parent, interview by author; Billig, interview by author.

52 Quoted in Grappo, interview by author.

53 Grappo, interview by author.

54 Wilkof, interview by author. Television producer Ernie Anderson was the father of filmmaker Paul Thomas Anderson, whose credits include *Boogie Nights* (1997) and *There Will Be Blood* (2007).

55 Ibid.

56 Kaplan, phone interview by author; Wilkof, interview by author.

57 Grappo, interview by author.

58 Quoted in Wilkof, interview by author.

59 Grappo, interview by author.

60 Wilkof, interview by author.

61 Ibid.

62 Grappo, interview by author. The story also appears in Cowan, interview by author; Kaplan, phone interview by author.

63 *Little Shop of Horrors* callback sheet, box 11, folder 6, LOC. Other contenders for Seymour and Audrey included Chip Zien and Randy Graff.

64 Grappo, interview by author; Rob Baker, "'Little Shop' Many Open *the* Door for Her," *Daily News* (New York), July 26, 1982.

65 Quoted in Grappo, interview by author.

66 Quoted in Scapperotti, "Off-Broadway Hit," 61.

67 Quoted in Tim Boxer, "Traveling with the Stars," *Jewish Week*, August 20, 1982, box 5, folder 1, NYPL.

68 Billig, interview by author.

69 Charles Abbott worked with Greene on a musical revue in the 1970s. "You couldn't rein her in," Abbott explained. One member of the cast told him, "Chuck, she's gonna be a star before any of us." Charles Abbott, conversation with author, October 11, 2019.

70 Gianfrancesco (aka Hawk), phone interview by author.

71 Sally Lesser, phone interview by author, November 13, 2020.

72 Ibid.

73 Paul Mills Holmes, phone interview by author, April 27, 2021.

74 Wilkof, interview by author.

75 *Little Shop of Horrors* "Production Information," 1986 film press kit, box 6, folder 7, page 5, NYPL.

76 "I remember we brought our own clothes," she said. McCarty and McGee, *Little Shop of Horrors Book*, 70.

77 *Little Shop of Horrors* "Production Information," 1986 film press kit, box 6, folder 7, page 5, NYPL.

78 Lesser, phone interview by author.

79 Quoted in ibid.

80 This description draws on Colker, "Old-Fashioned Monster Musical."

81 Menken, interview by author; Grappo, interview by author; Holmes, phone interview by author, January 22, 2019; Merkin, interview by author.

82 Howard Ashman, *Little Shop of Horrors* typescript, page 1-2-5. This is Leilani Jones's copy of the WPA script; I thank Donna Rose Fletcher for making it available to me.

83 Handwritten in ibid.

84 Howard Ashman, *Little Shop of Horrors* typescript, Orpheum draft, page 1-3-34. This is a draft from the subsequent Orpheum production; I thank Donna Rose Fletcher for making it available to me.

85 Quoted in Wilkof, interview by author.

86 Warren, phone interview by author.

87 Steve Gelfand, Zoom interview by author, February 23, 2021.

88 Jones, phone interview by author.

89 These comments are handwritten in Jones's copy of the WPA script.

90 Ashman, *Little Shop of Horrors* typescript, box 12, folder 1, n.p., LOC. An expanded version of this note appears in the Samuel French edition (7).

91 Vida Hope, preface to *The Boy Friend*, by Sandy Wilson (1953; New York: E. P. Dutton, 1955), 16.

92 Rick Besoyan, *Little Mary Sunshine* (1959; New York: Samuel French, 1999), 5. For comparison, see the "AUTHOR'S NOTE" in the Samuel French edition of *Little Shop*: the performers "should play with simplicity, honesty, and sweetness—even when events are at their most outlandish" (7).

93 *Little Shop of Horrors* rehearsal/performance schedule, March–May 1982, box 11, folder 6, LOC.

94 Cowan, interview by author.

95 *Little Shop of Horrors* rehearsal/performance schedule, March–May 1982, box 11, folder 6, LOC.

96 Holmes, phone interview by author, April 27, 2021.

97 *Little Shop of Horrors* schedule, January–May 1982, box 3, folder 22, NYPL.

98 Grappo, interview by author; Wilkof, interview by author.

99 Holmes, phone interview by author, April 27, 2021; Lesser, phone interview by author; Grappo, interview by author.

100 Holmes, phone interview by author, January 22, 2019; Robinson, interview by author.

101 Ellen Greene, quoted in Luz, interview by author.

102 Robinson, interview by author; Munderloh, phone interview by author.

103 Cowan, interview by author.

104 *Little Shop of Horrors* rehearsal/performance schedule, March–May 1982, box 11, folder 6, LOC.

105 Quoted in Holmes, phone interview by author, January 22, 2019.

106 Cowan, interview by author.

107 Clum, *Something for the Boys*, 7.

108 Grappo, interview by author.

109 *Little Shop of Horrors* rehearsal/performance schedule, March–May 1982, box 11, folder 6, LOC. The note for April 24, 1982 reads, "SEYMOUR + PLANT REH. RUN-THROUGH." The next day indicates, "AUDREY/PLANT REH. RUN-THRU." It's possible that Wilkof or Greene had another appointment, but this piece of scheduling looks deliberate.

110 Luz, interview by author.

111 Wilkof, interview by author.

112 Grappo, interview by author.

113 Wilkof, interview by author; Grappo, interview by author.

114 Grappo, interview by author; Wilkof, interview by author.

115 Robinson, interview by author; David Hutchings, "Critics Agree with the Man-Eating Plant in *Little Shop of Horrors*: Ellen Greene Is Delicious," *People Weekly*, January 12, 1987, 44.

116 Cowan, interview by author; Wilkof, interview by author.

117 Ashman, interview by Weitzman.

118 1977–78: *Gorey Stories* transferred to the Booth Theatre. 1978–79: *God Bless You, Mr. Rosewater* moved to the Entermedia (Off-Broadway). 1979–80: *Nuts* moved to the Biltmore; *Album* to the Cherry Lane (Off-Broadway). 1980–81: *The Freak* went to the Douglas Fairbanks and *Key Exchange* to the Orpheum (both Off-Broadway). WPA Theatre promotional brochure, 1983, box 2, folder 23, NYPL.

Chapter 4

1 Holmes, phone interview by author, January 22, 2019.

2 Grappo, interview by author; Menken, interview by author; Ashman Gillespie, interview by author, January 4, 2019.

3 Brent Spiner, email to author, February 18, 2021.

4 Quoted in Cowan, interview by author.

5 Jones, phone interview by author; Warren, phone interview by author; Wilkof, interview by author; Menken, interview by author.

6 *Little Shop of Horrors*, WPA Theatre, flyer, box 3, folder 22, NYPL.

7 Grappo, interview by author.

8 Brad Moranz, phone interview by author, December 1, 2020.

9 Alan Menken, quoted in Jerry Parker, "Greene Blossoms in London," *Newsday*, February 12, 1984; Howard Ashman, quoted in Scapperotti, "Off-Broadway Hit," 61. Channing created the role of Dolly Levi in *Hello, Dolly!*

10 Davis, phone interview by author.

11 Merkin, interview by author.

12 Quoted in Crossette, "Making a Plant Grow."

13 Wilkof, interview by author.

14 Luz, interview by author; Davis, phone interview by author.

15 Holmes, phone interview by author, January 22, 2019; Holmes, phone interview by author, April 27, 2021.

16 Holmes, phone interview by author, January 22, 2019; Luz, interview by author.

17 Marilyn Stasio, "Screaming 'Horrors' a Nifty Laugh Riot," *New York Post*, May 24, 1982.

18 Holmes, phone interview by author, January 22, 2019. For more, see chap. 2.

19 Mel Gussow, "Musical: A Cactus Owns 'Little Shop of Horrors,'" *New York Times*, May 30, 1982; Katie Kelly, WNBC-TV review of *Little Shop of Horrors*, transcript, May 25, 1982, box 5, folder 1, NYPL.

20 Donna Rose Fletcher, interview by author, July 13, 2019. Fletcher would remain with the show and eventually rise to the position of stage manager.

21 Renick, "How I Learned to Stop Worrying," 8. Elsewhere, Ashman recalled twenty-seven potential producers. Feldberg, "Uprooting a Budding Musical."

22 Quoted in Wells, phone interview by author, November 18, 2020.

23 Wells, phone interview by author, November 18, 2020.

24 Quoted in Wells, phone interview by author, November 18, 2020.

25 Wells, phone interview by author, November 18, 2020.

26 Ibid.

27 Poland, interview by author, October 7, 2019.

28 Ibid.

29 Cameron Mackintosh, phone interview by author, January 26, 2021.

30 Albert Poland, *Stages: A Theater Memoir* (N.p., 2019), 201.

31 Ibid.; Albert Poland, phone interview by author, May 21, 2021.

32 Cowan, interview by author.

33 Poland, interview by author, October 7, 2019.

34 Quoted in *Little Shop of Horrors: The Director's Cut*, behind-the-scenes featurette (Burbank: Warner Bros., 2017), Blu-ray disc.

35 Poland, *Stages*, 201.

36 Poland, interview by author, October 7, 2019; Mackintosh, phone interview by author. A version of this origin story appears in Riedel, *Razzle Dazzle*, 302–3.

37 Quoted in Wells, phone interview by author, November 18, 2020.

38 Wells, phone interview by author, November 18, 2020; agreement among the Shubert Organization, Inc.; Cameron Mackintosh; Geffen Records; and Workshop of the Players Art Foundation, Inc., June 1982, page 8, SA.

39 Wells, phone interview by author, November 18, 2020.

40 Poland, *Stages*, 201.

41 Robinson, interview by author; Poland, interview by author, October 7, 2019.

42 For details, see Hischak, *Off-Broadway Musicals*.

43 Grappo, interview by author.

44 Holmes, phone interview by author, January 22, 2019; Gianfrancesco (aka Hawk), phone interview by author.

45 Poland, interview by author, October 7, 2019.

46 Holmes, phone interview by author, April 27, 2021; Gianfrancesco (aka Hawk), phone interview by author.

47 Robinson, interview by author; Fletcher, interview by author, July 13, 2019. The third plant also remained in the air until it descended during the song "Don't It Go to Show Ya Never Know."

48 Moranz, phone interview by author.

49 Davis, phone interview by author; Warren, phone interview by author.

50 Fletcher, interview by author, July 13, 2019.

51 Agreement among the Shubert Organization, Inc.; Cameron Mackintosh; Geffen Records; and Workshop of the Players Art Foundation, Inc., June 1982, page 1, SA.

52 Bernard Rosenberg and Ernest Harburg, *The Broadway Musical: Collaboration in Commerce and Art* (New York: New York University Press, 1993), 17; *Little Shop of Horrors* Estimated Production Budget, June 14, 1982, box 13, folder 8, LOC.

53 Workshop of the Players Art Foundation, Inc., *The Little Shop of Horrors* [sic] budget, box 3, folder 22, NYPL. Hawk noted that the Equity Showcase cost $25,000, "more money than we had ever spent on one production." Quoted in Michael Burkett, "Just When You Thought It Was Safe to Go Back to the Theater," *Orange County Register*, May 1, 1983.

54 Poland, interview by author, October 7, 2019.

55 These points are extracted from *Little Shop of Horrors* Estimated Weekly Running Expenses, June 14, 1982, box 13, folder 8, LOC.

56 Mackintosh, phone interview by author.

57 Holmes, phone interview by author, January 22, 2019.

58 Kaplan, phone interview by author.

59 Grappo, interview by author.

60 Robinson, interview by author.

61 Merkin, interview by author; Holmes, phone interview by author, April 27, 2021.

62 Moranz, phone interview by author; Wilkof, interview by author; Robinson, interview by author.

63 Jones, phone interview by author.

64 Cowan, interview by author.

65 For more, see Joyce Wadler, "A Cat Now and for 17 Years (Nearly Forever)," *New York Times*, February 25, 2000.

66 Robinson, interview by author; Martin P. Robinson, email to author, November 10, 2021.

67 Poland, phone interview by author, May 21, 2021.

68 Warren, phone interview by author.

69 Poland, phone interview by author, May 21, 2021.

70 Warren, phone interview by author.

71 Poland, phone interview by author, May 21, 2021.

72 Ibid.

73 Poland, interview by author, October 7, 2019.

74 Holmes, phone interview by author, January 22, 2019.

75 Jones, phone interview by author.

76 Cowan, interview by author; Grappo, interview by author.

77 Robinson, interview by author.

78 Poland, interview by author, October 7, 2019.

79 Gianfrancesco (aka Hawk), phone interview by author; Poland, interview by author, October 7, 2019.

80 Don Nelsen, "Flytrap Catches Laughs," *Daily News* (New York), August 9, 1982; Howard Kissel, review of *Little Shop of Horrors*, *Women's Wear Daily*, August 13, 1982.

81 Mel Gussow, "In the Arts: Critics' Choices," *New York Times*, August 22, 1982.

82 Walter Kerr, "'Little Shop of Horrors' and the Terrors of Special Effects," *New York Times*, August 22, 1982.

83 Richard Corliss, "When Trash Is a Treasure," *Time*, August 23, 1982, 59.

84 Gillespie, interview by author, January 4, 2019.

85 Poland, interview by author, October 7, 2019.

86 Ibid.

87 Edith Oliver, review of *Little Shop of Horrors*, *New Yorker*, September 27, 1982, 118; Edwin Wilson, "Getting Away from the Season of Our Discontent," *Wall Street Journal*, September 1, 1982; Tommy Tune, quoted in Steyn, *Broadway Babies Say Goodnight*, 189.

88 Holmes, phone interview by author, January 22, 2019.

89 Frank Rich, "A Theatrical Mystery: The Missing Balconies," *New York Times*, September 9, 1982.

90 Poland, interview by author, October 7, 2019; Mackintosh, phone interview by author.

91 *Little Shop of Horrors* Production Reports, Orpheum Theatre, New York, 1982–87, DRF.

92 *Little Shop of Horrors* Production Report, February 27, 1983, DRF; Donna Rose Fletcher, telephone conversation with author, February 20, 2021.

93 Sideliners, *New York Post*, January 7, 1983; "They'll Visit Land of Merlin," *Daily News* (New York), January 7, 1983.

94 Fletcher, interview by author, July 13, 2019.

95 Quoted in Alvin Klein, "I Love Being Different Characters," *New York Times*, March 6, 1983. Robby Merkin explained that to Greene, "The wig was Audrey. She addressed it; she spoke to it; and she called it Audrey." Merkin, interview by author.

96 Luz, interview by author.

97 *Little Shop of Horrors* Production Report, November 13, 1982, DRF; Lee Wilkof, quoted in Luz, interview by author.

98 *Little Shop of Horrors* Production Report, August 31, 1982, DRF.

99 Corman, *How I Made a Hundred Movies*, 69.

100 Kyle Renick recalls this comment from Corman in the documentary *Howard*.

101 Ashman said, "I've been eating cast albums since I was 7." Quoted in Janice Arkatov, "Man-Eating Plant Hopes to Capture Los Angeles," *Los Angeles Times*, April 25, 1983.

102 Ashman, interview by Weitzman.

103 Many years later, *Rosewater* earned the distinction of a cast album, after the Encores! Off-Center production in 2016. The album was produced by Alan Menken and Michael Kosarin for Ghostlight Records.

104 Ian MacDonald, *Revolution in the Head: The Beatles' Records and the Sixties*, rev. ed. (London: Vintage Books, 2008), 212–50.

105 Mackintosh, phone interview by author.

106 David Geffen, quoted in Stephen M. Silverman, "Musicals Slip into the Groove on Cast Albums," *New York Post*, July 7, 1983; agreement among the Shubert Organization, Inc.; Cameron Mackintosh; Geffen Records; and Workshop of the Players Art Foundation, Inc., June 1982, page 13, SA.

107 Quoted in Craig Zadan, *Sondheim and Co.*, 2nd ed. (New York: Harper and Row, 1986), 173.

108 All these notes are in Howard Ashman, *Little Shop of Horrors* typescript, box 10, folder 2, page 54, LOC.

109 *Little Shop of Horrors* Production Report, August 9, 1982, DRF.

110 Holmes, phone interview by author, April 27, 2021; Holmes, phone interview by author, January 22, 2019.

111 Gelfand, Zoom interview by author; Merkin, interview by author.

112 Holmes, phone interview by author, April 27, 2021.

113 Billig, interview by author.

114 Holmes, phone interview by author, April 27, 2021; Billig, interview by author.

115 Holmes, phone interview by author, April 27, 2021.

116 Wilkof, interview by author.

117 *Little Shop of Horrors* Production Reports, August 11, 1982; August 16, 1982; August 23, 1982, DRF.

118 Wilkof, interview by author.

119 Quoted in Merkin, interview by author.

120 This conversation in Luz, interview by author.

121 Ibid.

122 Donna Rose Fletcher, email to author, June 13, 2021.

123 Luz, interview by author.

124 Poland, interview by author, October 7, 2019.

125 Ibid.; *Little Shop of Horrors* Production Report, September 7, 1982, DRF.

126 Grappo, interview by author; Holmes, phone interview by author, January 22, 2019.

127 Menken, interview by author.

128 The BMI Lehman Engel Musical Theatre Workshop survived him and trained future generations of librettists, lyricists, and composers, including creators of the musicals *Ragtime* (1998), *Avenue Q* (2003), *Next to Normal* (2009), *Fun Home* (2015), and more.

129 Poland, interview by author, October 7, 2019. This story also appears in Poland, *Stages*.

130 Poland, *Stages*, 204.

131 Poland, interview by author, October 7, 2019.

132 Wells, phone interview by author, November 18, 2020.

133 Wollman, *Theater Will Rock*, 6.

134 Clive Barnes, "'10 Best' Shows Are Really a Dynamic Dozen," *New York Post*, December 30, 1982.

135 Anthony Asbury, phone interview by author, December 7, 2020; Holmes, phone interview by author, April 27, 2021. *Gorey Stories*, from an earlier WPA season, played at the Booth.

136 Ashman Gillespie, interview by author, January 4, 2019; Grappo, interview by author.

137 Wells, phone interview by author, November 18, 2020; Munderloh, phone interview by author; Davis, phone interview by author.

138 Ashman, interview by Weitzman.

139 Ashman Gillespie, email to author, January 27, 2022; Ashman Gillespie, interview by author, July 15, 2011.

140 Quoted in Grappo, interview by author.

Chapter 5

1 Katherine Meloche, phone interview by author, March 2, 2021.

2 Holmes, phone interview by author, April 27, 2021.

3 Meloche, phone interview by author.

4 Ibid.

5 Moranz, phone interview by author.

6 Holmes, phone interview by author, April 27, 2021; Moranz, phone interview by author.

7 *Little Shop of Horrors* Production Report, December 29, 1982, DRF.

8 Holmes, phone interview by author, April 27, 2021.

9 Sharpe-Taylor, phone interview by author.

10 *Little Shop of Horrors* Production Report, October 24, 1982, DRF.

11 *Little Shop of Horrors* Production Report, August 8, 1982, DRF.

12 Fletcher, interview by author, July 13, 2019; Holmes, phone interview by author, April 27, 2021.

13 Holmes, phone interview by author, April 27, 2021; Fyvush Finkel, quoted in Robinson, interview by author.

14 Robinson, interview by author; *Little Shop of Horrors* Production Report, February 22, 1983, DRF.

15 Poland, *Stages*, 207–8.

16 Grappo, interview by author; Holmes, phone interview by author, January 22, 2019. In the 1990s, the Westwood Playhouse became the Geffen Playhouse.

17 Robinson, interview by author.

18 Asbury, phone interview by author.

19 Hippen, phone interview by author.

20 This story in Luz, interview by author.

21 *Little Shop of Horrors* Production Reports, January 25–February 1, 1983, DRF. Auditions were held on January 26–28 and February 1.

22 As Franc Luz later recalled, "I was defying Howard, David Geffen, Cameron Mackintosh, and the Shuberts. Other than that, I didn't have any enemies at all." Luz, interview by author. He rescinded his notice on Wednesday, February 2. *Little Shop of Horrors* Production Report, February 2, 1983, DRF.

23 *Little Shop of Horrors* Production Reports, March 18, 1983 and March 19, 1983, DRF.

24 Eydie Alyson, phone interview by author, April 14, 2021; Lesser, phone interview by author.

25 Holmes, phone interview by author, April 27, 2021; Billig, interview by author.

26 Holmes, phone interview by author, April 27, 2021; *Little Shop of Horrors* Production Report, March 20, 1983, DRF. This report would have been written by Peter Mumford, who took over as stage manager when Paul Mills Holmes traveled to LA.

27 Robinson, interview by author.

28 Holmes, phone interview by author, January 22, 2019.

29 Luz, interview by author.

30 Fletcher, interview by author, July 13, 2019.

31 Michael James Leslie, interview by author, October 7, 2019.

32 Lesser, phone interview by author.

33 Ibid.

34 Asbury, phone interview by author.

35 Holmes, phone interview by author, April 27, 2021.

36 *Little Shop of Horrors* Production Report, April 15, 1983, DRF. In New York, Katherine Meloche covered the role of Audrey until May. *Little Shop of Horrors* Production Report, May 3, 1983, DRF.

37 Quoted in Robinson, interview by author.

38 Grappo, interview by author.

39 Holmes, phone interview by author, January 22, 2019; Judi Davidson Publicity, memo, box 5, folder 5, NYPL. In the song "Git It," the plant offers Seymour "a guest shot on Jack Paar" (51). Paar hosted his late-night talk show from 1957 to 1962; Johnny Carson was his successor.

40 Drew Casper, review of *Little Shop of Horrors*, *Hollywood Reporter*, April 29, 1983, 7; Dan Sullivan, "The Not-Quite Purple People Eater," *Los Angeles Times*, April 29, 1983.

41 "Road Down," *Variety*, August 10, 1983. However, the LA production closed at a loss of $300,000 to $350,000, "which will be re-couped from New York." Board of Directors meeting, WPA Theatre, November 15, 1983, box 18, folder 6, NYPL.

42 Prince's last performance as Audrey at the Orpheum took place on Sunday, August 7. *Little Shop of Horrors* Production Report, August 7, 1983, DRF. Then Katherine Meloche went on once again.

43 Wilkof, interview by author; Grappo, interview by author; Spiner, email to author.

44 Fletcher, interview by author, July 13, 2019.

45 Mackintosh, phone interview by author.

46 Cowan, interview by author.

47 Asbury, phone interview by author.

48 The British equivalent to Actors' Equity permitted Asbury and Leslie to work in the UK because of their "special skills." Steve Grant, "Shop! Horror!," *Time Out*, October 6–12, 1983, 16.

49 Robinson, interview by author.

50 Leslie, interview by author.

51 Ibid.

52 Quoted in Lesser, phone interview by author.

53 Lesser, phone interview by author.

54 *Little Shop of Horrors* production schedule, London, 1983, box 13, folder 8, LOC; Howard Ashman, 1983 Diary Agenda, box 26, LOC.

55 Grappo, interview by author; Leslie, interview by author.

56 *Little Shop of Horrors* rehearsal call sheet, London, September 10, 1983, box 13, folder 8, LOC.

57 Grappo, interview by author.

58 "Glossary of Terms," in *Little Shop of Horrors* program, Comedy Theatre, London, box 5, folder 6, NYPL. Robert Weston Smith (aka Wolfman Jack) played himself in *American Graffiti*, the 1973 George Lucas comedy set in the year 1962. Donna Reed acted in the 1946 film *It's a Wonderful Life* before starring in *The Donna Reed Show*, an ABC television series that ran from 1958 to 1966.

59 Ibid.

60 Review of *Little Shop of Horrors*, *Punch*, October 19, 1983.

61 Quoted in Mackintosh, phone interview by author.

62 Joanna Lumley, "A Star Steps out of the Shadows," *The Times* (London), October 19, 1983.

63 Robert Cushman, review of *Little Shop of Horrors*, *The Observer*, October 16, 1983.

64 For example: "Unlike *The Rocky Horror Show*, it has no memorable songs." Michael Coveney, review of *Little Shop of Horrors*, *Financial Times*, October 13, 1983.

65 Michael Billington, review of *Little Shop of Horrors*, *The Guardian*, October 13, 1983.

66 Jack Tinker, review of *Little Shop of Horrors*, *Daily Mail* (London), October 13, 1983.

67 Asbury, phone interview by author.

68 Cameron Mackintosh to Eric Eisner, December 2, 1983, SA. Given that the British pound was then worth 1.4565 US dollars, the London production cost over $470,000.

69 Ibid.

70 Mackintosh, phone interview by author. By the end of its run, the show in London broke even. Steve Absalom, "Shutting Up the 'Little Shop' without a Profit," *Stage and Television Today*, no. 5448 (September 12, 1985): 1.

71 "Boffo 'Little Shop,'" *Variety*, January 18, 1984, 106. The exact figure reported was $3,181,161.

72 *Little Shop of Horrors* program, Comedy Theatre, London, box 5, folder 6, NYPL. For an affecting portrait of Stuart "Snooz" White, see the documentary *Howard*.

73 Joseph Church, phone interview by author, April 28, 2021; Holmes, phone interview by author, April 27, 2021.

74 Church, phone interview by author.

75 Alyson, phone interview by author.

76 Ibid.

77 Moranz, phone interview by author.

78 Menken, interview by author.

79 Wilkof, interview by author.

80 Ashman, *Little Shop of Horrors* typescript, Orpheum draft, page 1-3-33.

81 Ibid., page 1-3-32. This observation in Fletcher, interview by author, July 13, 2019.

82 Church, phone interview by author. I thank Joseph Church for making the sheet music available to me. The corrected version became incorporated into the text and has been performed since 1984.

83 Howard Ashman, printed invitation, box 14, folder 5, LOC; Sadowsky, phone interview by author.

84 Alyson, phone interview by author.

85 Joanna Connors, "'Little Shop of Horrors' Is a Monstrously Good Time," *Plain Dealer* (Cleveland), March 15, 1984.

86 Lloyd Grove, "Firmly Planted Cast Makes Big 'Little Shop of Horrors,'" *Washington Post*, May 4, 1984.

87 Church, phone interview by author; Alyson, phone interview by author.

88 Church, phone interview by author.

89 Mark Lipschutz to Esther Sherman, August 29, 1984, box 13, folder 8, LOC.

90 Quoted in Morley, "Voracious Appetite."

91 *Terrorsjappa* typescript, box 12, folder 9, LOC.

92 Ashman, 1983 Diary Agenda, box 26, LOC. According to the calendar, on October 24 he met the Norwegian company and saw the show.

93 Michael Evans to Esther Sherman, August 29, 1983, box 13, folder 8, LOC.

94 Cowan, interview by author; Asbury, phone interview by author.

95 Grappo, interview by author.

96 All quotes in ibid.

97 Ibid.

98 Ibid.

99 Adrian Monteath, "This Plant Is a Monster of a Hit Everywhere," *Sunday Times* (Johannesburg), August 26, 1984.

100 Holmes, phone interview by author, April 27, 2021.

101 Holmes, phone interview by author, January 22, 2019.

102 Ashman Gillespie, interview by author, July 15, 2011.

103 William (Bill) Lauch, interview by author, August 3, 2011.

104 Robert Barandos to Esther Sherman, August 2, 1984, box 12, folder 2, LOC; Esther Sherman to Robert Barandos, August 15, 1984, box 13, folder 9, LOC.

105 Esther Sherman to Claude Martinez and Paul Lederman, December 6, 1984, box 13, folder 9, LOC.

106 Tribunal de grand instance de Paris, *Boris Bergman v. Productions Paul Lederman et Claude Martinez*, legal filing, February 12, 1985, box 13, folder 9, LOC.

107 *La petite boutique des horreurs*, trans. Alain Marcel, box 12, folder 3, LOC.

108 "Liste des chansons," in *La petite boutique de l'horreur*, trans. Boris Bergman, box 12, folder 2, LOC.

109 "Numeros musicaux," no translator listed, box 12, folder 5, LOC.

110 The final version is available on the French cast album, produced by Martinez and Lederman in 1987.

NOTES TO CHAPTER FIVE

111 Lauch, interview by author, August 3, 2011.

112 *Little Shop of Horrors* Production Report, April 13, 1985, DRF.

113 Fletcher, interview by author, July 13, 2019; *Little Shop of Horrors* Production Report, July 30, 1985, DRF.

114 Fletcher, interview by author, July 13, 2019.

115 Hippen, phone interview by author.

116 Review of *La petite boutique des horreurs*, *Variety*, July 9, 1986, 86.

117 *La petite boutique des horreurs*, poster art, box 13, folder 13, LOC.

118 Patricia A. Bechtel to Howard Ashman, July 26, 1984, box 31, folder 9, LOC.

119 Colker, "Off-Broadway Play."

120 "'Little Shop' Scenarist Files Copyright Suit vs. Legit Production," *Variety*, October 20, 1982.

121 Steve Barnett, phone interview by author, June 22, 2021.

122 Gray, *Roger Corman*, 68.

123 Gray, phone interview by author.

124 Ira Hawkins's final performance as the voice of Audrey II was on February 2, 1985; Taylor resumed the role he created one day later. *Little Shop of Horrors* Production Reports, February 2, 1985 and February 3, 1985, DRF.

125 *Little Shop of Horrors* Production Report, August 25, 1984, DRF; Albert Poland, quoted in Davis, phone interview by author.

126 Wilkof, interview by author. Murphy was hired to cover for understudy Katherine Meloche, who was out for two weeks. Therefore, Murphy was available to rehearse with Wilkof. Decades later, he cast Murphy in a feature film that he directed, *No Pay, Nudity* (2016).

127 Ibid. The new, touring version of "Mushnik and Son" made its Orpheum début on April 4, 1984. Howard Ashman was in the audience that night. *Little Shop of Horrors* Production Report, April 4, 1984, DRF.

128 Fletcher, interview by author, July 13, 2019; Donna Rose Fletcher, telephone interview by author, November 13, 2021.

129 Marsha Waterbury (aka Skaggs), phone interview by author, April 1, 2021.

130 Andy Logan, "Around City Hall," *New Yorker*, March 25, 1985, 110; Marilyn Matlick, "The World's His Stage: Mayor Proves He's a Tough Act to Swallow," *New York Post*, March 11, 1985.

131 William (Bill) Lauch, interview by author, October 10, 2019.

132 *Little Shop of Horrors* Production Reports, March 6–March 8, 1985, DRF; Merkin, interview by author.

133 "City Hall of Horrors," the 1985 Inner Circle Show Rebuttal, program, March 9, 1985, box 4, folder 2, NYPL.

134 Ibid.

135 "Mayor Finds Himself 'Planted' inside . . . Jaws!," *Daily News* (New York), March 11, 1985; Matlick, "World's His Stage"; Logan, "Around City Hall," 110.

136 Fletcher, interview by author, July 13, 2019. There seems to be an affinity between the mayor's office and the musical stage. *Fiorello!*, a Broadway musical based on the life of Mayor Fiorello LaGuardia, won the Pulitzer Prize for drama after opening in 1959. Ten years later, *Jimmy* failed to do the same for an earlier mayor, Jimmy Walker. Even Ed Koch was musicalized, in a 1985 production called *Mayor*.

137 Holmes, phone interview by author, January 22, 2019.

138 Robinson, interview by author.

139 Lauch, interview by author, August 3, 2011.

140 Wilkof, interview by author; Alyson, phone interview by author.

141 Ashman and Menken, *Little Shop of Horrors*, 20, 46, 37, 91.

142 Quoted in Robinson, interview by author. By the 1990s, *Little Shop of Horrors* appeared on a list of the most popular plays (musical or otherwise) produced by American high schools. *Little Shop* ranked no. 8, tied with *A Midsummer Night's Dream*. "The Play Survey," *Dramatics*, October 1996, 12.

Chapter 6

1 Howard Ashman, *Little Shop of Horrors* Preliminary Notes, version 2, November 1982, box 13, folder 6, LOC.

2 Howard Ashman, *Little Shop of Horrors* Preliminary Notes, version 1, November 1982, box 13, folder 6, LOC.

3 Ashman, *Little Shop of Horrors* Preliminary Notes, version 2, November 1982, box 13, folder 6, LOC. This outline exists in three similar, overlapping versions, all dated November 1982. I have added the term "version" for clarification.

4 Ibid.

5 Fletcher, interview by author, July 13, 2019. This new version of "Audrey II" is an Ashman parody of a cut song. He wrote new lyrics for the occasion, with references to Orpheum cast and crew members. I thank Donna Rose Fletcher for making this available to me.

6 Ashman, *Little Shop of Horrors* Preliminary Notes, version 2, November 1982, box 13, folder 6, LOC.

7 Howard Ashman, *Little Shop of Horrors* Preliminary Notes, version 3, November 1982, box 13, folder 6, LOC.

8 Ashman, *Little Shop of Horrors* Preliminary Notes, version 2, November 1982, box 13, folder 6, LOC.

9 Quoted in Sasha Anawalt, "Ashman Prepares for New 'Little Shop' Movie," *Los Angeles Herald Examiner*, August 10, 1983.

10 Ashman, 1983 Diary Agenda, box 26, LOC.

11 Howard Ashman, *Little Shop of Horrors* typescript, first draft, December 1983, box 10, folder 4, pages 1, 3, 5, 9, 32, 34, 112, 122, LOC.

12 Photocopy of ibid., box 10, folder 5, pages 34, 90, LOC.

13 Ashman, *Little Shop of Horrors* typescript, first draft, December 1983, box 10, folder 4, page 65, LOC.

14 Howard Ashman, *Little Shop of Horrors* typescript, February 14, 1985, box 10, folder 4, page 67, LOC.

15 Quoted in Don Nelsen, "'Little Shop of Horrors' and Other Transitions from Movie to Stage," *Daily News* (New York), July 18, 1982.

16 On the Town, *New York Post*, March 28, 1983.

17 The Geffen Film Company had "virtual autonomy," according to its production head, Eric Eisner, although Warner Bros. "owned the worldwide distribution rights in perpetuity." Eric Eisner, phone interview by author, November 15, 2021.

18 *Little Shop of Horrors* Production Report, August 31, 1982, DRF; Merkin, interview by author.

19 Army Archerd, Just for Variety, *Daily Variety*, April 29, 1983, 3.

20 Howard Ashman to Harriet McDougal, August 7, 1983, box 13, folder 10, LOC.

21 Anawalt, "Ashman Prepares."

22 Bill Edwards, "Warners Buys 'Little Shop' Tuner for 500G," *Daily Variety*, August 9, 1983, 8; agreement among Workshop of the Players Art Foundation, Inc.; the Shubert Organization, Inc.; Ardentigh Enterprises, Inc. [Cameron Mackintosh]; Geffen Records, July 15, 1983, SA.

23 Anawalt, "Ashman Prepares."

24 "Hollywood Goes Shopping on Broadway," *New York Post*, March 14, 1984.

25 *Little Shop of Horrors* Production Report, March 4, 1984, DRF; Lauch, interview by author, October 10, 2019.

26 Robinson, interview by author.

27 Ibid. Two books cover this topic in detail: Stephen Farber and Marc Green, *Outrageous Conduct: Art, Ego, and the* Twilight Zone *Case* (New York: Arbor House/Morrow, 1988); Ron LaBrecque, *Special Effects: Disaster at* Twilight Zone; *The Tragedy and the Trial* (New York: Charles Scribner's Sons, 1988).

28 John Landis to Howard Ashman, June 29, 1984, box 13, folder 8, LOC.

29 All quotes from "Directors for LITTLE SHOP OF HORRORS—THE MOVIE," box 13, folder 8, LOC.

30 See chap. 2.

31 Diana Maychick, "Audrey II Has Roots in the Theater after 1000 Shows," *New York Post*, December 20, 1984.

32 Howard Ashman, 1982 Engagement Calendar, box 26, LOC.

33 Jeffrey Rubin, "'Little Shop' Blossoms into Big Hit," *Village Angle*, November 1984, box 4, folder 2, NYPL; Howard Ashman, *Little Shop of Horrors* typescript, Frank Oz Draft, November 1984, box 10, folder 7, LOC.

34 Leo Braudy, *The World in a Frame: What We See in Films* (Garden City, NY: Anchor Press/Doubleday, 1976), 109.

35 Parent, interview by author.

36 Ian Frazier, "Rereading 'Lolita,'" *New Yorker*, December 14, 2020, 35.

37 Janet Maslin connects the film version of *Little Shop* with *Gremlins* when she notes that Seymour purchases Audrey II "from the same sort of shady character as the one who peddled the first Gremlin." Both characters are depicted as Asian, with a suggestion of that which is alien or exotic. In fairness, the character played by Keye Luke in *Gremlins* refuses to sell the creature. Review of *Little Shop of Horrors*, *New York Times*, December 19, 1986.

38 Menken, interview by author.

39 This list is extracted from the Howard Ashman Archives, Audio Cassette Inventory, LOC.

40 For example: "CRYSTAL, RONETTE and CHIFFON enter the shot." Ashman, *Little Shop of Horrors* typescript, Frank Oz Draft, November 1984, box 10, folder 7, page 2, LOC.

41 Ibid., page 31.

42 Menken, interview by author.

43 Howard Ashman, "Some Fun Now" typescript, box 10, folder 7, LOC.

44 Howard Ashman, "Some Fun Now" typescript, with note to Frank Oz, box 12, folder 10, LOC.

45 Ibid.

46 Merkin, interview by author.

47 "Bad": Howard Ashman, *Little Shop of Horrors* typescript, July 1, 1985, box 11, folder 4, page 99, LOC; "Bad Like Me": demo recording, July 19, 1985, Howard Ashman Archives, Audio Cassette Inventory, LOC; "Mean Green Mother": Howard Ashman, *Little Shop of Horrors* typescript, September 27, 1985, box 11, folder 5, page 112, LOC.

48 Merkin, interview by author.

49 Don Shewey, "On the Go with David Geffen: Show Business Entrepreneur," *New York Times Magazine*, July 21, 1985; Merkin, interview by author. Shewey spent a week with Geffen in Los Angeles and attended a *Cats* touring premiere in January 1985.

50 Shewey, "On the Go."

51 John McClintock, "'Little Shop of Horrors' Is a Goofy Black Comedy," *Peninsula Times Tribune*, September 30, 1984. *Nerd* is an Americanism that emerged in the 1950s. The *Oxford English Dictionary* identifies an early appearance in *Newsweek* magazine, in 1951. A nerd was the equivalent to a "drip" or a "square."

52 Wilkof, interview by author.

53 Robinson, interview by author; Lauch, interview by author, October 10, 2019.

54 Poland, phone interview by author, May 21, 2021. Much later, Cyndi Lauper wrote music and lyrics for the 2013 Broadway musical *Kinky Boots*, based on the 2005 film.

55 Lauch, interview by author, October 10, 2019. Ashman owned the album *She's So Unusual*. I thank Bill Lauch for making this collection available to me.

56 Liz Smith, "Get This," *Daily News* (New York), April 23, 1985; Robinson, interview by author.

57 Harry Hahn, "Doctor, You've Got to Be Kidding," *Daily News* (New York), August 7, 1985; "Gardenia to Be Florist in 'Horrors,'" *Daily News* (New York), August 27, 1985.

58 It could be argued that the comedic cameos replace the comic potential of allowing the actor who plays Orin Scrivello to essay other roles, an idea dropped for the film.

59 Warren, phone interview by author; Davis, phone interview by author.

60 Jones, phone interview by author; Davis, phone interview by author.

61 Scapperotti, "Off-Broadway Hit," 61; Ashman Gillespie, interview by author, January 4, 2019.

62 *Little Shop of Horrors* Production Reports, September 23, 1985; October 14, 1985; November 25, 1985, DRF.

63 Quoted in Alan Jones, "Little Shop of Horrors," *Cinefantastique* 17, no. 1 (January 1987): 24; Merkin, interview by author; Billig, interview by author.

64 Menken, interview by author.

65 McCarty and McGee, *Little Shop of Horrors Book*, 161–2.

66 Robinson, interview by author.

67 Adam Pirani, "Remaking *Little Shop of Horrors*," *Fangoria*, no. 60 (January 1987): 37.

68 Quoted in Phil Koch, "Little Shop of Horrors," *Cinefantastique* 17, no. 5 (September 1987): 24.

69 A. Jones, "Little Shop of Horrors," 25, 55.

70 Quoted in McCarty and McGee, *Little Shop of Horrors Book*, 163–4.

71 Robinson, interview by author.

72 Before long, this animatronic technology would become outmoded: computer-generated imagery (CGI or CG) made an impact in the film *Young Sherlock Holmes*, released in 1985. Four years later, audiences were even more impressed by the shapeshifting CG creatures in *The Abyss*, the underwater adventure directed by James Cameron.

73 Merkin, interview by author.

74 Quoted in Koch, "Little Shop of Horrors," 28.

75 *Little Shop of Horrors: The Director's Cut*, alternate ending commentary (Burbank: Warner Bros., 2017), Blu-ray disc. Some scenes were shot at twelve frames per second.

76 Asbury, phone interview by author.

77 Merkin, interview by author.

78 Ibid.

79 Asbury, phone interview by author.

80 Quoted in Asbury, phone interview by author.

81 Asbury, phone interview by author.

82 McCarty and McGee, *Little Shop of Horrors Book*, 164.

83 Koch, "Little Shop of Horrors," 61.

84 A trade paper announced that *Little Shop* "started principal photography on Monday." "'Little Shop' Starts at Pinewood," *Screen International*, no. 520 (October 26, 1985): 6.

85 Quoted in *Little Shop of Horrors* "Production Information," 1986 film press kit, box 6, folder 7, page 4, NYPL.

86 Asbury, phone interview by author; Frank Oz, quoted in Michael Billington, "New Life for 'Little Shop,'" *New York Times*, December 8, 1985.

87 Billington, "New Life for 'Little Shop'"; Asbury, phone interview by author.

88 Merkin, interview by author.

89 Scapperotti, "Off-Broadway Hit," 55.

90 Aljean Harmetz, "'Little Shop' Is Returning to the Screen," *New York Times*, August 23, 1985.

91 Quoted in McCarty and McGee, *Little Shop of Horrors Book*, 161.

92 Asbury, phone interview by author.

93 Ibid.; Merkin, interview by author; Eisner, phone interview by author.

94 A. Jones, "Little Shop of Horrors," 18.

95 Lauch, interview by author, October 10, 2019; Merkin, interview by author.

96 Lauch, interview by author, October 10, 2019.

97 *Little Shop of Horrors: The Director's Cut*, original ending (Burbank: Warner Bros., 2017), Blu-ray disc; Asbury, phone interview by author. In June 1986, the studio announced that the film would not be a summer release; instead, it would appear before Christmas. *Variety*, June 11, 1986, 12.

98 Alan Jones, "The Lost Ending," *Cinefantastique* 17, no. 5 (September 1987): 34, 36.

99 Scapperotti, "Off-Broadway Hit," 61.

100 Holmes, phone interview by author, January 22, 2019; Lauch, interview by author, October 10, 2019.

101 Frank Oz said, "In the play, they're eaten by the puppet, but you know they're coming out for a curtain call." Quoted in McCarty and McGee, *Little Shop of Horrors Book*, 166. Eric Eisner made a similar point in Eisner, phone interview by author.

102 Lauch, interview by author, October 10, 2019.

103 Howard Ashman, quoted in Grappo, interview by author; Lauch, interview by author, October 10, 2019.

104 A. Jones, "Little Shop of Horrors," 19.

105 Howard Ashman, "Notes on Pages," box 12, folder 10, LOC; Howard Ashman, typescript pages, September 7, 1986, box 12, folder 10, LOC.

106 Fletcher, interview by author, July 13, 2019.

107 "On the twenty-third day of the month of September," begins the narrating voice in Ashman, *Little Shop of Horrors* typescript, Frank Oz Draft, November 1984, box 10, folder 7, page 1, LOC.

108 Bobbi Thompson to Howard Ashman, December 22, 1986, box 13, folder 10, LOC; Martin A. Grove, "Hollywood Report," *Hollywood Reporter*, December 18, 1986.

109 Maslin, review; Roger Ebert, "Amusing 'Little Shop' Plants Feet Firmly in the Cult Garden," *New York Post*, December 19, 1986.

110 Review of *Little Shop of Horrors*, *Variety*, December 10, 1986, 14; Ed Kaufman, review of *Little Shop of Horrors*, *Hollywood Reporter*, December 10, 1986, 3.

111 Weekend Film Boxoffice Reports, *Variety*, December 24, 1986, 4. On that first weekend, *Little Shop* earned $3,659,884 on 866 screens across the US. After two months of release, the film grossed more than $36 million. Weekend Film Boxoffice Reports, *Variety*, February 25, 1987, 39. *Three Amigos* was directed by John Landis.

112 Robert E. Wise to Howard Ashman, February 12, 1987, box 13, folder 10, LOC.

113 Later, the 1986 film expanded its audience through home video and cable television. In a way, the more intimate experience of a home viewing is a better approximation of the WPA and the Orpheum—again, in keeping with the kind of piece that Ashman wanted to create.

114 Robert Egan and Louise Egan, *Little Shop of Horrors*, based on the screenplay by Howard Ashman (New York: Perigee Books, 1986); McCarty and McGee, *Little Shop of Horrors Book*.

115 All quotes from Michael Fleisher et al., *Little Shop of Horrors: The Official Adaptation of the Movie* (New York: DC Comics, 1986). Three dancers—who may or may not be the film's Crystal, Ronette, and Chiffon—sing a few lines extracted from the song "Audrey II," including: "Who's the best, the beautiful green one?" and "Who's a star if ever I've seen one?"

116 Stephen M. Silverman, "This 'Little Shop' Builds Big Bucks Off-Broadway," *New York Post*, July 22, 1986.

117 Quoted in ibid.; Poland, interview by author, October 7, 2019.

118 This story in Meloche, phone interview by author.

119 Fletcher, interview by author, July 13, 2019.

120 Poland, interview by author, October 7, 2019.

121 Munderloh, phone interview by author.

122 Quoted in Poland, interview by author, October 7, 2019.

123 Albert Poland to the Little Shop Company, October 15, 1987, DRF.

124 Albert Poland to the Little Shop Company, October 27, 1987, DRF.

125 Peter Mumford to Donna Rose Fletcher and Paul Mills Holmes, October 30, 1987, DRF.

126 Many years later, Fletcher discovered an error in the production reports. There are two performances both identified as performance no. 1,262. So the grand total number of performances that has been reported (2,209) is incorrect. The correct number is 2,210. Donna Rose Fletcher to author, May 25, 2021.

127 Donna Rose Fletcher, phone interview by author, February 6, 2021. Szymanski was the understudy to plant puppeteer Lynn Hippen. She found more remunerative employment for that weekend and missed the final performances. It's worth noting that Meloche and Finkel joined the Off-Broadway production at the start (as understudies) and remained with the show.

128 This story in Fletcher, interview by author, July 13, 2019. By the end of its run, the New York production grossed approximately twenty million dollars. Stock and amateur rights were earning $80,000 to $90,000 every month. "'Little Shop' Winding Long Off-B'way Run," *Variety*, October 28, 1987, 103.

129 Fletcher, interview by author, July 13, 2019; Holmes, phone interview by author, January 22, 2019. In attendance: Ashman; Lauch; Marty Robinson; Ellen Greene; and stage managers Paul Mills Holmes, Elizabeth (Betsy) Nicholson, and Donna Rose Fletcher.

130 Lauch, interview by author, October 10, 2019.

Chapter 7

1 "Source of 'Horrors,'" *New York Post*, November 26, 1982; "Corman, WB Ink 'Little Shop' Deal," *Variety*, January 22, 1986, 7, 14.

2 Corman, *How I Made a Hundred Movies*, 69.

3 "Horizon Targets Illegal 'Horrors,'" *Variety*, July 3, 1985, 31. Among the companies offering *The Little Shop* were Budget Video, Discount Video Tapes, Movie Buff Video, Sheik Video, and Video Yesteryear. Further, Corman's film endured a cheap knock-off in the form of *Please Don't Eat My Mother!*, a 1973 "nudie-comedy" about a man and his talking plant. Mike Wathen, "The Damned and the Demented: Roger Corman and the Filmgroup," in *Shock Xpress*, ed. Stefan Jaworzyn (London: Titan Books, 1991), 152.

4 Barnett, phone interview by author.

5 Nasr, *Roger Corman*, 155; McCarty and McGee, *Little Shop of Horrors Book*, 114.

6 Lee Goldberg, Zoom interview by author, April 20, 2021.

7 William (Bill) Rabkin, Zoom interview by author, April 20, 2021.

8 Goldberg, Zoom interview by author.

9 Rabkin, Zoom interview by author.

10 Lee Goldberg and William Rabkin, *Little Shop of Horrors*, Writers' Draft, December 9, 1991. I thank Lee Goldberg for making this and other drafts available to me.

11 Lee Goldberg and William Rabkin, *Little Shop of Horrors*, Series Bible, September 18, 1991, 9; Lee Goldberg and William Rabkin, *Little Shop of Horrors*, Second Draft, February 10, 1992, 11, 13.

12 Goldberg, Zoom interview by author.

13 Quoted in Goldberg, Zoom interview by author .

14 Goldberg, Zoom interview by author.

15 Roger Corman, quoted in Rabkin, Zoom interview by author.

16 Don Hahn directed two documentaries that tell this story in detail: *Waking Sleeping Beauty* (2009) and *Howard* (2018).

17 Howard Ashman memorial program, May 6, 1991.

18 For more, see Jessica Sternfeld, *The Megamusical* (Bloomington: Indiana University Press, 2006).

19 Lesser, phone interview by author.

20 Robin Pogrebin, "The Show That Ate the Original Cast," *New York Times*, October 20, 2003.

21 See chap. 3.

22 Menken, interview by author.

23 Hunter Foster, phone interview by author, April 30, 2021.

24 Robinson, interview by author.

25 Asbury, phone interview by author.

26 Robinson, interview by author.

27 Wilkof, interview by author.

28 Menken, interview by author.

29 Robinson, interview by author.

30 Robert Hofler, "'Horrors' Closes Shop," *Variety*, June 2, 2003. This article quotes an official statement from the show's producers: "We feel an obligation to everyone involved with 'Little Shop,' and to the ticket-buying public, to insure that the work we present on Broadway represents the best work we can do. In spite of the great number of talented people involved, the elements of this production did not come together in the way we would have liked."

31 Pogrebin, "Show That Ate."

32 Quoted in Pogrebin, "Show That Ate."

33 Gelfand, Zoom interview by author.

34 Foster, phone interview by author.

35 Ben Brantley, "A Hungry Actor? Audrey II Is Back," *New York Times*, October 3, 2003.

36 Wilkof, interview by author.

37 Data extracted from the *Little Shop of Horrors* page on the website www.playbill.com.

38 Robinson, interview by author.

39 Pirani, "Remaking *Little Shop of Horrors*," 37.

40 Mayer, Zoom interview by author. *Hundreds of Hats* premiered at the WPA (at 519 West Twenty-third Street) on May 25, 1995.

41 Quoted in Lesser, phone interview by author.

42 Lesser, phone interview by author.

43 Asbury, phone interview by author; William (Bill) Lauch, telephone conversation with author, October 15, 2018.

44 Ben Brantley, "Reviving a Star's Signature Role and a Plant's Appetite for Blood," *New York Times*, July 2, 2015; Joe Dziemianowicz, "Jake Gyllenhaal and Ellen Greene Lead a Gleeful Revival at Encores!," *Daily News* (New York), July 2, 2015.

45 David Rooney, review of *Little Shop of Horrors*, *Hollywood Reporter*, July 2, 2015, www.hollywoodreporter.com; Jeremy Gerard, "Jake Gyllenhaal and Taran Killam Serenade Ellen Greene in *Little Shop of Horrors*," www.deadline.com, July 2, 2015.

46 Ellen Greene, quoted in Wilkof, interview by author.

47 Joey Nolfi, "*Little Shop of Horrors* Team on Failed Stage Revival: It 'Broke My Heart,'" *Entertainment Weekly*, October 13, 2017, www.ew.com.

48 Undated photograph, circa 1983, box 3, folder 25, NYPL.

49 Merkin, interview by author.

50 Gelfand, Zoom interview by author; Merkin, interview by author.

51 Oliver, review of *Little Shop of Horrors*, 118; Hischak, *Off-Broadway Musicals*, 199.

52 Nancy Nagel Gibbs, phone interview by author, November 12, 2021.

53 Hischak, *Off-Broadway Musicals*, 400.

54 "A NOTE ABOUT THE PLAY," in the printed version, recalls Ashman's note in the Samuel French edition of *Little Shop*. "*Weird Romance* takes its speculative fiction seriously. It is never to satirize the genre or degenerate into camp." Alan Menken, David Spencer, and David Brennert, *Weird Romance: Two One-Act Musicals of Speculative Fiction* (1992; New York: Samuel French, 1993), viii.

55 Bob Carlton, *Return to the Forbidden Planet* (1989; New York: Samuel French, 1998), 38.

56 Ibid., 30. All capitals in the original.

57 Charles Isherwood, review of *Little Shop of Horrors*, *Variety*, October 2, 2003; Viertel, *Secret Life*, 194.

58 Holmes, phone interview by author, January 22, 2019.

59 Henry Jenkins, *Textual Poachers: Television Fans and Participatory Culture* (1992; New York: Routledge, 2013), 18.

60 Catawba Valley Community College, "*Little Shop of Horror* [sic] 'Dentist' Parody by the CVCC Dental Hygiene Class of 2020," October 24, 2019, www.youtube.com.

61 R2ninjaturtle, "Feed Me (Git It!) Scene Reenactment," February 12, 2014, www.youtube.com. Subsequent entries include "Suppertime" (April 18, 2014), "Suddenly, Seymour"

(July 3, 2014), "Suppertime" Reprise (November 14, 2014), "Mean Green Mother from Outer Space" (May 23, 2015), and "Dentist!" (September 23, 2017).

62 Phyllis A. Ehrlich, "A Christmas Bounty for Youngsters," *New York Times*, December 24, 1982; Howard Ashman, quoted in Arkatov, "Man-Eating Plant."

63 "Little Shop of Horrors: Mmm, Mmm, Good!," *Los Angeles*, June 1983, box 5, folder 7, NYPL; Robert Scott, review of *Little Shop of Horrors*, *Yorkshire Post*, October 18, 1983, box 5, folder 6, NYPL.

64 Quoted in Chris Archer, "Secret of 'Little Shop of Horrors': An Off-Broadway Hit Revisited," *Villager*, September 5, 1985, box 4, folder 2, NYPL.

65 Michael Quintos, "Gloriously Reimagined *Little Shop of Horrors* Kills at Pasadena Playhouse," www.broadwayworld.com, October 7, 2019; Dino-Ray Ramos, "Campy Classic Devours Pasadena Playhouse with Soul, Heart and Inclusivity," www.deadline.com, October 1, 2019.

66 Charles McNulty, "'Little Shop of Horrors' at Pasadena Playhouse Finds Humanity amid the Musical Camp," *Los Angeles Times*, September 27, 2019, www.latimes.com.

67 Diep Tran, "A Tale of Two 'Little Shop(s) of Horrors,'" *American Theatre*, October 18, 2019, www.americantheatre.org.

68 Ibid.

69 Tom Kirdahy, Zoom interview by author, February 5, 2021.

70 Ibid.

71 Mayer, Zoom interview by author; Kirdahy, Zoom interview by author.

72 Kelsey O'Connor, "Bool's Will Be Stage for Special 'Little Shop of Horrors' Production," *Ithaca Voice*, February 18, 2019, www.ithacavoice.com.

73 Kirdahy, Zoom interview by author.

74 Jonathan Groff, Zoom interview by author, January 8, 2021.

75 Mayer, Zoom interview by author.

76 Groff, Zoom interview by author.

77 Kirdahy, Zoom interview by author; Mayer, Zoom interview by author.

78 Tammy Blanchard, phone interview by author, February 18, 2021.

79 Mayer, Zoom interview by author.

80 Blanchard, phone interview by author.

81 Will Van Dyke, phone interview by author, July 30, 2020.

82 Quoted in Groff, Zoom interview by author.

83 Mayer, Zoom interview by author; Van Dyke, phone interview by author.

84 Groff, Zoom interview by author.

85 Kirdahy, Zoom interview by author.

86 Quoted in Mayer, Zoom interview by author.

87 Alexis Soloski, "Gory Musical Blooms Again Off-Broadway," *The Guardian*, October 17, 2019, www.guardian.com; David Rooney, review of *Little Shop of Horrors*, *Hollywood Reporter*, October 17, 2019, www.hollywoodreporter.com; Ben Brantley, "A Delicious Revival for a Grisly Shop," *New York Times*, October 17, 2019.

88 Groff, Zoom interview by author.

89 R. Eric Thomas, "Getting a Disaster Do-Over in *Little Shop of Horrors*," *Elle*, March 25, 2020, www.elle.com. This article also points out that the musical has three openings. The spoken prologue, the song "Little Shop of Horrors," and "Skid Row (Downtown)" introduce three aspects of the piece: the science-fiction genre, the music of the era, and the central characters.

90 Blanchard, phone interview by author.

91 Mayer, Zoom interview by author; Kirdahy, Zoom interview by author.

92 Jack Viertel, "'Little Shop': Horror Spoof with a Song in Its Heart," *Los Angeles Herald Examiner*, April 29, 1983.

93 Van Dyke, phone interview by author; Mayer, Zoom interview by author.

94 Blanchard, phone interview by author.

95 Quoted in Groff, Zoom interview by author.

96 Groff, Zoom interview by author.

97 Mackintosh, phone interview by author.

Bibliography

Absalom, Steve. "Shutting Up the 'Little Shop' without a Profit." *Stage and Television Today*, no. 5448 (September 12, 1985): 1.
Anawalt, Sasha. "Ashman Prepares for New 'Little Shop' Movie." *Los Angeles Herald Examiner*, August 10, 1983.
Archer, Chris. "Secret of 'Little Shop of Horrors': An Off-Broadway Hit Revisited." *Villager*, September 5, 1985, 15, 17.
Archerd, Army. "Just for Variety." *Daily Variety*, April 29, 1983, 3.
Arkatov, Janice. "Man-Eating Plant Hopes to Capture Los Angeles." *Los Angeles Times*, April 25, 1983.
Ashman, Howard. "A Musical about a Man-Eating Plant?" www.howardashman.com. Originally published in *Playbill*, c. 1983.
Ashman, Howard, and Alan Menken. *Little Shop of Horrors*. 1982. New York: Samuel French, 1985.
Ashman, Howard, and Alan Menken. *Little Shop of Horrors: A New Musical*. Garden City, NY: Nelson Doubleday, 1982.
Ashman, Howard, Alan Menken, and Dennis Green. *Kurt Vonnegut's God Bless You, Mr. Rosewater*. 1979. New York: Samuel French, 1980.
Baker, Rob. "'Little Shop' May Open *the* Door for Her." *Daily News* (New York), July 26, 1982.
Barnes, Clive. "A Clear and Sparkling 'Rosewater.'" *New York Post*, May 29, 1979.
Barnes, Clive. Review of *Dreamstuff. New York Times*, April 5, 1976.
Barnes, Clive. "'10 Best' Shows Are Really a Dynamic Dozen." *New York Post*, December 30, 1982.
Beaufort, John. Review of *Little Shop of Horrors. Christian Science Monitor*, August 26, 1982.
Besoyan, Rick. *Little Mary Sunshine*. 1959. New York: Samuel French, 1999.
"Big Rental Films of '87." *Variety*, January 20, 1988, 19.
Billington, Michael. "New Life for 'Little Shop.'" *New York Times*, December 8, 1985.
Billington, Michael. Review of *Little Shop of Horrors. The Guardian*, October 13, 1983.
Blau, Eleanor. "Howard Ashman Is Dead at 40; Writer of 'Little Shop of Horrors.'" *New York Times*, March 15, 1991.
Blau, Eleanor. "Making a Vonnegut Novel Sing." *New York Times*, September 24, 1979.
Block, Geoffrey. *Enchanted Evenings: The Broadway Musical from* Show Boat *to* Sondheim. New York: Oxford University Press, 1997.
"Boffo 'Little Shop.'" *Variety*, January 18, 1984, 106.

Botto, Louis. "Little Shop of Horrors." *Playbill: The National Magazine of the Theatre*, January 1983, 19–22.
Bottoms, Stephen J. *Playing Underground: A Critical History of the 1960s Off-Off-Broadway Movement*. Ann Arbor: The University of Michigan Press, 2004.
Boxer, Tim. "Traveling with the Stars." *Jewish Week*, August 20, 1982, 23.
Brantley, Ben. "A Delicious Revival for a Grisly Shop." *New York Times*, October 17, 2019.
Brantley, Ben. "A Hungry Actor? Audrey II Is Back." *New York Times*, October 3, 2003.
Brantley, Ben. "Reviving a Star's Signature Role and a Plant's Appetite for Blood." *New York Times*, July 2, 2015.
Braudy, Leo. *The World in a Frame: What We See in Films*. Garden City, NY: Anchor Press/Doubleday, 1976.
Burkett, Michael. "Just When You Thought It Was Safe to Go Back to the Theater." *Orange County Register*, May 1, 1983.
Carlton, Bob. *Return to the Forbidden Planet*. 1989. New York: Samuel French, 1998.
Carter, Tim. *Oklahoma! The Making of an American Musical*. New Haven: Yale University Press, 2007.
Casper, Drew. Review of *Little Shop of Horrors*. *Hollywood Reporter*, April 29, 1983, 3, 7.
Cedrone, Lou. "'Little Shop' Is Enjoyable Camp and Fun." *Baltimore Evening Sun*, April 12, 1984.
Christon, Lawrence. "A Stage Prop Buts Bite on 'Shop.'" *Los Angeles Times*, June 2, 1983.
Clarke, Arthur C. *Tales from the White Hart*. New York: Ballantine Books, 1957.
Clum, John M. *Something for the Boys: Musical Theater and Gay Culture*. New York: St. Martin's Press, 1999.
Colker, David. "Off-Broadway Play Stems from 1960s Cult-Horror Film." *Los Angeles Herald Examiner*, April 19, 1983.
Colker, David. "An Old-Fashioned Monster Musical." *Los Angeles Herald Examiner*, April 19, 1983.
Collier, John. *Fancies and Goodnights*. Garden City, NY: Doubleday, 1952.
Connors, Joanna. "'Little Shop of Horrors' Is a Monstrously Good Time." *Plain Dealer* (Cleveland), March 15, 1984.
Corliss, Richard. "Dream Girls." *Time*, January 3, 1983, 80.
Corliss, Richard. "When Trash Is a Treasure." *Time*, August 23, 1982, 59.
Corman, Roger, with Jim Jerome. *How I Made a Hundred Movies in Hollywood and Never Lost a Dime*. New York: Random House, 1990.
"Corman, WB Ink 'Little Shop' Deal." *Variety*, January 22, 1986, 7, 14.
Coveney, Michael. Review of *Little Shop of Horrors*. *Financial Times*, October 13, 1983.
Crossette, Barbara. "Making a Plant Grow: A Hidden Art on Stage." *New York Times*, October 8, 1982.
Cushman, Robert. Review of *Little Shop of Horrors*. *The Observer*, October 16, 1983.
Czarnecki, Mark. "The Plant That Ate New York." *Maclean's*, July 1, 1985. www.archive.macleans.ca.
Demme, Jonathan. "Roger Corman." *Interview*, April 2014. www.interview.com.
Dziemianowicz, Joe. "Jake Gyllenhaal and Ellen Greene Lead a Gleeful Revival at Encores!" *Daily News* (New York), July 2, 2015.

Ebert, Roger. "Amusing 'Little Shop' Plants Feet Firmly in the Cult Garden." *New York Post*, December 19, 1986.
Edelstein, David. "I Drink Your Blood." *Village Voice*, December 23, 1986.
Edwards, Bill. "Warners Buys 'Little Shop' Tuner for 500G." *Daily Variety*, August 9, 1983, 8.
Egan, Robert, and Louise Egan. *Little Shop of Horrors*. Based on the Screenplay by Howard Ashman. New York: Perigee Books, 1986.
Ehrlich, Phyllis A. "A Christmas Bounty for Youngsters." *New York Times*, December 24, 1982.
Engel, Lehman. *Their Words Are Music: The Great Theatre Lyricists and Their Lyrics*. New York: Crown Publishers, 1975.
Engel, Lehman. *This Bright Day: An Autobiography*. New York: Macmillan, 1974.
Engel, Lehman. *Words with Music*. New York: Macmillan, 1972.
Farber, Donald C. *From Option to Opening*. 3rd ed. New York: Drama Book Specialists, 1977.
Farber, Stephen, and Marc Green. *Outrageous Conduct: Art, Ego, and the* Twilight Zone *Case*. New York: Arbor House/Morrow, 1988.
Feldberg, Robert. "Uprooting a Budding Musical." *Sunday Record*, July 25, 1982.
"Film Company News." *Film Journal* 89, no. 3 (March 1, 1986): 21.
Fischer, Dennis. "Little Shop of Horrors." *Cinefantastique* 14, no. 2 (December 1983/January 1984): 12.
Fischer, Dennis. "Roger Corman's *Little Shop of Horrors*." *Cinefantastique* 17, no. 1 (January 1987): 27–31, 60–1.
Fleisher, Michael, et al. *Little Shop of Horrors: The Official Adaptation of the Movie*. New York: DC Comics, 1986.
Flinn, Denny Martin. *What They Did for Love: The Untold Story behind the Making of* A Chorus Line. New York: Bantam Books, 1989.
Fosdick, Scott. "Scream Play." *Baltimore News American*, April 8, 1984.
Frazier, Ian. "Rereading 'Lolita.'" *New Yorker*, December 14, 2020, 30–5.
"From Trade Paper Reviews Roger Corman's 'Cheapie' Film Rates Cannes Bid." *Variety*, May 17, 1961, 17.
"Gardenia to Be Florist in 'Horrors.'" *Daily News* (New York), August 27, 1985.
Gerard, Jeremy. "Jake Gyllenhaal and Taran Killam Serenade Ellen Greene in *Little Shop of Horrors*." www.deadline.com, July 2, 2015.
Grant, Steve. "Shop! Horror!" *Time Out*, October 6–12, 1983, 14–16.
Gray, Beverly. *Roger Corman: An Unauthorized Biography of the Godfather of Indie Filmmaking*. Los Angeles: Renaissance Books, 2000.
Green, Dennis. "Saying Goodbye to Howard." In *Queer Stories for Boys: True Stories from the Gay Men's Storytelling Workshop*, edited by Douglas McKeown. New York: Thunder's Mouth Press, 2004.
Grove, Lloyd. "Firmly Planted Cast Makes Big 'Little Shop of Horrors.'" *Washington Post*, May 4, 1984.
Grove, Martin A. "Hollywood Report." *Hollywood Reporter*, December 18, 1986, 3.
Guernsey, Otis L., Jr., ed. *Broadway Song and Story: Playwrights/Lyricists/Composers Discuss Their Hits*. New York: Dodd, Mead, 1985.
Guffey, Elizabeth E. *Retro: The Culture of Revival*. London: Reaktion Books, 2006.

Gussow, Mel. "In the Arts: Critics' Choices." *New York Times*, August 22, 1982.
Gussow, Mel. "Musical: A Cactus Owns 'Little Shop of Horrors.'" *New York Times*, May 30, 1982.
Hahn, Harry. "Doctor, You've Got to Be Kidding." *Daily News* (New York), August 7, 1985.
Haimsohn, George, Robin Miller, and Jim Wise. *Dames at Sea*. 1966. New York: Samuel French, 1969.
Harmetz, Aljean. "'Little Shop' Is Returning to the Screen." *New York Times*, August 23, 1985.
Heilpern, John. "Musical Jaws." *Tatler* 278, no. 9 (1983): 150–151.
Hischak, Thomas S. *Off-Broadway Musicals Since 1919: From* Greenwich Village Follies *to* The Toxic Avenger. Lanham, MD: Scarecrow Press, 2011.
Hoberman, J. *Vulgar Modernism: Writing on Movies and Other Media*. Philadelphia: Temple University Press, 1991.
Hoffman, Warren. *The Great White Way: Race and the Broadway Musical*. New Brunswick: Rutgers University Press, 2014.
Hofler, Robert. "'Horrors' Closes Shop." *Variety*, June 2, 2003. www.variety.com.
"Hollywood Goes Shopping on Broadway." *New York Post*, March 14, 1984.
Hope, Vida. Preface to *The Boy Friend*, by Sandy Wilson. 1953. New York: E. P. Dutton, 1955.
"Horizon Targets Illegal 'Horrors.'" *Variety*, July 3, 1985, 31.
Horn, Barbara Lee. *The Age of* Hair: *Evolution and Impact of Broadway's First Rock Musical*. Westport, CT: Greenwood Press, 1991.
Hunter, Stephen. "'Shop of Horrors': The Film behind the Musical." *Baltimore Sun*, April 20, 1984.
Hutchings, David. "Critics Agree with the Man-Eating Plant in *Little Shop of Horrors*: Ellen Greene Is Delicious." *People Weekly*, January 12, 1987, 43–4.
International Box Office. *Screen International*, no. 588 (February 21, 1987): 248.
Isherwood, Charles. Review of *Little Shop of Horrors*. *Variety*, October 2, 2003. www.variety.com.
Jenkins, Henry. *Textual Poachers: Television Fans and Participatory Culture*. Rev. ed. New York: Routledge, 2013.
Jenkins, Philip. *Decade of Nightmares: The End of the Sixties and the Making of Eighties America*. Oxford: Oxford University Press, 2006.
Jones, Alan. "Little Shop of Horrors." *Cinefantastique* 17, no. 1 (January 1987): 16–21, 24–5, 55.
Jones, Alan. "The Lost Ending." *Cinefantastique* 17, no. 5 (September 1987): 32–7.
Jones, Kenneth. "He's a Guest: Composer Alan Menken Shares Thoughts at BMI Master Class." *Playbill*, December 21, 1998. www.playbill.com.
Jones, Tom, and Harvey Schmidt. *The Fantasticks: Thirtieth Anniversary Edition*. 1960. Lanham, MD: Applause Theatre Book Publishers, 1990.
Kaufman, Ed. Review of *Little Shop of Horrors*. *Hollywood Reporter*, December 10, 1986, 3, 22.
Kerr, Walter. "'Little Shop of Horrors' and the Terrors of Special Effects." *New York Times*, August 22, 1982.
Kerr, Walter. Review of *Oh, Captain!* *New York Herald Tribune*, February 5, 1958.

Kissel, Howard. Review of *Little Shop of Horrors. Women's Wear Daily*, August 13, 1982.
Klein, Alvin. "I Love Being Different Characters." *New York Times*, March 6, 1983.
Knapp, Raymond. *The American Musical and the Performance of Personal Identity.* Princeton: Princeton University Press, 2006.
Knapp, Raymond, and Mitchell Morris. "Tin Pan Alley Songs on Stage and Screen before World War II." In *The Oxford Handbook of the American Musical*, edited by Raymond Knapp, Mitchell Morris, and Stacy Wolf. New York: Oxford University Press, 2011.
Knapp, Raymond, Mitchell Morris, and Stacy Wolf. *The Oxford Handbook of the American Musical.* New York: Oxford University Press, 2011.
Koch, Phil. "Little Shop of Horrors." *Cinefantastique* 17, no. 5 (September 1987): 24–6, 28–30, 61.
Koch, Phil. "The Man behind the Plant." *Cinefantastique* 17, no. 5 (September 1987): 27.
Kramer, Elizabeth. "Tavares Inspires IU Production." *Indiana Daily Student*, April 17, 1987.
Kreuger, Miles. *Show Boat: The Story of a Classic American Musical.* 1977. New York: Da Capo, 1990.
LaBrecque, Ron. *Special Effects: Disaster at* Twilight Zone; *The Tragedy and the Trial.* New York: Charles Scribner's Sons, 1988.
Leaman, Kristin. "Sincerely Yours: Howard Ashman, Making IU Part of His World." *Blogging Hoosier History*, January 18, 2017. blogs.libraries.indiana.edu.
"Little Shop of Horrors: Mmm, Mmm, Good!" *Los Angeles*, June 1983.
"'Little Shop of Horrors' Set for Art Theatres Booking." *Boxoffice* 79, no. 2 (May 1, 1961): W2.
"'Little Shop' Scenarist Files Copyright Suit vs. Legit Production." *Variety*, October 20, 1982.
"'Little Shop' Starts at Pinewood." *Screen International*, no. 520 (October 26, 1985): 6.
"'Little Shop' Winding Long Off-B'way Run." *Variety*, October 28, 1987, 103.
Logan, Andy. "Around City Hall." *New Yorker*, March 25, 1985, 110–117.
Lumley, Joanna. "A Star Steps out of the Shadows." *The Times* (London), October 19, 1983.
MacDonald, Ian. *Revolution in the Head: The Beatles' Records and the Sixties.* Rev. ed. London: Vintage Books, 2008.
Majchrzak, Ben. "Remembering Howard Ashman in Vermont." Goddard College Alumni News, n.d. www.goddard.edu.
Maslin, Janet. Review of *Little Shop of Horrors. New York Times*, December 19, 1986.
Mast, Gerald. *Can't Help Singin': The American Musical on Stage and Screen.* Woodstock, NY: Overlook Press, 1987.
Matlick, Marilyn. "The World's His Stage: Mayor Proves He's a Tough Act to Swallow." *New York Post*, March 11, 1985.
Maychick, Diana. "Audrey II Has Roots in the Theater after 1000 Shows." *New York Post*, December 20, 1984.
"Mayor Finds Himself 'Planted' inside . . . Jaws!" *Daily News* (New York), March 11, 1985.
McCarty, John, and Mark Thomas McGee. *The Little Shop of Horrors Book.* New York: St. Martin's Press, 1988.
McClintock, John. "'Little Shop of Horrors' Is a Goofy Black Comedy." *Peninsula Times Tribune*, September 30, 1984.
McGee, Mark Thomas. *Roger Corman: The Best of the Cheap Acts.* Jefferson, NC: McFarland, 1988.

McHugh, Dominic. *Loverly: The Life and Times of* My Fair Lady. Oxford: Oxford University Press, 2012.

McNulty, Charles. "'Little Shop of Horrors' at Pasadena Playhouse Finds Humanity amid the Musical Camp." *Los Angeles Times*, September 27, 2019. www.latimes.com.

Menken, Alan, David Spencer, and David Brennert. *Weird Romance: Two One-Act Musicals of Speculative Fiction*. 1992. New York: Samuel French, 1993.

Monteath, Adrian. "This Plant Is a Monster of a Hit Everywhere." *Sunday Times* (Johannesburg), August 26, 1984.

Moore, Ward. *Greener Than You Think*. New York: William Sloane, 1947.

Morigi, Gilda. "Broadway Jottings." *American-Jewish Life*, June 29, 1984.

Morley, Sheridan. "Voracious Appetite." *The Times* (London), October 6, 1983.

Most, Andrea. *Making Americans: Jews and the Broadway Musical*. Cambridge, MA: Harvard University Press, 2004.

Nashawaty, Chris. *Crab Monsters, Teenage Cavemen, and Candy Stripe Nurses: Roger Corman; King of the B Movie*. New York: Abrams, 2013.

Nasr, Constantine, ed. *Roger Corman: Interviews*. Jackson: University Press of Mississippi, 2011.

Nelsen, Don. "Flytrap Catches Laughs." *Daily News* (New York), August 9, 1982.

Nelsen, Don. "'Little Shop of Horrors' and Other Transitions from Movie to Stage." *Daily News* (New York), July 18, 1982.

Nichols, Lewis. "'Oklahoma!' a Musical Hailed as Delightful, Based on 'Green Grow the Lilacs,' Opens Here at the St. James Theatre." *New York Times*, April 1, 1943.

Nolfi, Joey. "*Little Shop of Horrors* Team on Failed Stage Revival: It 'Broke My Heart.'" *Entertainment Weekly*, October 13, 2017. www.ew.com.

O'Brien, Richard. *The Rocky Horror Show*. 1973. New York: Samuel French, 1999.

O'Connor, Kelsey. "Bool's Will Be Stage for Special 'Little Shop of Horrors' Production." *Ithaca Voice*, February 18, 2019. www.ithacavoice.com.

Oliver, Edith. Review of *Little Shop of Horrors*. *New Yorker*, September 27, 1982, 118.

On the Town. *New York Post*, March 28, 1983.

"Oscar Winners Help Boost LA Scores." *Boxoffice* 79, no. 2 (May 1, 1961): W4.

Parker, Jerry. "Greene Blossoms in London." *Newsday*, February 12, 1984.

Pearson, Mike. "Shop Talk." *Sunday Herald-Times*, April 12, 1987.

Peary, Danny. *Cult Movies: The Classics, the Sleepers, the Weird, and the Wonderful*. New York: Delacorte Press, 1981.

Picture Grosses. *Variety*, September 7, 1960, 18.

Picture Grosses. *Variety*, September 14, 1960, 9.

Pirani, Adam. "Remaking *Little Shop of Horrors*." *Fangoria*, no. 60 (January 1987): 34–8.

"The Play Survey." *Dramatics*, October 1996, 12.

Pogrebin, Robin. "The Show That Ate the Original Cast." *New York Times*, October 20, 2003.

Poland, Albert. *Stages: A Theater Memoir*. N.p., 2019.

Quintos, Michael. "Gloriously Reimagined *Little Shop of Horrors* Kills at Pasadena Playhouse." www.broadwayworld.com, October 7, 2019.

Ramos, Dino-Ray. "Campy Classic Devours Pasadena Playhouse with Soul, Heart and Inclusivity." www.deadline.com, October 1, 2019.

Renick, Kyle. "How I Learned to Stop Worrying and Love the Shubert Organization." *Theatre Times* 2, no. 3 (January 1983): 1–2, 8.
Review of *La petite boutique des horreurs*. *Variety*, July 9, 1986, 86.
Review of *Little Shop of Horrors*. *Punch*, October 19, 1983.
Review of *The Little Shop of Horrors*. *Variety*, May 10, 1961, 6.
Review of *Little Shop of Horrors*. *Variety*, December 10, 1986, 14.
Rich, Frank. Review of *Real Life Funnies*. *New York Times*, February 12, 1981.
Rich, Frank. "A Theatrical Mystery: The Missing Balconies." *New York Times*, September 9, 1982.
Riedel, Michael. *Razzle Dazzle: The Battle for Broadway*. 2015. New York: Simon and Schuster, 2016.
"Road Down." *Variety*, August 10, 1983.
Rodgers, Richard. *Musical Stages: An Autobiography*. New York: Random House, 1975.
Rooney, David. Review of *Little Shop of Horrors*. *Hollywood Reporter*, July 2, 2015. www.hollywoodreporter.com.
Rooney, David. Review of *Little Shop of Horrors*. *Hollywood Reporter*, October 17, 2019. www.hollywoodreporter.com.
Rosenberg, Bernard, and Ernest Harburg. *The Broadway Musical: Collaboration in Commerce and Art*. New York: New York University Press, 1993.
Rousuck, J. Wynn. "Howard Ashman's Greenery Knocks 'Em Dead on Stage." *Baltimore Sun*, April 8, 1984.
Rubin, Jeffrey. "'Little Shop' Blossoms into Big Hit." *Village Angle*, November 1984.
Sarris, Andrew. "The Myth of Old Movies: An Interpretation of Dreams." *Harper's Magazine*, September 1975, 38–42.
Scapperotti, Dan. "Frank Oz on Directing." *Cinefantastique* 17, no. 5 (September 1987): 31, 55.
Scapperotti, Dan. "The Off-Broadway Hit." *Cinefantastique* 17, no. 1 (January 1987): 22–3, 61.
Scott, Robert. Review of *Little Shop of Horrors*. *Yorkshire Post*, October 18, 1983.
Shewey, Don. "On the Go with David Geffen: Show Business Entrepreneur." *New York Times Magazine*, July 21, 1985.
"Showcase: Issues and Answers." *Show Business*, November 23, 1978, 4.
Shukat, Scott. Letter to the Editor. *Theater Week*, September 26–October 2, 1994, 4.
Sideliners. *New York Post*, January 7, 1983.
Silverman, Stephen M. "Musicals Slip into the Groove on Cast Albums." *New York Post*, July 7, 1983.
Silverman, Stephen M. "This 'Little Shop' Builds Big Bucks Off-Broadway." *New York Post*, July 22, 1986.
Simon, John. "Campsites." *New York*, August 23, 1982, 82, 85.
Singular, Stephen. *The Rise and Rise of David Geffen*. Secaucus, NJ: Birch Lane Press, 1997.
Smith, Liz. "Get This." *Daily News* (New York), April 23, 1985.
Soloski, Alexis. "Gory Musical Blooms Again Off-Broadway." *The Guardian*, October 17, 2019. www.guardian.com.
Sontag, Susan. *Against Interpretation and Other Essays*. New York: Farrar, Straus and Giroux, 1966.

"Source of 'Horrors.'" *New York Post*, November 26, 1982.
"Srs. to Present 'The Brat's Meow.'" *Mill Wheel* 17, no. 5 (January 12, 1967): 1.
Stanley, J. N. "'It's Very, Very Odd' Says *Little Shop* Creator." *Arts Insight* 9, no. 5 (June 1987): 12–13.
Stasio, Marilyn. "Screaming 'Horrors' a Nifty Laugh Riot." *New York Post*, May 24, 1982.
Sternfeld, Jessica. *The Megamusical*. Bloomington: Indiana University Press, 2006.
Sternfeld, Jessica, and Elizabeth L. Wollman, "After the 'Golden Age.'" In *The Oxford Handbook of the American Musical*, edited by Raymond Knapp, Mitchell Morris, and Stacy Wolf. New York: Oxford University Press, 2011.
Steyn, Mark. *Broadway Babies Say Goodnight: Musicals Then and Now*. 1997. New York: Routledge, 2000.
Sullivan, Dan. "The Not-Quite Purple People Eater." *Los Angeles Times*, April 29, 1983.
Sullivan, Dan. "Spoofs for, and by, the Totally Hip." *Los Angeles Times*, June 19, 1983.
"They'll Visit Land of Merlin." *Daily News* (New York), January 7, 1983.
Thomas, R. Eric. "Getting a Disaster Do-Over in *Little Shop of Horrors*." *Elle*, March 25, 2020. www.elle.com.
Tinker, Jack. Review of *Little Shop of Horrors*. *Daily Mail* (London), October 13, 1983.
Topor, Tom. "'Off-Off' Spells Success." *New York Post*, January 19, 1979.
Tran, Diep. "A Tale of Two 'Little Shop(s) of Horrors.'" *American Theatre*, October 18, 2019. www.americantheatre.org.
Variety, June 11, 1986, 12.
Viertel, Jack. "'Little Shop': Horror Spoof with a Song in Its Heart." *Los Angeles Herald Examiner*, April 29, 1983.
Viertel, Jack. *The Secret Life of the American Musical: How Broadway Shows Are Built*. 2016. New York: Sarah Crichton Books/Farrar, Straus and Giroux, 2017.
Vonnegut, Kurt, Jr. *God Bless You, Mr. Rosewater; or, Pearls before Swine*. 1965. New York: Dial Press, 2006.
Wadler, Joyce. "A Cat Now and for 17 Years (Nearly Forever)." *New York Times*, February 25, 2000.
Wall, Mick. *Tearing Down the Wall of South: The Rise and Fall of Phil Spector*. 2007. New York: Vintage Books, 2008.
Wardle, Irving. "Movable Feast." *The Times* (London), October 13, 1983.
Wathen, Mike. "The Damned and the Demented: Roger Corman and the Filmgroup." In *Shock Xpress*, edited by Stefan Jaworzyn. London: Titan Books, 1991.
Weekend Film Boxoffice Reports. *Variety*, December 24, 1986, 4.
Weekend Film Boxoffice Reports. *Variety*, February 25, 1987, 39.
Weldon, Michael, et al. *The Psychotronic Encyclopedia of Film*. New York: Ballantine Books, 1983.
Wells, H. G. *The Stolen Bacillus and Other Incidents*. 1895. London: Macmillan, 1904.
Wells, Stephen. "The Other Side of Broadway." Unpublished manuscript, October 12, 2020. Microsoft Word file.
Wilson, Edwin. "Getting Away from the Season of Our Discontent." *Wall Street Journal*, September 1, 1982.
Wilson, Sandy. *The Boy Friend*. 1953. New York: E.P. Dutton, 1955.

Wolf, Stacy. *A Problem Like Maria: Gender and Sexuality in the American Musical*. Ann Arbor: The University of Michigan Press, 2002.

Wolfe, Tom. "The First Tycoon of Teen." In *The Kandy-Kolored Tangerine-Flake Streamline Baby*. 1965. New York: Picador, 2009.

Wollman, Elizabeth L. *A Critical Companion to the American Stage Musical*. London: Bloomsbury Methuen Drama, 2017.

Wollman, Elizabeth L. *The Theater Will Rock: A History of the Rock Musical, from* Hair *to* Hedwig. Ann Arbor: The University of Michigan Press, 2006.

Zadan, Craig. *Sondheim and Co*. 2nd ed. New York: Harper and Row, 1986.

Index

NOTE: Songs in *Little Shop of Horrors* appear in published and unpublished editions under various titles (e.g. "Closed for Renovation" or "Closed for Renovations"). Significant variants are listed below. Page numbers in italics refer to illustrations.

A and R Recording 90
Actors' Equity Association 15–16, 57–8, 83–4, 131
Actors Playhouse (Coral Gables) 149–51
After Hours (1985) 124
Ahrens, Robert 160
Ailes, Roger 62
AIP *see* American International Pictures
Aladdin (1992) 148
Albee, Edward 18
Allen, Marit 132
Alley Theatre (Houston) 149
Allied Artists 5
"All Gone" 32, 44, 45
Alyson, Eydie 108–9, 110, 111
American Graffiti (1973) 40, 199 n.58
American International Pictures (AIP) 2, 5
Andersen, Hans Christian 10
Anderson, Ernie 62, 188 n.54
Annie (1977) 54, 56, 85
Anything Goes (1934) 78
Anzell, Hy 82, 99, 109
Applause (1970) 27
Aquino, Virginia 16
Aristotle 165
Aronson, Henry 151
Asbury, Anthony
   and Ashman 94
   and Broadway 150
   and film adaptation 134, 135, 136, 137, 138

and Greene 153
on *Little Shop* 113
and London 105, 107
and Orpheum, 100 101
ASCAP (American Society of Composers, Authors and Publishers) 12
Ashman, Howard *8, 71, 89*
   and Actors' Equity 84
   and adaptation 27, 165
   and amateur rights 120
   and Broadway 94, 149
   and cast albums 88–90, 92–3, 195 n.101
   casting 58–63, 98, 101, 108, 130, 141–2
   contract with 57, 81, 83
   and Dale, Grover 52–3
   and designers 64–5, 105
   developing *Little Shop* 27–33, 35–40, 55
   as director 52–4, 65–9, 85, 104, 119, 135
   and *Dreamstuff* 16
   early works of 23–4, 25
   early years of 6–10
   and family entertainment 158
   and film adaptation 121–5, 127–9, 130, 131, 136–9
   on Greene 74
   hires staff 56, 63–4, 116
   and horror films 6, 127

and international productions 111, 113, 115–16
and *The Little Shop* 6, 8–9, 24–6, 27–32, 34, 42, 66, 123, 155
and London 104–6, 108
and Los Angeles 99, 100–1, 102–4
memorial 148
and memory 163, 165
and Menken 14–15, 19–20, 42–5
and the Muppets 24, 126, 146
and musical style 34–6
and nostalgia 40–2
and Orpheum 85, 86, 142, 143
as parodist 119
and performance 67, 98, 189 n.90, 190 n.92
and producers 77, 79
and race 31
and reviews 25, 75, 104, 107
revising *Little Shop* 45–8, 66, 109–10
and Robinson 50, 60, 83
and *Rosewater* 18–19, 20–2
and songwriting 19–20, 24, 70–1
success of 120
and tour 108–10
at university 9–10
and Walt Disney Pictures 148
and Waters, John 156
and WPA Theatre 15, 16–17
see also titles of individual works
Ashman, Raymond 6
Ashman, Sarah
  on Ashman 7, 40, 94
  on Ashman and Menken 19–20
  and Broadway 94, 149
  early years of 6
  and film adaption 131
  on *Little Shop* 73
  on *The Little Shop* 25–6
  marriage of 86
  and revival 160
  on *Rosewater* 20, 21, 22
  on WPA Theatre 17, 18, 45
Ashman, Shirley 6, 110

"Audrey II" (song) 33, 122, 141, 154, 203 n.5, 209 n.115
Australia 111, 114

Babe (1981) 23–4, 26, 45
"Bad" 123, 127, 129
"Bad Like Me" 127, 129
Ball, Lucille 88, 101
Ballad of the Sad Café, The (1963) 18
Barnes, Clive 16, 21, 94
Barnett, Steve 145–6
Bartlett, Rob 151
Bat Boy: The Musical (1997) 155
"Be a Dentist" *see* "Dentist!"
Beatles 17, 34, 89–90
Beauty and the Beast (1991) 148, 177 n.82
Bechtel, Patricia A. 117
Beehive: The '60s Musical (1986) 156
Belushi, James 138
Bentley, Mary Denise 143
Bergman, Boris 115
Besoyan, Rick 67, 79–80
Best Little Whorehouse in Texas, The (1978) 21, 54, 93
Big River (1985) 117
Billig, Robert (Bob) 71
  auditions 58–9, 62
  and Audrey's look 101
  and cast album 91
  and London 104
  and WPA Theatre 54, 67
Black Sunday (1960) 5
Blaisdell, Paul 132
Blanchard, Tammy 161–2, 163, 165
BMI (Broadcast Music, Inc.) 12–13, 76
BMI Musical Theatre Workshop 12–14, 16, 42–5, 177 n.80, 196 n.128
Bool's Flower Shop 160–1
Born Yesterday (1946, 1950) 65
Boyd, Gregory 149
Boy Friend, The (1953) 41, 67
Boyle, Barbara 25
Brantley, Ben 151–2, 153, 162–3
Brat's Meow, The (1967) 7–9, 176 n.46
Brigadoon (1947) 7, 12, 48

Brown, David 91
Brown, Lenora (Cookie) 65, *71*
Bucket of Blood, A (1959) 2–3, 42, 174 n.13
Butler, Kerry 151–2, 155
Byrd, David Edward 84, 120

Cabaret (1966) 6, 12, 79
Calandra, Pete, 116
"Call Back in the Morning" 121
Camelot (1960) 6, 12
Cameron, James 157, 207 n.72
Canada 114
Candy, John 130
Candy Shop, The (1967) 9, 42, 50, 66, 87, 184 n.82
Cannes Film Festival 5
Carlton, Bob 155–6
Carousel (1945) 159
Cats (1981) 78, 79, 81, 83, 93, 94, 111, 148
Chicago (1975) 149
Chiffons 34, 185 n.107
Children's Theatre Association (CTA) 6–7
Chiume, Connie 114
Chorus Line, A (1975) 18, 85, 93
Church, Joseph 108, 110, 111
City Center 152–3
Clarke, Arthur C. 174 n.12
Cleese, John 107
"Closed for Renovation" 121, 123, 127
Coffin, Frederick 23
Collier, John 174 n.12
Colonial Theatre (Boston) 111
Comedy Theatre (London) 104, 108, 200 n.70
Conn, Didi 63
Conway, Lyle 132–3, 134, 137
Conway, Richard 137
Cooper, Eddie 153
Corliss, Richard 86, 89, 155
Corman, Gene 146
Corman, Roger *89*
 advertising art of 4, *5*
 and copyright 42, 145
 early years of 1–2
 and film adaptation 125
 and *Little Shop* 30, 81, 88, 117, 145
 and *The Little Shop* 2–5, 145–6
 production methods of 3, 132
 and television 146–8
 and WPA Theatre 25, 42
Cowan, Edie *71*
 auditions 58–9
 choreography of 67–9, 82, 85, 97
 contract with 81
 and costumes 64
 and *Dames at Sea* 9–10, 56
 and London 104, 105
 on songwriting 57, 70
 and WPA Theatre 56–7, 73, 78, 113
Creamer, Robert W. 23
"Crystal, Ronette, and Chiffon" 127
Crystals 34, 36, 39, 123, 185 n.107

"Da-Doo" 55, 90, 157
Dale, Grover 52–3
Dames at Sea (1966) 9–10, 41, 56, 57
Damn Yankees (1955) 23, 26
Danese, Connie 102–3
Dangerfield, Rodney 138
Danielle, Marlene 82–3, 84
Dante, Joe 2, 157
 see also Gremlins
Dark Crystal, The (1982) 126, 129, 132, 134
Davis, Sheila Kay *71*
 auditions 58–9
 and concert 154
 and film adaptation 131
 and Orpheum 80, 117–18
 on title 94
 and WPA Theatre 74
Day in Hollywood, A/A Night in the Ukraine (1979) 98
DC Comics *140*, 141, 147
Debbie Reynolds Dance Studio 102
Denmark 111, 113
"Dentist!" 40, 57, 136, 141, 158, 187 n.34
Derricks, Marguerite 149
Diamonds (1984) 180 n.1
Dice Incorporated 3
"Dick Whittington and His Cat" (tale) 7

Dlanga, Mandisa 114
"Don't Feed the Plants" *see* "Finale (Don't Feed the Plants)"
"Don't It Go to Show Ya Never Know" 46, 50, 90, 121, 127–8, 193 n.47
Dooley, Paul 138
Douglas, Suzzanne 108
Drake, Donna 142
Dreamgirls (1981) 78–9, 85, 87, 94, 101
Dreamstuff (1976) 16
Dr. Strangelove (1964) 76
Dumas, Alexandre 110, 117

Eating Raoul (1992) 155
Eckstein, Eddie 114
Egan, Louise 139
Egan, Robert 139
Eisner, Eric 129
Eisner, Michael D. 40
Eliot, T. S. 93
Empire Strikes Back, The (1980) 126, 129
Encores! 149
Encores! Off-Center 152–3
Engel, Lehman
   advice of 27
   and BMI Musical Theatre Worshop 12–13
   early years of 11–12
   and *Little Shop* 44, 93
   and *Their Words Are Music* 14
Entermedia Theatre 21–2, 40, 54
Equity *see* Actors' Equity Association
Evans, Craig 18, 64
Evans, Michael 113
Evil Dead: The Musical (2003) 155

Family Guy (1999–) 157
Farber, Donald C. 21, 93
Fatone, Joey 152
Faust (legend) 23, 26, 32, 75, 85, 156
"Feed Me" (first version) 33, 55
"Feed Me" (second version) *see* "Git It"
Feinstein's/54 Below 154
Ferrera, Steve 56, *71*
Filmgroup 2, 4, 5

"Finale (Don't Feed the Plants)" 45, 73–4, 137
Finkel, Fyvush 99, 143
Finley, Carole *71*
Fitzgerald, John F. 110
Fleisher, Michael *140*, 141
Fletcher, Donna Rose *71*
   corrects production reports 209 n.126
   and film adaptation 138–9
   and Paris 116
   on performance 99, 118
   as stage manager 142, 143
   and WPA Theatre 76
"Flowering of the Strange Orchid, The" (1894) 174 n.12
Forbidden Broadway (1982) 101
Forbidden Planet (1956) 156
Forever Plaid (1987) 156
Fosse, Bob 97
Foster, Hunter 150, 151–2
France 115–16
Frankel, Richard 149
Frisch, Robert 101
Fugard, Athol 113, 114

Gale, David 16
Gardenia, Vincent 130
Gaudio, Robert (Bob) 128–9
Geffen, David
   and Ashman 148
   and cast album 90, 91, 92
   and *Cats* 93
   and film adaptation 122, 123–4, 129, 130, 136–7
   and Los Angeles 99
   and Orpheum 78–9, 81, 85, 86
Geffen Film Company 124, 204 n.17
Geffen Records 78, 90
Gelfand, Steve 91, 151, 154
Ghostbusters (1984) 126, 130
Gianfrancesco, Edward T. (Hawk)
   early years of 17
   and Houston 149
   and Orpheum 80

and set design 63–3, 68, 85
and WPA Theatre 17
Gibbs, Nancy Nagel 155
Gillespie, Ron 25–6, 86
Gillespie, Sarah *see* Ashman, Sarah
"Git It" ("Feed Me")
   analysis of 55
   and cast album 91
   and City Center 153
   fan video of 158
   and film adaptation 133, 134
   and musical style 60, 102
   and Paar, Jack 198 n.39
God Bless You, Mr. Rosewater (1965)
   14–15, 20
God Bless You, Mr. Rosewater (1979)
   and cast albums 89, 195 n.103
   and cast size 30, 57
   and Coffin, Frederick 23
   at Entermedia 21–2, 71
   failure of 22
   and Greene 63
   revival of 160
   at WPA 18–21
Godspell (1971) 93
Goldberg, Lee 147–8
Goodchild, Tim 105
Goodspeed Opera House 59
Gorey, Edward 18
Gorey Stories (1977) 18, 179 n.111
Grappo, Constance (Connie) *71*
   and Ashman 65, 73, 94
   auditions 58, 61, 62, 63
   and cast album 92
   as director 104, 113–14, 149–51
   early years of 56
   and film adaptation 138
   and Greene 74, 153
   and London 104, 105–6
   and Los Angeles 99, 103–4
   and Orpheum 80
   in rehearsal 68–70
   and Wilkof 70, 120
Gray, Beverly 2, 3, 42
Grease (1971) 35, 40, 87, 97

Grease (1978) 40, 134
Great Scott Advertising 84
Green, Dennis 16, 17, 19, 20–1, 189 n.129
Greene, Ellen *71, 103*
   auditions 63
   and Audrey's look 65, 88, 105, 153,
     195 n.95
   and cast album 91
   as celebrity 154
   contract with 83
   as diva 69
   early years of 63
   and film adaptation 125, 130, 133, 136,
     138
   and London 104, 105, 106–7
   and Los Angeles 100, 101, 102–3, 104,
     108
   and Meloche 98
   and Orpheum 80, 118, 142, 143
   as performer 74
   in rehearsal 68–9
   returns to role 152–4
   and reviews 86, 87, 107, 153
   and Robinson 70
   and *Weird Romance* 155
   and Wilkof 148
Greener Than You Think (1947)
   174 n.12
"Green Thoughts" (1931) 174 n.12
Gremlins (1984) 127, 159, 205 n. 37
Griffith, Charles B. (Chuck)
   as actor 29, 31, 33
   directing second unit 3
   lawsuit of 117
   and sequel 146
   writing *The Little Shop* 2–3, 174 n.12
Grind (1985) 117
Groff, Jonathan 161, 165
Grosset and Dunlap 10
"Grow for Me" 29, 37–9, *38*, 55, 141
"Growing Boy" 24
Guest, Christopher 130
Guys and Dolls (1950) 149
Gyllenhaal, Jake 153
Gypsy (1959) 9, 87, 88–9, 90

Hadary, Jonathan 81
Hagen Uta, 56, 70
Haggadah, The (1980) 50, 100
Hair (1967) 18, 102
Hairspray (1988) 156
Hairspray (2002) 156–7
Hamlisch, Marvin 131
Hammerstein, Oscar, II 10, 11, 27, 41, 59, 159, 181 n.19
Happy Days (1974–84) 40
Hart, Lorenz 59
Harvey (1944) 26
Hastings, Hal 12
Hawk *see* Gianfrancesco, Edward T.
Hawkins, Ira 202 n.124
Haze, Jonathan 3, 103, *103*
"He Hit Me (And It Felt Like a Kiss)" 39
Heilbron, Medora 147–8
"Hello, Dolly!" 29, 33, 122, 141
Henson, Brian 134
Henson, Jim 24, 50, 60, 87, 100, 125, 126, 134
Herman, Jerry 29
"Hero" 24
Hersey, David 105
Hippen, Lynn 100, 116, 209 n.127
Holliday, Judy 65
Holmes, Paul Mills *71*
  and Anzell 99
  and Ashman 65, 94
  and Audrey's look 101
  and cast album 93
  as director 114–15, 118
  and film adaptation 137–8
  and Greene 68, 91
  and Los Angeles 101–2
  and midnight shows 75
  and Orpheum 80, 82, 98, 119, 142, 143
  and tour 108
  and WPA Theatre 18, 58, 73
Hope, Vida 67
Houseman, John 119
House of Usher (1960) 4
Hudson, Walter 143
Hundreds of Hats (1995) 152, 211 n.40

"I, Eliot Rosewater" 19
"I Found a Hobby" *see* "Just a Hobby"
I Love Lucy (1951–7) 48, 88, 186 n.114
"In the Midnight Hour" 134
Invasion of the Body Snatchers (1956) 76, 123
Invasion of the Body Snatchers (1978) 44
Israel 111, 114–15

Jackson, Chelli 143
Jacobs, Bernard B. (Bernie) 77–9, 93, 99
James, Barry 106
Japan 111, 114, 115
Jaws (1975) 55, 157
Jefferson, B. J. 102, 108
Jim Henson Company 150
Jim Henson's Muppet Babies (1984–91) 146
Joel, Billy 87, 90, 91
Jones, Leilani *71*
  absence of 84, 99
  auditions 58–9
  and film adaptation 131
  and *Grind* 117
  and Orpheum 82
  in rehearsal 66
  and WPA Theatre 74
Jordan, Jeremy 163
Joseph, Jackie 39, 65, 103, *103*, 189 n.76
Jujamcyn Theaters 77, 79, 150
"Just a Hobby" 57, 187 n.34

Kaplan, Darlene 58, 60, 61, 62, 63, 64, 82
Katzenberg, Jeffrey 148
Kennedy, John Fitzgerald 123
Kennedy, Rose Fitzgerald 110
Key Exchange (1981) 80
King, Carole 54, 187 n.23
Kirdahy, Tom 160, 163
Kline, Kevin 88, 165
Koch, Edward I. 118–19, 203 n.136
Koerner, Carl Seldin 117
Khumalo, Sheila 114
Kosarin, Michael 195 n.103
Kubrick, Stanley 132, 136

Kushnick, Beth Anne *71*
Kyte, Mary 56

Labyrinth (1986) 134
Land, Ken 109
Landiş, John 98, 124–5, 132, 209 n.11
Lane, Nathan 61–2, 149
Last Woman on Earth (1960) 4, 42
Lauch, William (Bill)
    and Ashman 115, 120
    and Broadway 149
    and City Center 153
    and film adaptation 125, 130, 136–7, 138
    and Orpheum 143
    and revival 160, 162
Lauper, Cyndi 130, 206 n.54
"Leader of the Pack" 40, 165, 184 n.82
Leader of the Pack (1984) 156
Lederman, Paul 115
Lehrer, Tom 81
Leigh, Mitch 108
Lerner, Alan Jay 12, 87
Leslie, Michael James 102, 105, 108, 151
Lesser, Sally
    and Greene 68, 152–3
    and Houston 149
    and London 105
    and Los Angeles 102
    and Prince, Faith 101
    and WPA Theatre 64–5, 132
Lieberson, Goddard 90
Linowitz, Debi (Delin Colon) 8
"Little Bit Anemic, A" 37, 41, 44
"Little Dental Music, A" 41, 44
Little Mary Sunshine (1959) 41, 67, 79–80
Little Mermaid, The (1989) 148
Little Night Music, A (1973) 27
"Little Shop of Horrors" (song) *see* "Prologue (Little Shop of Horrors)"
Little Shop of Horrors Book, The (1988) 141
Lloyd Webber, Andrew 93
Loewe, Frederick 12
London *see* Comedy Theatre
Los Angeles *see* Westwood Playhouse

Lucas, George 40, 199 n.58
Luz, Franc *71*
    absence of 98
    versus Ashman 92, 100–1, 106, 198 n.22
    early years of 61
    and film adaptation 88, 131
    and Los Angeles 102
    and midnight shows 75
    in rehearsal 69

Macbeth (Shakespeare) 160, 165
McCullers, Carson 18
McDougal, Harriet 10, 124
McGee, Mark Thomas 2, 6, 42
Mackintosh, Cameron
    and *Cats* 93
    and film adaptation 124
    and Geffen 90
    on *Little Shop* 87, 165
    and London 104, 105, 106, 107–8
    and Orpheum 78–9, 81
Madonna 124
Magic Show, The (1974) 52, 54
Mailman, Bruce 84
Malamet, Marsha 16, 19
Manhattan Theatre Club 25
Man of La Mancha (1965) 12, 108
Marcel, Alain 115–16
Marry Me a Little (1980) 84
Marshall, Kathleen 151
Martin, Steve 88, 130, *135*, 135–6, 139
Martinez, Claude 115
Marvel Comics 131, 134
Mayer, Michael 152, 160, 161, 162, 163, 165
"Mean Green Mother from Outer Space" 127, 129, 132–3, 134, 139
"Meek Shall Inherit, The" 68, 121, 123, 139
Meloche, Katherine 97–8, 101, 141–2, 143, 198 n.36
Menken, Alan *71, 89*
    and adaptation 165
    and Ashman 14–15, 19–20, 42–5, 65, 73
    and Broadway 149, 150–1, 177 n.82
    and cast albums 91, 92, 93, 195 n.103

casting 58–60, 63
and concert 154
contract with 57, 81, 83
and Dale, Grover 52–3
early works of 23–4, 25, 26, 62
early years of 13–14
and film adaptation 127–9, 131, 139
and Greene 74
as lyricist 14, 15
and Merkin 54–5, 74
and musical style 31, 32, 34–6, 85, 102, 165
and music department 54–6
and nostalgia 40–2
and reviews 25, 58, 75, 86, 107
revising *Little Shop* 46, 109–10
and revival 162
and Robinson 50–1
and *Rosewater* 19, 20–2, 57
songwriting of 37, 39, 55, 70
at university 13, 54
and Walt Disney Pictures 148
and *Weird Romance* 155
and WPA Theatre 74
see also titles of individual works
Menken, Janis (née Roswick) 13, 15, 23, 55
Menken, Judith 13
Menken, Norman 13
Mercury, Freddie 129
Merkin, Robert (Robby) *71*
  and Ashman 65
  and cast album 91
  casting 128–9
  and concert 154
  as conductor 116, 119
  early years of 54
  and film adaptation 131, 133–4, 136
  and Greene 195 n.95
  and Menken 54–5, 74
  and Vale 61, 82
  and WPA Theatre 55–6
Merman, Ethel 9, 87, 89
Mertz, LuEsther T. 18
Mikado, The (1885) 4, *5*
Milford Mill High School 7–9

Miller, Dick 6, 42
Minnelli, Liza 130
Monat, Phil 56
Moore, Claire 106–7
Moore, Susan 100
Moore, Ward 174 n.12
Moranis, Rick 130, 133, 138, 157, 158, 161
Moranz, Brad 98, 101, 109
Morris A. Mechanic Theatre (Baltimore) 110
Mumford, Peter 143, 198 n.26
Munderloh, Otts 7, 16, 94, 142
Muppet Show, The (1976–81) 24, 126, 129, 132
Muppets Take Manhattan, The (1984) 126, 132, 146
Murphy, Donna 118, 202 n.126
Murray, Bill 130, *135*
"Mushnik and Son"
  allusions in 106, 109–10
  and cast album 109
  early reference to 29
  and film adaptation 121
  and revival 162
  staging 85, 162
  versions of 109–10, 118, 202 n.127
My Fair Lady (1956) 11, 12, 48

Nachamie, Stephen 154
Nederlander Organization 77
Nelson, Jerry 50
Nelson Doubleday 120
Newman, Andrew Hill 154
New World Pictures 42
Nicholson, Elizabeth (Betsy) *71*
Nicholson, Jack 3–4, 123
Nichtern, Claire 21–2
Nicola, James 16
Nightmare on Elm Street, A (1984) 127
Nine (1982) 14, 85
No, No, Nanette (1925) 9
Norway 111, 113
"Now (It's Just the Gas)" 90, 121
Nussbaum, Jeremy 76
Nuts (1979) 25

Oh, Captain! (1958) 27
One Mo' Time (1979) 84
"On the Day That It Started" *see* "All Gone"
Orpheum Theatre
    and Ashman memorial 148
    box office 108, 141, 210 n.128
    and cast album 92–3
    closing at 141–3
    and *Little Shop* 79–81, 94, 95
    long run at 117–18, 119, 122, 209 n.126
    opening at 85
Orzello, Harry 16
Oz, Frank
    casting 130–1
    early years of 24, 125–6, 146
    and fan videos 158
    and film adaptation 129, 132, 133, 134–6
    and Greene 153
    and musical numbers 128
    and reshoots 137, 138

Palace Theatre (Cleveland) 110
Paramount Pictures 1, 76
Parent, Nancy 10, 21, 22, 23, 25–6, 58, 62, 127
Pasadena Playhouse 159–60
Pask, Scott 151
Paynter, Robert 132
Personal Best (1982) 124
Pickwick Players 6
Pinewood Studios 132
Pix Theatre (Los Angeles) 4
"Plain, Clean, Average Americans" 22
"Plant Who Loves You, The" 44
Please Don't Eat My Mother! (1973) 210 n.3
Ploog, Mike 131
Poland, Albert
    and cast album 92
    as general manager 81, 83–4, 98, 118
    and Los Angeles 99
    and Orpheum 77–9, 85, 86, 87
    and Orpheum business 141, 142–3, 158
    and revival 162
    and Shubert Organization 93
Porter, Billy 150
Porter, Cole 11, 27, 35, 177 n.69
Potter, Dennis 158
Present Tense, The (1977) 62
Price, Vincent 1
Prince, Faith
    and *Guys and Dolls* 149
    and Los Angeles 103, 104, 108, 118
    and Orpheum 101, 199 n.42
    and WPA Theatre 63, 82
Prince, Harold S. 12, 180 n.1
"Prologue (Little Shop of Horrors)"
    and cast album 92
    and choreography 58, 68
    development of 35–6
    and film adaptation 137, 139
    as opening number 44, 214 n.89
    on television 85
    title of 35, 41
Public Theater 18, 50
"Purple People Eater, The" 3
Pushing Daisies (2007–9) 152
Put Them All Together (1980) 77

Rabkin, William (Bill) 147–8
Ramone, Phil 90–1
Ramsey, Marion 102
Real Life Funnies (1981) 25, 75
Reed, Donna 106, 115, 199 n.58
Reefer Madness (1998) 155
"Reluctant Orchid, The" 174 n.12
Renick, Kyle
    and Corman 25, 42
    and Dale, Grover 53
    and pop culture 123
    as producer 76–7, 81, 82, 83
    and revival 162
    on *Rosewater* 22
    and WPA Theatre 17, 18, 20, 50, 56
Return to Oz (1985) 132
Return to the Forbidden Planet (1989) 155–6
Revenge of the Nerds (1984) 129–30

Ricamora, Conrad 163
Rice, Tim 27
Rich, Frank 25, 75, 86–7
Rifkin, Robert 115
Ripley, Alice 150
Risky Business (1983) 124, 125, 129, 137
Robber Bridegroom, The (1975) 61
Robinson, Louise 102, 108
Robinson, Martin P. (Marty) *71*
  and Ashman 50, 79, 120
  auditions 60
  and Broadway 149, 50, 151, 152
  builds Audrey II 50–2, 55, 85, 100
  and concert 154
  early years of 49–50
  and film adaptation 125, 132–3
  and Greene 68, 70, 130, 153
  and Houston 149
  and Los Angeles 100, 101
  and Mushnik 82, 99
  and ownership of Audrey II 83
  as performer 68
  success of 119–20
  and Taylor 60
  and WPA Theatre 132
Rocky Horror Show, The (1973) 24, 75, 99, 107, 200 n.64
Rodgers, Richard 10, 11, 27, 41, 59, 159, 181 n.19
Rodriguez, Mj 159
Rogers, Reg 150
Ronettes 34, 46, 185 n.107
Roosevelt, Franklin D. 12, 16
Routh, Marc 149
Ruth, Babe *see* Babe

Sadowsky, John 7–8, *8*
Salazar, George 159
Sallow, Jackie (aka Jacky) 8
Samuel French, Inc. 120
Samuels, Gayle 143
Saturday Night Live (1975–) 125, 130
Scanlan, Dick 152
Schlamme, Thomas 84–5
Schoenfeld, Gerald 77

Schwartz, Norman 7–9, *8*
Scorsese, Martin 124
SCTV (Second City Television) (1976–84) 130
Serling, Rod 44
Serrian, Michael 25, 127
Sesame Street (1969–) 24, 50, 100, 105, 126, 131
Sgt. Pepper's Lonely Hearts Club Band (1967) 89–90
Shakespeare, William 27, 156
Sha Na Na 40, 111, 184 n.85
Shangri-Las 34, 40, 165, 184 n.82
Sharpe-Taylor, Deborah 60, 98–9
Shea's Buffalo 108
Sherman, Esther 25–6, 50, 78, 83, 111, 113, 115
Shop around the Corner, The (1940) 4
Shubert Organization 77, 78, 79, 81, 85, 93, 124, 179 n.123
Shubert Theatre (Philadelphia) 117
Shukat, Scott 25, 54
Side by Side by Sondheim (1976) 78
Silk Stockings (1955) 27
Sills, Douglas 151
"Since You Came to This Town" 19
Skaggs, Marsha (née Waterbury) 118
"Skid Row (Downtown)"
  and cast album 91
  and concert 154
  development of 36–7, 55
  early reference to 29
  and film adaptation 123
  and Groff 161
  and *Hairspray* 157
  as opening number 44, 214 n.89
  parody of 119
  and Seymour 109
  staging of 68–9
Skid Row (Los Angeles) 181 n.28
Sleep No More (2011) 160
Smile (1975) 131
Smokey Joe's Cafe (1994) 156
Snow Queen, The (1973) 10
Sokolov, Elliot 56, *71*

"Some Fun Now" 127–8
"Somewhere That's Green"
  allusions in 106
  analysis of 46–8
  as ballad 70
  and Blanchard 162
  and cast album 90, 91
  development of 169–70
  and film adaptation 121–2, 123, 128
  in French 115
  and Greene 63, 88, 143
  parody of 157
  and reviews 87
"Sominex" 121
Sondheim, Stephen 24, 25, 27, 32
Sour, Robert 12
South Africa 111, 113–14
Spain 112
Spector, Phil 34, 35, 36, 39, 40, 55
  incarceration and death of 183 n.59
Spencer, David 155
Spielberg, Steven 88, 124
Spiner, Brent 73, 104
Streisand, Barbra 130
Stubbs, Levi 133–4, 158
Studio 54 154
"Suddenly, Seymour" 43
  as ballad 70
  and Blanchard 161–2
  and cast album 91
  and film adaptation 127
  and Los Angeles 109
  parody of 157
  and Pasadena 159
Sunlight Studios 162
Sunset Boulevard (1950) 152
Sweden 111, 113
Sweeney Todd (1979) 24, 32, 87
Sweet Charity (1966) 27
Szymanski, William 143

Taylor, Ron *71*
  later career of 117–18
  and Orpheum 143
  as performer 68
  and prologue 92
  and reviews 86
  and *Trading Places* 98
  and WPA Theatre 60, 74–5
Taymor, Julie 50
Tempest, The (Shakespeare) 16, 156
Tempo Books 10
Tesori, Jeanine 152
"Thank God for the Volunteer Fire Brigade" 19
Then She Fell (2012) 160
Three Musketeers, The (1844) 110
Three Musketeers, The (1984) 117–18
"Thundercrash" 123, 127–8
Time Machine, The (1895) 134
Toerien, Pieter 114
To Kill a Mockingbird (1960) 7
Tomfoolery (1980) 81, 84
Tonight Show, The (1954–) 104, 198 n.39
Topps Company 139
Torch Song Trilogy (1981) 70
Towb, Harry 106
Toxic Avenger, The (2008) 155
Trading Places (1983) 98, 132
Troob, Danny 151
Tune, Tommy 75, 87
Twilight Zone, The (1959–64) 44
Twilight Zone: The Movie (1983) 125

"Uptown" 36, 123
Urdang Studios 105
USA Network 147–8
Uthaugh, Geir Håvard 111

Vale, Michael 60–1, *71*, 82
Van Dyke, Will 162, 165
Velardi, Valerie 88
Virginia Theatre 150, 151, 156
Vonnegut, Edith 21
Vonnegut, Kurt, Jr. 15, 21, 27, 93
  see also *God Bless You, Mr. Rosewater*

"Waitin' for My Dearie" 48
Walker, Roy 132

Walt Disney Company 148
Ward, Ken 109
Warfield Theatre (San Francisco) 111
WarGames (1983) 129–30
Warner Bros. 21, 124, 137, 141, 145, 159
Warner Theatre (Washington, DC) 111
Warren, Jennifer Leigh *71*
  auditions 58–9
  and *Big River* 117
  and concert 154
  and film adaptation, 130–1
  and Orpheum 80
  and race 83–4
  in rehearsal 66
  and WPA Theatre 74, 132
Waterbury, Marsha *see* Skaggs, Marsha
Waters, John 110, 156
Weird Romance (1992) 155, 212 n.54
Welles, Mel 2, 5, 6, 103
"We'll Have Tomorrow" 70, 148
Wells, H. G. 134, 174 n.12
Wells, Stephen G.
  and *Dreamstuff* 16
  on Green 19
  as negotiator 76, 79
  and Orpheum 94
  on producing 93
  on White 18
West, Robert 105
Westheimer, Ruth 119
Westside Theatre 161, 162, 163, 165
Westwood Playhouse (Los Angeles) 99, 103, 197 n.16, 199 n.41
Whales of August, The (1980) 56
What Would Jeanne Moreau Do? (1982) 67–8
Wheeler, Hugh 24, 27
Whelton, Clark 119
White, Jesse 102, *103*
White, R. Stuart
  death of 108
  as director 18, 67–8
  early years of 9–10, 56
  reminiscence of 200 n.72
  and WPA Theatre 15, 17, 20

Whitham, Sarah *71*
Wilkof, Lee *71*, *103*
  on Anzell 82
  auditions 61–3
  on Brown, Lenora 65
  and cast album 91
  early years of 62
  and film adaptation 88, 130, 131
  and Grappo 63, 70, 120
  and Greene 148, 153
  later career of 202 n.26
  and Los Angeles 100, 103, 104, 109
  as Mushnik 150, 151
  and "Mushnik and Son" 109
  and Orpheum 118
  in rehearsal 66, 68–70
  and reviews 86, 152
  and WPA Theatre 74, 132
Williams, Robin 88
Wilson, Sandy 67
Wiz, The (1975) 60
Wolff, Richard G. 77, 79
Wolfman Jack (Robert Weston Smith) 106, 199 n.58
Wooley, Michael-Leon 151
Wooley, Sheb 3
Works Progress Administration (WPA) 12, 16
"Worse He Treats Me, The (The More He Loves Me)" 29, 39–40, 46, 154
"Wouldn't It Be Lovely" 48, 186 n.115
WPA Theatre (Workshop of the Players Art Foundation) *164*
  on Fifth Avenue 17
  and film adaptation 124
  financial limitations of 30, 41, 65, 179 n.109
  hires staff 50
  later years of 155, 211 n.40
  origins of 15, 16–18
  as producer 57, 81
  qualities of 56, 132
  success of 71
  and understudies 97

Yankovic, "Weird Al" 157
Yeston, Maury 14, 185 n.104
"You Never Know" *see* "Don't It Go to Show Ya Never Know"
Young Sherlock Holmes (1985) 207 n.72
"Your Day Begins Tonight" 127

Zagnit, Stuart 143
Zaks, Jerry 149, 151, 156
Zombie Prom (1993) 155
Zombies from the Beyond (1995) 155
Zuckerman, Steve 62, 64